CW01663093

First published in 2001

Published By:
Islamic Academy London
PO Box 42240
London
E7 8WQ
Tele: + 44 (0) 7940 479 665
E-Mail: antidajjal@hotmail.com

Freemasons and Dajjal (The Antichrist)
Author: Kamran R'ad

Reprinted in 2003

A catalogue record for this book is available from the British Library

ISBN 0-9545734-0-4

اعوذ باالله من ا لشيطن الرجيم

AAOOZO BILLAHE MINASH SHAYETANIR RAJEEM

I seek Refuge with Allah from Shayetan Ar Rajeem

بسم الله الرحمن الرحيم

BISMILLAHIR RAHMANIR RAHEEM

With the Name of Allah, The Rahman, The Raheem

اشهد ان لآ إله الآ الله

ASH-HADO ANLLA ILAHA ILLALLAH

I bear witness that there is none worthy of worship except Allah

واشهد ان محمدًا عبده و رسوله

WA ASHHADO ANNA MOHAMMADAN ABDOHOO WA RASULOH

And I bear witness that Mohammad (PBUH) is his slave and messenger

ACKNOWLEDGEMENT

In the Name of Allah, The Rahman, The Raheem

I thank everyone who helped and encouraged me in this humble effort. There were times when I was on the verge of giving-up this task because of the worldly obstacles and financial problems, then came the help from Allah (SWT). This reassured my confidence in the work and firmed my faith in Allah (SWT).

I thank all the authors and publishers from whosever book I have taken quotations.

It would be appropriate to mention a few names to show gratitude for their efforts. Hafiz Mumtaz of Southall, London, for his supplication. Brothers Sabeeh Mian, Munir Hussain and Fahad Mihyi, for the motivation. My Turkish brother Yasser for informative sittings regarding Ottoman Empire, brother Abdullah Actha, for long and knowledgeable discussions on Ahadith and editing the book. My elder brother Farooq Matloob, for his unvarying confidence and faith in my research. Brother Arshad Mahmood and his family for providing me a proper atmosphere and out-of-way support to complete the project. Dr. Allama Khalid Mahmood of Islamic Academy Manchester, UK, for his priceless guidance in the form of his own-written books and personal teachings, also his attention towards the urgency and importance of the subject.

Above all I thank Allah (SWT), Who enabled me to complete this work entirely by His Mercy. I pray Him to guide us all to "The Straight Path", "Al Sirat Al Mustaqim".

FOREWORD

Dear brothers and sisters in Islam

Assalam O Alaykum

I am sure every sensible person wonders that why there is so much injustice in the world? Why Muslims especially are weak and oppressed? Why are they fighting each other like crazy? Are all Muslims unintelligent, fools and really foes to each other? Why Western countries are in peace and harmony? Is the West gifted with intellect? Finally has Islam gone old and do we need to separate Islam from our day-to-day practical life? Is "Secularism" the solution to all the problems?

The answers to these questions are hidden in last 1000 years history. The actual history with a different aspect! The aspect, that was never enlightened or if enlightened, on a very small scale. This research is an effort with a view to reveal this conspiracy and the actual conspiracy is far bigger and greater than ever known.

This is not something that was revealed to only me, overnight. Many other people also know the exact nature of this conspiracy specially those on higher level of executiveship; Leaders, Ministers, Prime Ministers and Presidents but unfortunately either they are brainwashed or part of it, with a very few exceptions. These exceptional people never get a chance to overthrow the corrupt. Because corrupts have media in their hands. Through media they manipulate the masses and mass manipulation is called "Democracy".

The chapters in this work of "Research" are designed to give an outlay of how, when and where the so-called "Modern History" began, arose and has now established itself as the defining "moment of mankind".

The object in this research is to report, encourage and open-up the true skeletons that discarded the "Flesh" and took the guise of "Democracy". They used "Democracy" to defeat God's given law and replace it systematically, chronologically, step by painful step, genealogically and steadfastly in order to pave the way for the coming of the "master of the darkness". This "master of the darkness" is the "Antichrist", better known to Muslims the world over as the "Dajjal".

This is a true, sincere heartfelt endeavour and attempt to open bare the conspiracy that began in 1095 AD. This conspiracy has taken hold of every single sector and section of the human way of life that is "GOVERNED" by Godly laws. This "Plot", was set by a deadly poisonous group that initiated in the guise of "KNIGHTS" and now operate as the "MEN IN GREY SUITS"! Their aim is to disrupt the course of Godly Divine Rule and replace it with satanic inhumane way of life. So they can avail the right suitable conditions to enable the advent of the **"Antichrist", "Ad-Dajjal"!**

How did they achieve their target and have they really achieved their target, if not then how close are they...are the objectives of this research. With a few exceptions, most of the books I have used for reference are written by Freemasons. This hardly leaves them any chance but to accept the outcome and be responsible for the consequences. I sincerely hope that every Muslim and Non-Muslim reader benefits from it, opens his eyes in order to view the severity of dangers, overwhelming the entire society.

That time is not too far when we will not be able to do anything. We will be densely stressed and strained in the mitt of the **"New World Order"** which is marching towards us discreetly, silently and constantly.

Still there is some time…before this "Satanic Order" is fully implemented. Time is now to wake-up! Wake-up now… before put asleep in sleep!

Sincerely,
KAMRAN R'AD

CONTENTS

Part-1

Part-2

FREEMASONS

CH-1 HOLY LAND

Khosrau II, the King of Persia captured Jerusalem in 614 CE. His reign did not last more than 14 years and in 628 CE Heraculius the Byzantine king recovered Jerusalem this time only for 9 years though. Umar (RA) the second Caliph of Islam conquered it in 637 CE. A shrine was built between CE 685 and 691 by the caliph "Abdul Malik ibn Marwan". We know this shrine today as the **'Dome of the Rock'** or **"Bait-al-Muqaddas"**.

Jerusalem has always been a sacred city for all three religions of the Book. Muslims believe in all the prophets so any place related to any prophet is sacred for them. According to the Old Testament the 'Dome of the Rock' relates to Solomon (AS) so there is no doubt in its religious status. Christians believing in Solomon (AS) as well as in Jesus (AS) have a great respect for the land as Jesus (AS) was born in Bethlehem, Jerusalem.

After Muslims established their rule in Jerusalem they understood its religious importance to all three religions so they did not prohibit any pilgrims either Christians or Jews to benefit from. This practice carried on for centuries till Turk Seljuks overtook the control in 1071 CE. Whether they stopped the pilgrims or not and if they did then for what reasons, is not the question. The fact is that in 1095 CE Pope "Urban II" called upon Christian Europe to re-capture the Holy Land from the pagans (Muslims). Who according to Pope Urban had slaughtered thousands of their Christian brothers and occupied most of the world leaving only a small part of the globe for Europeans to live and rule (radical Christian historians believe that this sermon of Pope Urban was nothing but a pack of lies as for as slaughter of Christians is concerned).

Why is it so that Muslims are invincible and ready to give their life in the cause of their God and such is not the case with Christians? This was the major question facing Pope Urban or them who were behind this school of thought of the time. The answer was very simple; Muslims fight to sacrifice their lives because they are promised Paradise in the life hereafter. What could be the promise to the Christians that they shouldn't hesitate to give their lives for the Cross? The answer came as a promise of salvation and forgiveness of all the sins of the participants, fighting for the cause of the Cross. Pope Urban gave this promise on his own authority; which was contradicting to the Bible on the first place. According to Bible, Jesus (AS) has already shed his blood for all the sins of the sons of Adam (AS). This promise also nullified the concept of Confession.

However the first response came from a fanatical group of poor men and women who poured across Hungary to Constantinople and Asia Minor. These warriors were only disorganized civilians just to be slaughtered by Hungarians; the Turks completed rest of the job.

KNIGHTS

A second wave of crusade and attack was launched by a group called **Knights,** who stormed Jerusalem and established a Latin kingdom. This was the first successive attack under the flag of the Cross-, which not only gave courage to Europeans against invincible Muslims but also started a new era of bloodshed, which followed for centuries and is still carrying on. This attack was named **"Crusade"** meaning **"Holy War against Infidels".** To look at the motive behind this first Crusade we look at the actions of the Knights along the way to Jerusalem.

"Along the way they massacred Muslims, Jews and dark skinned Christians".
(Encyclopaedia Encarta- Crusades)

Actions speak louder than words! Was this really a sacred religious war? No! Not at all but a racial crusade, the very first of its kind and these crusades are still carrying on---even today, as we shall prove Inshallah.

As the time passed and crusades grew in quantity, so did Knights in both, quality and quantity. In regard to different backgrounds and duties they were named and titled different to each other, amongst them were,

1- Teutonic Knights.
2- Spanish Knights or Spanish Orders.
3- Portuguese Knights.
4- Knights of St John or Hospitallers
5- Templars Knights.

Several crusades and countless loss of lives proved to the Christian world that Muslims are invincible as long as they have a concept of *Ummah (Muslim Brotherhood)* and follow the sacred law of *Shariah (Islamic Law)*. To overcome their only enemy, Christians changed their concept of victory. Battlefields changed---so did the strategy. Deception, took over bravery, politics replaced the sword. Soon they were able to occupy the Holy Land of Jerusalem without any war with Muslims. At this point, the Muslim world was threatened on one side by Mongols, and on the other by Christians. Descendants of "Salah-ul-Din Ayyubi" decided to fight one at a time, so they signed a treaty with Christians. According to that treaty the Christian king will rule Jerusalem protecting Muslim population and their mosques. Soon these condition were forgotten and as ever before Muslims were tortured and *Moazzens (the one who calls for prayer)* were banned to recite *Azan (the call for prayer)*.

This condition did not stay for long,*Khwarzemie* Muslims who were defeated by Mongols, gathered around this side of the peninsula. The then Muslim Sultan faced a problem to populate these *Khwarzemies,* so he decided to use their aggression of defeat, at the hands of Mongols to re-occupy Jerusalem. Years of fighting experience with ferocious Mongols made this conquest one sided for Muslims. Jerusalem was once again in Muslims hands, this time until the 20th century.

The fall of Jerusalem into the hands of Muslims was followed by the fall of Acre (Akka) in 1291 CE, and with the fall of Acre, fell all the hopes of establishing a Christian Holy Land dominion. All these orders of Knights seemed to be rendered aimless and useless (though not very much so; as we will find out). With no more crusades on the line, different Knights' groups went different directions.

Teutonic Knights: found their way into the Baltic, exterminating the pagan tribes there and establishing a Christian rule, which extended from Prussia, through Latvia, Lithuania and Estonia, to the Gulf of Finland.

Spanish Knights: went to expel Moors from the Iberian Peninsula.

Portuguese Knights: took over the duty to protect and explore the nearby waters.

Hospitaller Knights:decided to establish first as **Knights of Rhodes**, then as **Knights of Malta** and spent next three centuries controlling Mediterranean with more interest and hold of mercantile. Nowadays they are working under the name of **Knights of St John from Jerusalem.**

Templars Knights:were the only ones, apparently with no aim and cause. They seem to disappear from all visible aspects. But they were actually working for a bigger cause, a very big agenda in corroboration with other Knights' Orders. They had the whole world in front of their eyes, and the biggest dominion. To understand their strategy, we have to go into detail of their foundation and mottoes.

CH-2 KNIGHTS TEMPLARS

Although Christian rule over the Holy Land was short, but this little occupation of Jerusalem was actually a turning point of the whole world's history. During this short period, a special order of Knights was formed to protect Christian pilgrims from Muslim attacks. This order was a religious order to protect the Holy Temple from pagans, so they became respectable to the rest of the Christians. According to their religious duties and their Christian way of dewelling they were called **Monks.** Afterwards this title was abandoned and they became **Templars**, soon they became a proper military order and adopted the name '**Knights Templars'**.

'The Penguin Dictionary of Religions' defines Knights Tamplars as,

"A religious military order founded in 1119 at Jerusalem to protect Christian pilgrims against Muslim attacks. Quartered originally near the site of the Temple. They lived under the monastic rule, but their activities were mainly military and administrative. Important in maintaining the Latin Kingdom in the Holy Land, they also held properties in Europe and acted as international bankers. ***Conducting their internal affairs with strict secrecy". (Emphases added)***

There are different legacies about their formal foundation and actual existence. Many legends tell us that Templars actually existed 4 years prior to their official announcement. As we have checked, Templars were formed to protect the pilgrims in Holy Land, but from whom? Was this protection from Muslims? If that was the actual case then they should have been a group of few hundreds, if not a few thousand. Amazingly for the first nine years they were only nine:

Hugues de Payen*- a vassal lord to Hugh of Champagne.*
Geoffrey de St Omer*- the son of Hugh of St Omer.*
Andre de Montbard*- a vassal lord to Hugh of Champagne and uncle of Bernard of Clairvaux.*
Payen de Montdidier*- related to the rulers of Flanders.*
Achambaud de St-Amand*- related to the rulers of Flanders.*
Gondemare*- no details known.*
Rosal*- no details known.*
Godefroy*- no details known.*
Geoffroy Bisol*- no details known.*

The knights of whom, little is known are believed to have been representatives of the ruling families of Champagne, Anjou, Gisors, and Flanders. The leader of the Templars was Hugues de Payen, a middle-ranking nobleman in Champagne who married Catherine St Clair, the niece of his crusading partner Baron Henri St Clair of Roslin, in 1101. (19-97)

So what were they protecting and from whom? On this point some researchers believe that Templars, the 'Nine Templars' were actually guarding some treasure or some sacred manuscripts found from the 'Holy Temple' (Bait-al-Muqaddas), 'King Solomon's Temple'. Others believe that they were formed as protectors and military wing of a secret society called the '**Order of Sion**' or '**Priory of Sion**' and Sion means **Sun**. The greatest of ancient Egypt's many gods was the sun god, the 'Ra'! Pharaohs, gods themselves, were sons of 'Ra'.

We can't claim that Templars did guard some ancient manuscripts or treasure but we certainly know that they vowed:

"To hold all property in common". (The Mysteries of Charters Cathedral. A quote from 19-30)

If they were merely treasure hunters, they would vow to "share property", not to *"hold property in common"*. This phrase explicitly demonstrates their objectives for a long term planning, which we know today as: the **"New-World-Order"**! In the following years their wealth and property grew enormously. They had minimum seventy-four major properties, including thirty full-scale preceptories and literally hundreds of small belongings, including villages, hamlets, churches and farms. This was only in England---! Their properties and lands were everywhere, France, England, Scotland, Spain and Portugal. Templars don't deny having these properties but say 'all these properties and lands were donated to them by 300 recruits from noble families, who joined Templars in return'.

Obviously these noble family people paid a very high price only to become recruits, not even knights and they belonged to wealthy families themselves, yet they donated their whole wealth just to become recruits. If this is true, they must have been given a definite promising future, so definite that they prepared to bet all their wealth. If this is not true, then we can understand this story as a cover-up and the reason of ***'conducting their internal affairs with strict secrecy'***. Within next ten years, their properties extended to Italy, Austria, Germany, Hungary and Constantinople.

RAIDERS OF THE LAST ARKS

In ancient times when Jews settled down in Jerusalem, they brought the Ark of Moses (PBUH) with them. Centuries passed but nothing was ever heard about the Ark. The Old Testament describes that the Ark was built with pure gold, specifying its measurements and geometrical angles. According to the Old Testament this Ark contained the original tablets given to Moses (AS) on the mount Sinai, Rod of Aaron (actually Mosses', according to Qur'an) and a pot of Manna. The Ark was kept in the 'Temple of the Dome' but nothing is written in history suggesting what happened to it after that. In the time of the Templars, the Dome was prohibited to pilgrims for some time for an "apparent" reason of repair.

Jerusalem is built on top of a net of tunnels built for the purpose of hiding, storing wealth and escaping in case of enemy attack. It was a general idea that the Ark was hidden in the maze of these tunnels because it was sacred and untouchable by other than Rabies. The Ark was hidden for the mere purpose of its sacredness so in case of enemy invasion it would not be disrespected. In 1948 (after the foundation of Israel) many archaeologists excavated the underground tunnels of Jerusalem with that times modern equipment and whole world had high hopes. Only one group already knew the results because that group had had not only the Ark---but---'Arks' for centuries, which they dug out during the Dome's confiscation, and that group is Templars, the Knights Templars! This is exactly what "Christopher Knight" and "Robert Lomas" (modern Knights Templars themselves) who went all the way to investigate the origins of "Templars" write:

"We know that the first Knights Templars had excavated the site of the last Temple". (9-33)

They also found another four Arks with the original, which were made by early Judaic descendents. Beside many legends of their whereabouts experts have strong evidences that these Arks are still safe and kept in **'Roselyn Chapel'** in Scotland built between 1440 and 1490. The name Roselyn, according to Scottish Gaelic dictionary is a combination of two syllables:

Ros: A noun meaning "knowledge".

Linn: A noun meaning "generation".

When these two words are combined, they mean as "knowledge of the generations".

According to Gaelic speakers; the word "Ros" means "ancient knowledge", so the translation precisely phrases;

"Ancient knowledge passed down the generations". (19-43)

EARLY BANKING SYSTEM

'Goldsmiths' introduced the first system of 'safes'; with their own amount of gold they started safekeeping public's gold and ornaments. For safety reasons this deposit system was liked and became popular. Gradually goldsmiths introduced a slight change to it, in case of deposit gold's sale from one client to another, rather than actually returning it to former and new owner; an 'exchange chit' was introduced. This transfer system saved all the hassle of drawing and re-depositing gold.

Some people had to travel distances; it worried them about their safety as well as their goods'. Templars found an alternate way for these people to travel empty handed, yet carrying their valuables. Templars collected gold, silver, etc and issued a chit to clients in Templars code words, de-codable by Templars only. These chits had description and name of the client and details of deposits, which were obtainable from the other end. Not long afterwards they started granting loans on behalf of these deposits. Gold stored with these artisans for safekeeping was; expected to be returned to the owners on demand.

The goldsmiths soon discovered that the amount of gold actually removed by owners was only a fraction of the total stored. Thus, they could temporarily lend out some of this gold to others, obtaining a promissory note for principal and interest. In time, paper certificates redeemable in gold coin were circulated instead of gold. Consequently, the total value of these banknotes in circulation exceeded the value of the gold that was exchangeable for the notes.

This safeguarding fund, granting and guaranteeing loans is the foundation of modern banking system. Templars had a credibility of religious background and access to all European countries even to Middle East and Holy Land, with their offices established around the globe! Wealthy families of Renaissance such as the Medicis in Florence (Italy) also supported this system and gradually established the first modern bank of Sweden, the 'Riksbank' in 1656 and the Bank of England in 1694. Seventeenth-century English goldsmiths provided the model for contemporary banking.

According to the Bible, usury is prohibited, so it was strictly forbidden in those days. Templars, the "Holy Templars" were least bothered about it. They not only took interest on loans but a very high interest. On one occasion, the borrower had to pay 60% interest. With modern banking system in ancient times, they soon became modern capitalists of ancient times!!!

Most of the monarchs were under their debts. Leave alone the Europeans; even the English crown was chronically in debt to the "Temple". King John, Henry the 3rd, Edward the 1st, all borrowed money from Temple. Between 1260 and 1266, King Henry pawned the English crown jewels to Templars. With the Crown under their debts, Templars did not waste time and restricted tax collection from the public only by Templars! Tax collections excessively grew their power and they not only collected Papal donations but also revenue on behalf of monarchs. Beside so much wealth they themselves were tax exempted. Doesn't this sound familiar? Something like modern MPs? Same as today's tax exempted organisations are working, who makes the decision to exempt them from tax? Of course the law and who makes the law? We shall find out---Inshallah!

All Knights were working in corroboration with each other, Richard "the Lionheart", had very close relations with Templars. He was not officially a Templar, but used their ships frequently and received instructions from them. There was a time when he was under threat from his brother John; he escaped from England in guise of a Templar---with Templars---! This is the same John who owed money to Templars. This incident establishes a fact, a conspirational theology: "if you want to monitor the consequences, make sure that leftists and rightists are your people". This theology is working in Democratic countries right in front of our eyes, yet hidden from us in the forms of "ruling party" and "opposition".

Templars were dictating to Richard, as well as his opponent and brother John. When John was King of England, his adviser was Aymeric de St Maur, a Templar and Grand Master.

Templars increased their wealth and power rapidly. They controlled both sides, exploited them, created a coup, and provided both sides with arms, which brought both sides under their debts and order. With majority of European kings under their debts they could even manipulate the consequences.

FRIDAY THE 13TH

This rapid progress of the Brotherhood, their control on the monarchs and economy of the whole of Europe went well hidden from public eye. Even kings themselves were not aware for a long time, till King Philippe IV of France sensed this conspiracy. He; with the Church on Templars side, could not break their monopoly. So, first he got rid off the Pope, Boniface the 8th and then his successor Benedict, the 11th.

In 1305, king Philippe installed Pope Clement the 5th. With Papacy more radical he decided to thoroughly investigate Templar's affairs. The extent of danger compelled him to take severe and sudden action. As a result he sent sealed orders to bailiffs and other officers throughout the country to be opened all at the same time, "at dawn---**Friday the 13th ---Oct 1307---!**"

According to the orders, all Templars in France were suddenly to be seized, arrested, and their belongings to be confiscated. Templars were accused of "homosexuality, blasphemy and idolatry". Those who were proved guilty were executed. These charges brought enormous hate and disgust for the Templars throughout Europe. They were suspected and arrested everywhere.

Pope Clement dissolved the "Temple" in 1312 officially. The last Grand Master of the order, "Jaques de Molay" was burnt at the stake on a slow fire, in 1314. This sacrifice of their Grand Master is still remembered by Templars and is an essential ritual in their ceremonies.

Once public opinion was against them and the church was hostile, "Brotherhood" could not do much to defend themselves against these allegations. Their properties were confiscated all over Europe, though most of these properties in Europe were given to their rivals, "The Hospittelars", who publicly opposed Templars. Apparently this was the end of Templars but they learnt a lesson from this, "power in one hand can be dangerous so divide it".

Apparently this was the end of Templars, at least officially. Considering a few facts, this was not! This was the start of a new era, "Democracy", was the alternate system. What Brotherhood learnt from this was that "covert control" is the best guise for a secret society like theirs, more "confusion" is more safety for them. If an enemy is known he can be stopped, but if you don't know the source of trouble you blame yourself or say, "times are bad".

What king Philippe found was very little, the actual treasure of Templars was never found. The wealth that made the Monks---kingmakers---was never re-covered. Rather this is very susceptible weather Philippe's surprise coup was as unexpected as, he or subsequent historians thought. Evidence shows that Templars did receive some kind of advance warning. For example,

"Shortly before the swoop the Grand Master, Jaques de Moley, called in many of the order' book and extant rules and had them burnt". (3-84)

A Knight who withdrew from the Temple around this time, was told by the Temple's treasurer that,

"He was extremely wise." (3-84)

These evidences show that Templars were aware of some sort of crises is imminent. Moreover, an official edict was circulated to all French perceptories stressing,

"That no information about the Order's rites or rituals was to be released." (3-84)

Weather the Templars were warned in advance or weather they simply sensed, what was in the wind, certain precautions were definitely adopted. In the first place, many Knights fled and those who were captured seemed to have submitted passively, as if under instructions to do so. At no point in the record of historians show that French Templars resisted the King's seneschals, rather there is a record of:

"An organised flight by a particular group of Knights, virtually all of whom were in some way associated with the Order's treasure". (3-84)

This escape was carried out in a fleet of ships and there is no evidence in the history about their fleet of ships, ever seized by king Philippe. Even there is no definite evidence of the fleet to be found anywhere. Absolute mystery, only assumptions have been made. It strengthens the idea, that enormous treasure and fleet was taken out safely.

Another thing bothers mind: what was so secretive about those "order books" and "extent rules" that were burnt. Why not 'to release any information about rites and rituals'? Certainly the allegations on Templars had some credibility. If not all of them were true at least some of them were. Remembering that Templars were accused of "blasphemy, idolatry and homosexuality". (Ibid.)

When we talk about these charges, we have to understand, to what extent these charges meant. With the idols of Jesus and Mary in every church all over the world, what idolatry were they being accused of? Answer lies in the question. What was the blasphemy according to church? Finally were they really practicing homosexuality?

On 30th of March 2000, a film festival for "Gays & Lesbians" was held in London, appropriate media coverage was provided even discussions were held on the BBC. This festival was sponsored by the London City's big institution called "J P Morgan", a subsidiary Knight's institute. Ten fifteen years before from now, gays and lesbians were a rejected lot of society; labelled as sinners. Now they hold all the rights to practice their "genetically inherited" attraction to their own sex. This "scientific invention" of genetic inheritance gives them an excuse to spare their own filthy lust and to blame it on the nature. If this is a genetic disease, then this gene was supposed to disappear after one or two generations, with no re-production ability.

"Section 28" is a restriction on "homosexual" education in British schools. British Government has pre-decided to lift this section and to introduce "homosexual education" in the classrooms. The first attempt to promote homosexuality failed in the "House of Commons" with a heavy opposition, second attempt failed with a narrow contest. Tony Blair the British Prime Minister, apparently criticising homosexuality announced:

"People can say whatever they want to say but the truth is that no parent is going to be ***forced*** *to have their children take part in gay sex lessons in schools.* ***No child is going to be forced*** *to take part in homosexual role-play. It is complete and total nonsense". (The Daily Telegraph-11/3/00)* ***Emphases*** *added.*

This statement looks like that it is apparently opposing the gay sex education, but let us look at the emphasised words. *No parent is going to be forced,* means they will have an option, that clearly indicates the presence of this lethal, satanic education in schools. Again children are given an option by *no child is going to be forced.* Let me tell you what does this politically phrased comforting statement means! This means that this education will be there for sure, but with extra optional marks and then innocent children will join in voluntarily, in greed of extra marks. Thus: *not being forced!*

Britain's most senior family law judge and President of the High Court's Family Division, with a salary of £139,931 "Dame Elizabeth Butler Sloss" backed adoption by gays saying:

"It is a different world from when I started in the law. I was, when I started, surprised and dubious about the stability of children living in a family with two parents of the same sex.... It would be 'quite wrong' not to recognise that different children need different types of home." (The Times London Saturday October 16 1999)

At the time when Dame made this statement in 1999 she was 66. That makes her birth of 1933. She must be in her early 20s when she started law. This brings us into the early 1950s. Can you imagine a young female student in early 1950s introduced with gay couples living as a family! I am sure no one from general public had this concept---only the elite. Dame has a law-family background. Her father, Sir Cecil Havers was also a judge. As a young barrister, it is stated in the Times that:

*"She set up and ran a **nursery for toddlers** in a **basement** in **Temple.** (The Times London Saturday October 16 1999)*

Alas---! Dame is also the first woman to reach this level of seniority in the judiciary---now you know ---why---!

GAY SEX 'TO BE LEGAL IN PUBLIC'

Parents in fury over latest threat to kids

Gays will be free to have sex in public loos; under an astonishing plan to "modernise" indecency laws, it emerged last night. (The Sun, July 27, 2000)

Who is behind all these promotions, and who is responsible for making these laws. Usually we don't go beyond a certain boundary when investigating these things, maximum we can see a few responsible faces for these changes in the society, the elected members. But this is a vaster field of conspiracy that is going to cause unprecedented chaos. We will disclose these conspiracies as much as we can Inshallah!

*"The Prophet (PBUH) said: 'By Him Who sent me with the truth, this earth will not pass away until people are afflicted with landslides, are pelted with stones, and are transformed into animals'. The people asked, 'when will that be, O Messenger of Allah?' He said: 'When you see women riding in the saddle, when singers are common, when bearing false witness becomes widespread, and **when men lie with men and women with women'** " (Reported by Abu Hurayrah- al-Haythami, Kitab al Fitan. Quote from 20-93)*

A close look at the results of the French coup on Friday the 13th shows that this coup was availed by the elite group of Templars as an opportunity to get rid of the extra burden. They were looking forward to dominate the Globe and elite order did not need an extra army because they were moving to an economic control. Although their next step was a war a historical war!

Ch-3 KING ROBERT THE BRUCE (1306-1329)

Robert The Bruce was descendent of Malcom the 3rd, king of Scotland. He became prominent in 1292, when he was fighting for the independence of Scotland from the British monarchy.

Alexander the 3rd was seated on Scotland's throne in 1249. Alexander had no sons, his only daughter Margaret was married to the King of Norway. If Alexander dies, he would leave no heir to the throne of Scotland, as the Scots had no desire for a Norwegian ruler. Alexander's death could create a civil disorder, with chances of foreign (English) interference. Guess what? This is what exactly happens. On a stormy night in March 1286, separated from his guards, on the way back from a council at Edinburgh he disappeared. The following morning, he was found dead with his neck broken... an accident! Perhaps!

A caretaker government was formed in Scotland, consisting of six people, named as "Guardians of the Peace". This council decided to confer the throne to the "rightful owner", the daughter of Margaret also called Margaret and an infant at that time. It was decided that Margaret, reaching the age of maturity, would marry Prince Edward of England, subsequently Edward the 2nd of England. But in 1290 coming home from Norway, the young Margaret died... Another accident perhaps!

This death of the young princess caused dangers of civil war, because more than a dozen candidates presented themselves for the throne. This included "Robert Bruce", named as "The Competitor". According to the Brotherhood's plan the Bishop of St. Andrews invited Edward the 1st of England to arbitrate. Edward eventually claimed the throne himself as suzerain over Scotland. Monkey business, isn't it? This decision caused what it was supposed to prevent---a civil war---! Rebels in Scotland formed an alliance with France. At that time the monarchy of France was already in the hands of Templars, Friday the 13th hadn't come yet. So whom do these rebels unite with? Of course with the Templars!

In the mean time, Edward had already advanced with his army into Scotland. The second full-scale invasion took place on 19/20 July 1298, with 2000 horsemen and 12000 footmen. Keeping in mind that Edward's army included Templars too, in fact "Master of England" and "Preceptor of Scotland". "Utter control" of the situation! Knights Templars on both sides!

King Robert The Bruce emerges from this background, when he was made "Earl of Celtic", the most powerful leader of the time. Still with limited resources he could not afford an open battle because battle needed financiers, financiers could only be Templars and Templars had their own terms and conditions. Till 1310 Robert The Bruce had to rely on guerrilla attacks, this brought him no success against the English. After 1310, he suddenly started getting equipment and armour from Ireland. Whereas; at that time poor Ireland, was not capable of providing such heavy aid. So where was Ireland getting all this equipment, from? At this point, historians suggest that the fleet of ships, vanished from France in the 1307 coup was safely downloaded and stored in Ireland for the future "Battle of Bannockburn".

BATTLE OF BANNOCKBURN

Bruce's brother Edward besieged a small English garrison toward the end of 1313. Edward did not want to lose his men, according to him "on such unstratigic operation". As the siege prolonged, both sides agreed on condition that: If by midsummer next year no English army appears within three miles of the castle, the

English garrison will surrender. What a hoax! In fact this was a background being created for the actual battle.

King Edward's integrity could not decline this challenge and he had to walk into this trap to save the dignity of English. Edward gathered around 3,000 knights, with their own-trained soldiers; an estimated number of 20,000 formed his army. On the other hand Bruce's forces were around 7'000 to 10'000' out numbered by half or one third and far less armoured than English.

The battle continued for a full day with no result and not much loss on both sides. Suddenly a fresh force appeared to confront English. This force was called "The Mysterious Horsemen". Edward and his Templars were defeated and forced to retreat. Amazingly the number of casualties of the retreating English army was next to none. Historians, like Bernard Jones and Michal Baigent believe that the fresh force or the mysterious horsemen were actually Templars.

This was a decisive battle between England and Scotland, which liberated Scotland from England for the next 289 years. A long time for Templars to prosper and plan, the world-wide dominion.

Question arises that why Brotherhood Selected particularly Scotland as the platform to launch their mission? Could they not carry on with their secret mission anywhere else in Europe? The answer is very simple; Scotland was the only place in the world free from the Church or religious obligations. Templars were hurt once they could not afford to lose their wealth and supremacy once more. There was no "Law of God" in Scotland so the law of Fraternity could fill the gap---"Freedom"---! King Robert The Bruce was not recognised as King by the Church so Scotland did not come under any law unless a recognised government was established.

DECLERATION OF ARBROATH

King Robert The Bruce died in October 1318, on 6th of April 1320; an extra ordinary document was issued. This document explained the terms and conditions on which the troubled Bruce was helped by Templars. This was the "Declaration of Arbroath".

*"The divine providence. The right of succession by the laws and customs of the kingdom, and the due and lawful consent and assent of all the people made him our king and prince. To him we are obliged and resolved to adhere all things, both upon his account of his right and his own merit, as being the person who restored the people's safety in defence of their liberties. But after all, if this prince shall leave these principles he has so nobly persued, and consent that; we or our kingdom be subjected to the king or people of England. **We** will immediately endeavour or expel him as our enemy, and as the subverters both of his own and our rights, and will make another king, who will defend our liberties". (3-66)**(Emphasis added)***

It simply means as long as Templars were favoured and free to carry on their activities, Bruce was a king. If he becomes a threat like Philippe of France, he would be expelled. This document speaks in favour of the public and illustrates the power of the public. Whereas; the public was not even aware of its existence, until it was necessary to make it public for the interest of the elite group. This declaration; was signed on behalf of the public, without the public's knowledge, by eight Earls and thirty-six other Nobles. Noticeable is the word "**We**", who did this "We" represent and who does this "We" represent? **The first parliament in the modern history of peoples freedom was enforced not elected and is still not elected.** This parliament was also called "**Round Table".** We don't have to be extra intelligent to understand that who were "We" and who was sitting on the **corner of this "Round Table".**

Templars became very expert and experienced to deceive the general public. They began to hide behind different names and myths, one after the other, names, signs, societies. "Skull & Bones Society" was formed which was another name for the same people to spread confusion and maintain secrecy. This **"Skull & Bones Society"** still exists and has presidents and ministers as members. George Bush and Bill Clinton are the fresh flesh on the old Templar's **Skulls & Bones.**

In the early 19th century, King Robert The Bruce's grave was dug open and bones of his legs were found carefully crossed immediately under his skull. This is not the only evidence, of Templars presence in Scotland; there are other graves still in Argyll, Scotland with Templars monograms and swords engraved on them. With no other historic evidence of Templars migration to Scotland, this is the only plug that fit's the socket.

TEMPLARS' LAND

After the Church's allegations of blasphemy and homosexuality on the Templars a general hatred grew among the public and governments started confiscating Templars' properties. While Templars' properties were being confiscated all over the Europe, actual story was different. All these properties were in fact conferred to their apparent rivals, "The Hospittelars", who are called by the late historians, "the trusties of Templars properties". These lands and hamlets were given back to the Templars one by one on their demand, reluctantly or promptly. Why were these lands given to Hospittelars on the first place any way? Logically these should be included into relative government's ownership if not publicly auctioned.

In fact, Hospittelars were another shield used by the Brotherhood just to confuse people; apparently rivals on the general level, yet absolutely one on the elite level. Another case of grasping both sides to monitor the results. Can you imagine when you go to vote and there are two big political parties raising slogans against each other, insinuating rival leaders, yet when you look closely there is no big difference between their mottoes. This is called freedom of choice, freedom to chose between two heirarchical leaderships, which are in place since generations. This is freedom---this is **Democracy** or any other electing system. Any poor man cannot stand for elections unless he is financially supported by any big fish and taking money from these filthy rich resources means to bow down to their demands, to say yes Sir. It is going on in every country, in every Muslim country when the public raise voices for freedom and Democracy they are actually asking to enslave themselves with their own hands. They don't know that the elected Mayor has no part in policy making, the **Cabinet is not elected---it is selected.** Yes it is selected or recommended by already Cabinet Ministers, these cabinet Ministers who are there to make sure that new comers are no strangers to their ideology and if they are, then they are not recommended, simple as that.

This freedom of choice was---and is used by Templars to fool the public, to make sure people are satisfied with the right to question the government. Yet government... sorry, the **selected group** carries on making policies to their own benefit, in fact to their financier's benefit. They never lose; they are never in debts. The famous poems written in 1843 and a quote in 1896 by Seton (a genealogist) convey the same message:

"But the Templars felt no loss".

Why would they lose if they control every source of information? Their enormous amount of wealth is a tool used by them to manipulate the history. These transfers of lands are excellent examples showing Templars control on information. When these incidents were taking place, these should have been headlines in the news but never mind the news---even history is totally silent in this regard! It is only until the late research found out that only in Scotland, altogether 579 properties were held by the Templars and only now this record is in the National Library of Scotland!!

We must know that this is not the only case of manipulating history and records, rather this happened everywhere, in England, Scotland, the European continent and all parts of the world where ever Colonial influence (or should we say Templars) have been. Let it be Turkey, Africa, Arab or the Indian sub-continent:

"Freemasonry, the teachings and practices of the secret fraternal order of Free and Accepted Masons, the largest worldwide secret society. Spread by the advance of the British Empire, Freemasonry remains most popular in the British Isles and in other countries originally within the empire." (Britannica Micropaedia)

Still pupils in the schools read their national history, written by western scholars. Normally this is thought that Western historians are radical and portray a fair picture of incidents, I found it altogether a whole load of nonsense. We should feel sorry for our children who read about Islam and Islamic history written by these biased writers. Only now when ancient documents are approachable, can we find some filtered truth. Still you will find very limited research available in the market, done by Muslim scholars. Because the Brotherhood still dominates the information market. They realised this long ago that, the best way to enslave a people is not to fetter or chain their limbs but to **Control their Minds.** Feed them the false news from all sources and they will believe it. We always think, "they are all saying it, it must be true". Not realising that it is only one source behind all these channels. The matters they don't want us to know; they keep silent about them. As the saying goes, "**No news is good news".**

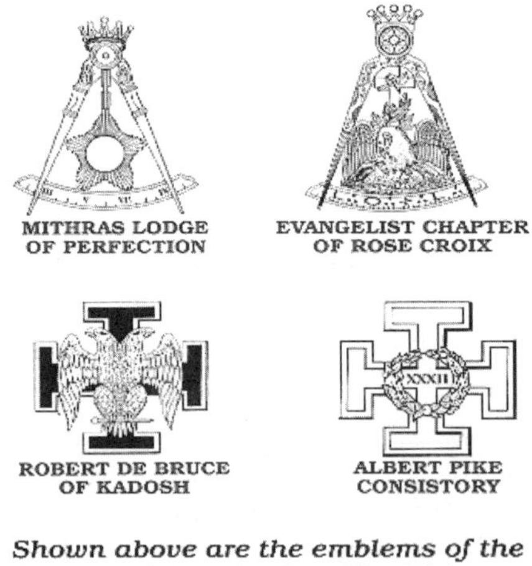

Shown above are the emblems of the four coordinate bodies. The Mithras Lodge of Perfection No. 2 was chartered in 1870, Evangelist Chapter of Rose Croix in 1872; Robert de Bruce Council of Kadosh in 1874; and Albert Pike Consistory in 1876.

CH-4 TEMPLARS' AMERICA

The success of Battle of Bannockburn gave Templars or Skull & Bones society a home, a country. With no threat to their activities they could sit back and carefully plan ahead. If Templars were ordinary people, they should have been content with what they had but just Scotland did not fulfil their greed. Their eyes were set on the whole world.

During this time Templars had guised themselves under various names and societies like, Round Table, Skull & Bone, Scottish Guards, Black Nobility and Hospittelars. England had remained no threat to them and finally they had formed their basis in English Monarchy within less than fifty years. More they expanded----more land was required. With a vast experience of navigation and sea knowledge, they knew where to look for it. The noble signatories (**We**) of the Declaration of Arbroath had amongst them, Sinclair, Seton and Montgomery, which appear in future history on prominent occasions.

"When the Scottish lodges decided to elect a Grand Lodge to administer them, they went back to their traditional loyalty and agreed that Sir William Sinclair of Roslin was their hereditary Grand Master. He was a direct male line descendent of the Lord William St Clair who had built Rosslyn [Roslyn Chapel]*". (19-76)*

Ros: A noun meaning "knowledge".
Linn: A noun meaning "generation".

Amongst the others were the immigrants from France such as Stuart, Hamilton, Hay, Cunningham and Cockburn. Under the title of "Scottish Guards" all these people and other Templars re-united (or more accurately, we should say pre-planned) to adopt a new title.

COLUMBUS'S STORY

We all are familiar with the world known phrase that " Columbus was looking for another route to India and accidentally discovered America". What an accident! Do we really believe it?

Well, the first thing is that if this land was invented by Columbus, then how come people, the so-called "Red Indians", already populated it? The actual Americans! They were there first and living for centuries. They had their own calendar, culture, language and religions. In this case how is it not possible that not even a single person in the whole world knew about the "Land of Freedom".

In fact many explorers had been there prior to Columbus. In 1395, Sir Henry Sinclair the Earl of Orkney, with Antonio Zeno (a very active member of Black Nobility) reached **"Greenland"**. Zeno's explorer brother had already been there in 1391, only four years before them. One hundred years before Christopher Columbus (real name Colon) who also was a Templar. Columbus had flags of Red Cross in white background on his ships when he officially sailed to find America, a sign of Templars!

"Order of the Knights of the Red Cross of Babylon". (19-66)

What was this **Greenland** and where was it?

" In 'Massachusetts' at a place called 'Prospect Hill' in 'Westford', 25miles from 'Boston', a representation of a sword and an armoured Knight has been found in the rock. T C Lethbridge, the curator of the 'University Museum of Archaeology and Ethology' at Cambridge, England said that the arms, armour and heraldic emblems were those of a late century knight, north Scottish and a "kin to the first Sinclair, Earl of Orkney". (5-179)

John Cabot, an Italian explorer, set off from the port of Bristol, England to discover Asia five years after Columbus' discovery. Bristol was the centre of Templars activities. Cabot's journey to Asia ended finding North America. What a series of accidental journeys. Apparently there was no link between Columbus and Cabot but "Givonni Caboto" (Cabot's real name) comes from Genoa, the very city where Columbus operated, from!

Manly P Hall, a high degree Freemason himself says: "They were both connected with the same secret societies". In his book "America's Assignment with Destiny" he writes,

"The explorers, who opened New World, operated from a master plan and were agents of a re-discovery rather than discoverers". (5-180)

Twenty years later in 1519 another Spanish explorer Hernando Cortes, takes over Central America with only 580 men. The natives of Central America were waiting for the second coming of a Messiah or white god called "Quetzalcoatl", who was heralded by another white god who preceded him. How long ago? We don't know because Americans had their own calendar.

Cortes ashored at the predicted spot and time of "Quetzalcoatl"---fitted the description with blue eyes and blond hair, wearing foretold dress and even nicknamed as "Plumed Serpent", already predicted by his herald.

Natives had no doubts in believing their "white god". When the Aztec king, "Montezuma" realised the fiddle, it was too late. They had lost all their power to their "white gods". According to one Spanish historian, estimated 12 millions natives of South America alone were killed and even more were enslaved, after Europeans arrived.

Twenty years after Columbus, an Ottoman Turkish Admiral, "Piri Reis", drew a map of what the landmass of Antarctica looked like 300 years before it was officially discovered. Piri Reis actually copied this map from an ancient map he had an access to. The authenticity of Piri's map has been confirmed by modern techniques.

Ericcson Leif was a Norse explorer, he traditionally sailed from Greenland (Denmark) in 1000 AD to find a country which was first sighted by one of his predecessors in 986 AD This country was no other than America. He landed in North America and named it "Vinland" because he found grapevines growing and spent a whole winter there along with his 35 companions who accompanied him in the journey.

"Ericcson leif's story was confirmed in 1963 when a Norwegian expedition led by Helge Ingstad discovered remains of a Viking settlement (dated C 1000) near the fishing village of L' Anse-aux-Meadows, at the northern tip of 'Newfoundland'. Eric Thered, the alleged discoverer of Greenland. According to a 13th century saga, he was the sun of a Norwegian chieftain, was banished from Iceland c 982 for homicide, sailed westward and discovered a land, which he called Greenland". (The New Hutchinson 20th Century Encyclopaedia-Ericcson)

What we find out is that the world already knew about America but opportunists were the Templars, they knew what to do with her, they waited for the right time when they could hold power over her. Finally when the time was right, they actually announced America. Columbus was just an icon used to open a long planned game.

It took them nearly 80 years to clear up the "native mess" to introduce "Freedom" and "Knowledge". Christianity was to be the religion of that "Freeland" and any one opposed the law of the Freeland was to be crucified. Paganism or idol worshipping was strictly forbidden, any one caught worshipping local idol was prosecuted and hung. The only idol allowed to be worshipped; was that of Jesus Christ's. Locals were so terrified that they shifted their altars and built their temples in hidden places out side the towns.

FIRST STATE OF USA

In the early 17th century, at Jamestown, Virginia the first English settlement was founded. This town Virginia was said to be named after Queen Elizabeth the 1st.

"It has one of the longest continues histories among the American states, dating from the settlement of Jamestown in 1607. It was named for Elizabeth I, the virgin Queen..." (16)

There is a difference between "not getting married" and "deciding to stay virgin". Elizabeth did not decide to stay a spinster, rather she did not find a suitable match as Queen of England. Philip II of Spain, Archduke of Austria and Erik XIV king of Sweden, were among many of her candidates.

"Many scholars think it unlikely that Elizabeth ever seriously intended to marry any of these aspirants to her hand, for the dangers always outweighed the possible benefits, but she skilfully played one off against another and kept the marriage negotiations going for months, even years, at one moment seeming on the brink of acceptance, at the next veering away toward vows of perpetual virginity". (16)

Describing her English suitors:

"Most assiduously by her principle favourite, Robert Dudley, Earl of Leicester. As master of the horse and a member of the Privy Council, Leicester was constantly in attendance on the queen, who displayed toward him all the signs of an ardent romantic attachment". (16)

So, according to Modern English language she was a "Flirt", and inappropriate for the name and symbol of "virgin". In fact this title "virgin" has nothing to do with Queen Elizabeth, nothing to do with even Christianity. This title goes back to Babylonian, Nimar and Pharaoh's time. In human history many tyrants and kings have claimed to be "gods". Question arises when these so-called "gods"---die! According to Allah's word:

"Every living soul has to taste death".

If even "gods" die, where do they go? Who takes their lives away and collects their souls? Who runs the world when they are dead or in the womb? To answer these questions, the philosophy of "re-incarnation" was introduced. These allusions comply with the self-created images of desired gods but only for the people who are induced or who want to choose a god that fits their desires. To have a selected god does not mean that one is worshipping the "Actual Deity" rather one affirms, "worshipping his own desires" in shape of a self-encarved statue.

This ideology of re-incarnation made a difference between "ordinary human beings" and "god human beings". This baseless faith raised another question, if god was created by a human being i.e., father then what is the difference between an ordinary human and a god human's birth? This vital question was the basic factor that introduced the necessity of a virgin mother. This concept goes back to ancient religions times and later was introduced to Christianity.

A virgin mother is actually married to her husband but the first son (the first born) is not of her husband's but of a god or the spirit of god. This is the root of "Trinity". "The god, the son, and the holy-spirit"--- never mind about the vital donation of mother baring the child for nine months.

Trinity was introduced, rather, forced upon Christianity in the time of "Constantine". In 324AD the Roman emperor "Constantine" who selected the ancient city of

"Byzantium" as the site of his new capital, which he later named "Constantinople". "The New Catholic Encyclopaedia", in vol 14, p.295 describes Trinity as:

"...One should not speak of Trinitarianism in the New Testament without serious qualifications. There is also the closely parallel recognition on the part of historians of dogma and systematic theologians that when one does speak of an unqualified Trinitarianism, one has moved from the period of Christian origins to, say, the last quadrant of the 4th century. It was only then that what might be called the definitive Trinitarian dogma 'One God in Three Persons' became thoroughly assimilated into Christian life and thought...It was the product of 3 centuries of doctrinal development". (A quote from "What did Jesus really say? By Mishal ibn Abdullah")

In 325AD, the council of Nicea was held. Christians in need of a strong back up had to accommodate with pagan Romans, so they adopted the idea of Trinity from them on condition that Romans will call themselves Christians and free to carry on practicing Trinity. All conanical Gospels from before this period were destroyed. A new list of acceptable Gospels was drawn up. With different alterations on different occasions the present Bible is printed, that we know as, the New Testament with Trinitarianism (Although there is no explicit evidence of Trinity in present Bible as well).

The name Virginia not only had this Trinitarian back ground but behind this was a corporation called "Virginia Company" which was formed in 1604 in Greenwich, England. This company was founded by then leading bankers, politicians, businessmen, manufacturers and merchants (in simple words Templars). The original charter of the company was completed on 10th April 1606 and updated later. King James the 1st was the main stockholder of the company a Templar himself:

"...The Freemason king, James VI of Scotland, succeeded Queen Elizabeth to become James I of England". (19-68)

We will explain the connection between Freemasons and Templars in later chapter. The Virginia Company consisted upon two branches. The London Company and the Plymouth or New England Company. The latter arrived at Cape Cod (USA) in the ship, then Mayflower in November 1620 and went on to land on Plymouth Harbour on December 21st. They were the so-called "Pilgrim Fathers" and this is the myth behind the Pilgrims of American history. They were actually members of New England Company. According to "Virginia Company's" charter:

"Virginia Company owned any lands upto 900 miles off shore in USA.
Virginia Company had rights to 50% of all the gold and silver, mined on its land.
After the 21st year from the formation of V. Company, all duties, excise and imports were directly to be paid to British Crown through Crown treasurer.
All ownership of the Freeland was retained by British Crown and was only to be leased to the colonies, under a "Deed of Trust".
The colonial lands were to be governed by two colonial councils each with 13 members, but the Kings Council in London had the final say. The sitting British King also chose the Governor of the American colonies, who we would today call the President
The monarch, through his council, insisted that the members of the colonies impose the Christian religion on all the people. (As we have explained before)
The criminal courts on the lands of the Virginia Company were to be operated under Admirately Law, the law of the sea, and the civil courts under common law."
(5-188/189)

We still can see the signs of this Admirately Law, Maritime Law or British Law in every Criminal Court and many official buildings, yes...the "Gold Fringe" is their sign! USA is still under British Law. The above rules still apply today, even after the "War of Independence". Actually this war of independence was a change of policy, not of the controlling hands. It was a change from an overt control to a covert control, as we shall see further, Insha Allah.

Vicar Of Christ "Claims" Dominion

Pope as a vicar of the Christ claimed a dominion over the world. On 3rd October 1213 "King John" as "King of England Corporation Sole", claimed autonomy over all the sovereign rights of England and assigned them to the Pope. In return, Pope granted executiveship to the English Crown over all the dominions. In other words the Crown is the chief executive and the Vatican is the real owner.

We shall discuss "American War of Independence" in a later chapter because it is still a century and a half away. In the mean time we will concentrate on other contributions of Templars around the continent and abroad and emergence of a new order combined with a mythical organization.

Masonic Temple, Northwest Corner Ninth and F Streets, N. W.
Home of the Grand Lodge and a majority of the subordinate Lodges from 1870 to 1908.

Temple of Scottish Rite Freemasonry 1007 G Street Washington 1870 Through 1908

Cathedral Of The Ancient And Accepted Scottish Rite
Third and E Streets N.W.

Temple of Scottish Rite Freemasonry 433 Third Street Washington 1909 through 1940

CH-5 FREEMASONS

"There will be a special group who will pave the way for Al-Masih Ad-Dajjal (The Anti Christ)". (Tarjuman Al Sunnah. Vol 3, p-587)

ROSICRUCIANS

The order "Rosicrucian" started in Germany, when a man called "Rosenkreuze", a possible Christian or may be a Jew, traveled to "Holy Land" in around 1393 to collect the legends of Biblical myths. He returned to Germany in 1402 and many disciples gathered around him to learn his mythical research. Rosenkreuze died in 1484 at least at the age of 111 years. A legend tells about his preserved corps in a secret vault with an everburning magical lamp. In Rosicrucian's myths this story is described as "He, who was taken to a secret vault".

Other scholars believe that this "Fraternity" actually developed after the publication of the "Fama Fraternitatis and the Confessio Rosae Crucis" (1614, 1615; The Fame and Confession of the Fraternity of the Rosy Cross; translated in 1652). These pamphlets record a journey to the Orient made by Rosenkreuz. In the USA there are still two orders of this society, and these both, claim to belong to the ancient Order. One is the "Rosicrucian Fraternity" with their known headquarters in San Jose, California. Other is the "Ancient Mystical Order Rosae Crucis", usually abbreviated AMORC and their known international headquarter is in Quakertown, Pennsylvania.

"*These both groups hold that the order been in remote antiquity in Egypt and continued in existence through periods of deliberate secrecy. Rosicrucian teachings combine elements of Egyptian Hermetism, Gnosticism, Jewish Cabalism (Kaballa) and other occult beliefs and practices". (Encyclopaedia Encarta 96)*

The symbol of the Rosicrucians is a combination of the rose and the cross, from which the Order takes its name. This society also believed in transmutation of metal into gold. This cult: is described by the Muslim scholar "Ibne-Kathir", as "a group of Jews who believed in such transmutation". This society said to devote her for the search of truth; its members included philosophers, artists and most prominently, Chemists. These are the "Chemists", known as Al-Chemists" in history zone.

MASONS

When the name Templars, became infamous, Templars needed to adopt some new identity, which should be absolutely irrelevant to their prior field and expertise, yet give them all the freedom to move around unsuspected. Some thing that could shelter their secrecy. What could be better than adopting the name Masons? This could give them freedom to carry their affairs not only in privacy but provided a reason for this privacy in shape of Mason's secrecy about their hierarchy trade secrets, which they always used to hide from non masons. But how could someone be a Mason when he doesn't know any thing about masonry? For this reason the term **"Speculative Mason"** was introduced which, with the time converted into **"Freemason",** meaning a Mason that does not have to have skills. When exactly it happened is a question hidden behind many myths but we can still have an answer.

ELIAS ASHMOL

In the town of Lichfield, England, Elias Ashmole was born in the year of 1617. His father was a soldier and a saddler. First Ashmol joined Lichfield Cathedral but moved down to London afterwards. There he studied Law and became a solicitor at the age of 21. Later he joined the "Brasenose College of Oxford" and made a sound career. In London he became friendly with three most famous astrologers of that time, Moor, Lilly and Booker. This friendship built his interest in astrology and later he even wrote few books on the subject. This was his introduction to Rosicrucians. This was the time when Templars had already adopted the name "Freemasons" and were active on a different scale than Rosicrucians. Besides the Modern Freemasons deny any claims of their existence prior to their actual announcement but Elias Ashmole left a proof, which they could not deny.

Ashmole was in a habit of writing diary not consistently but enough to leave a proof for historians. In his diary on Oct 16 1646, he writes,

"4.H.30: PM. I was made a freemason at Warrington in Lancashire with Col, Henry Main Waring of Karincham in Cheshire. The names of those That were of the Lodge: Mr Rich: Penket Warden, Mr Janes Colleir, Mr Rich: Sankey, Henry Litter, John Ellam, Rich: Ellam and Hugh Brewer".

Another note of 1682, nearly 30 years after records: March 10 and 11.

"About 5 H.PM. I received a summon to appear at the Lodge to be held at the next day, at Mason Hall London..."

And then he carries on to describe how; new accepted Masons treated them with a dinner at Half Moon Tavern in Cheapside.

He really gave the game away, didn't he? This was the proof that Freemasonry existed well before 1646, and was active on full scale; they had their ranks and posts, (the Degrees) and offices (lodges), as we shall see in next chapter Inshallah. Free masons had no choice but to accept the fact that Ashmole was a Freemason, so he is listed as the *"First Speculative Mason"* in their book (2-226).

At this point we realise the fact that Ashmole joined Freemasonry in 1646 and the pamphlet "Fama Fraternitatis and the Confessio Rosae Crucis" was translated in 1652. This forms a strong base to the idea that "Ash-mole" was one of the responsible people to bring "Rosicrucians" and "Freemasons" together. This blend of two societies was the substance, later to be shaped into "Modern Freemasonry". Other evidence comes from other Freemasons of high degree, "Christopher Knight" and "Robert Lomas"; both Freemasons and recognised historians of Fraternity revealed in 1997 that; "Templars" and "Freemasons" are two sides of the same coin. They also revealed about the Scottish and British that:

"The two crowns had been combined in 1603 when the Freemason king, James VI, of Scotland, succeeded Queen Elizabeth to become James I of England...Freemasonry had first come to London at least as early as in 1603 with James VI". (19-68,71)

When "Ash-mole" was accepted as a Freemason he was given all prosperities. Charles the 2nd, a Rosicrucian, was deeply interested in Al-Chemy. In his first appointment as restored king he appointed Ashmole as "Windsor Herald". Numerous other offices were given to him in short time. In 16th and 17th centuries many organisations and brotherhoods joined together that shared some magical or mythical interests. Another vital link between Rosicrucians, Templars and/or Freemasons was James VI of Scotland, who succeeded Elizabeth the 1st and became James the 1st of England. This was the real amalgam of high breed societies.

Another name Rosicrucians used was**"Invisible College"**, which begun in 1648, just after two years Ashmole joined Freemasonry. The members of this college held their meetings in Oxford. Invisible College subsequently formed the **"Royal Society"**, which is the mother society of other societies like, **"Royal Society of Arts"**, and **"Royal Society of Science".**

ESTABLISHMENT OF THE MODERN FREEMASONRY

The "Freemasonry" as we know it now and Masonic writers accept as "Modern Freemasonry" was established on papers in 1723 in London. This is called the "First Constitution". Beside the official document shows the actual foundation took place in 1723, does not deny the fact that, unofficially its mottoes and postulates were agreed upon since a long time.

"The engraved list of 1725 shows the total number of Lodges was 64. Of these Lodges 50 were in London (modern Central London) and others were in Edgworth, Acton, Richmond, Bath, Bristol, Norwich, Chichester, Chester, Fulham, Greenwich, Branford and Reading". (1-72)

According to Freemasons own history.

"The one fixed point in the early history of Freemasonry is 24 June 1717, (The Feast of St John the Baptist). This was the day when four previously established London Lodges met together to constitute the 'Grand Lodge of England'". (2-13)

"With the founding of the 'Premier Grand Lodge', on 24th June 1717, Organised Freemasonry was born". (2-27)

As we find out from this "Brotherhood" existed prior to the establishment of the "Premier Grand Lodge", how long ago, is behind countless myths and legends according to their record-keeper,

"London had a strong Freemason and Mason Company. There is evidence of It before 1376, but how far long it had been in existence we do not know" (1-70).

Rendle Holme was author of a book called "Academy of Armory", published in 1688, a scrap of paper in his own handwriting notes,

"There is sure all words and signs of a Free Mason to be revailed to you, which as you will answer: before God at the Great and Terrible day of Judgement, you keep secret and not revail the same to any in the heares of any person but to the Masters and Fellows of the said society of Free Masons so help me God".

According to the British Museum authorities this scrap was written in 1640-50.

In Freemasons' own book, explaining about their history they claim;

"*But the traditional history goes back even further, to the Biblical Patriarchs (notably Noah and Moses) and then (by way of Nineveh, Egypt and worthy Clarke Euclid) to King Solomon and the building of the Temple of Jerusalem". (2-13)*

Dr Dodd, Grand Chaplain of Masonry, in his oration at the dedication of Freemason's Hall, London, traces Masonry through different stages.

"Masons, are well informed from their own private and interior records that the building of Solomon's Temple is an important era, from whence they derive many mysteries of their art. Now be it remembered that this great event took place above 1000 years before the Christian era and consequently more then a century before Homer, the first of the Grecian Poets, wrote; and above five centuries before Pythagoras brought from the East his sublime system of truly Masonic instruction to illuminate our Western world.... We trace its footsteps in the most distant, the most remote ages and nations of the world. We find it among the first and most celebrated civilizers of the East. We deduce it regularly from the first astronomers of the plains of Chaldea, to the wise and mystic kings and priests of Egypt, the sages of Greece and the Philosophers of Rome". (Origin of Freemasonry. Thomas Paine)

Also Thomas Pains in his "Origin of Freemasonry" proves from these reports and declarations of Masons of the highest order in the institution that:

"Masonry is derived and is remains of the religion of the ancient 'Druids'; who like the Magi of Persia and the priests of Heliopolis in Egypt, were priests of the Sun.

They paid worship to this great luminary, as the great visible agent of a great invisible first cause whom they styled 'Time without limits'".

This helps us to establish a fact that:

Anas ibn Malik said, "The Prophet (SAW) said, 'there has never been a Prophet who did not warn his people against that one-eyed liar'. (Ad-Dajjal, The Antichrist)." (Muslim, Bukhari)

No doubt the words of Prophet Mohammad (SAW) are true and like the choronics of the prophets have reached us and a true Muslim follows them, "Kuffar" are aware of "Dajjal" and follow his system. We can also establish the fact that as the gospel of "Dajjal (The Anti Christ)" existed, so existed in some form: the order and means that will be used to establish his rule. This must have been in shape of documentation. Taking in account, the confiscation of the 'Dome of Rock' and Templars excavation this is clear that they did find something from there.

"We had speculated that the Templars may have found a cache of writings which changed their world-view and in an attempt to find out what they had found we had looked into a collection of early writings collectively known as the "Gnostic gospels". We conclude that the concept of 'gnosis' (knowledge) is the opposite of the church's concept of 'faith' and that it is a type of thought process that fits well with 'Freemasonry'". (9-55)

A few questions arise at this point, if Freemasonry existed long time ago, why no one other than Freemasons knew about them? How could they survive amongst people without being pointed out? Were they practicing the same rituals and had the same Satanic practices as Templars had, when they were accused in 1307? Or was this a totally different Order? The answer is in the scrap of paper mentioned above and in a leaflet published in 1698 in London, calling Freemasonry a:

" Devilish sect of men, Anti Christ, Evil doers, Corrupt people. It is need full to warn all godly people in the city of London of the mischiefs and evils practiced in the sight of God by those called Freemasons. I say take care lest their Ceremonies and secret swearings take hold of you; and be wary that none causes you to err from Godliness". (1-114)

Says it all doesn't?

GREAT FIRE OF LONDON

After Rosicrucians and Templars/Freemasons merger, and USA near enough under their control, they needed a base, which could provide for their headquarters and as a centre of the world affairs. In other words slowly stepping towards "One World Government" or "New World Order". For this reason, London was the most suitable place for them, a homeland with English monarchy under their thumbs and also easily accessible from other continents. So followed the **"Great Fire of London".** It is said that it started, in a bakery on Pudding Lane on 2nd Sep 1666 and burnt most of what now is the City area of London. We can imagine how cheap were the uninsured burnt properties after the fire. Who else could avail this opportunity and buy these burnt properties, other than the people who knew what to do with the future's "Richest Square Mile" on earth. Yes it is "City of London" which has this title, beside all Shaikhs of Middle East, and Queen's extra-ordinary treasure, it is City of London that issues the rate of gold every evening.

The modern "City of London" was planned and built, not by Masons but Freemasons. Sir Christopher Wren, the main architect of the "City of London" was a high initiate of the Brotherhood.

EXPANSION OF MASONRY

The "Grand Lodge of London" was followed by masonic expansion around the world. First of all they founded "Grand Lodges" in different countries and continents and then invited local masons to join in with them. It served them two purposes. First; automatic expansion and second; a shelter for their actual activities. There is no harm having countless members in a political party as long as the real agenda is not exposed to them. In other words they shouldn't know, what they are being used for.

"Scottish Grand Lodge" followed 13 years later in 1736, after the Grand Lodge of London was founded. Invitations were issued to about 100 lodges (local mason's lodges that perhaps had nothing to do with Freemasonry), 33 responded. This was probably the first chain of trade formed, which we see today in forms of big chains of super markets and food chains like Mc Donald's, Shell and Tesco. As it is hard today for a little food store to survive next door to "Tesco", must have been very hard for little lodges next to a "Grand Lodge".

"By 1728/29, lodges were founded in Madrid, Gibraltar and Bengal, all three are now extinct" (1-79,80)

"Military Lodges" were founded in the same era with a view to conquer the world and bring "One World Government". Cadwallader the 9th Lord Blaney was "Grand Master" and a soldier from a "Military Lodge", his ambitions were:

"To erect 'English Grand Lodge' as the supreme masonic authority in the world" (1-208).

"He constituted 74 lodges, of which nineteen are alive even today, all baring honoured names" (1-209).

These "Military Lodges" played a vital part in British rule over the world and dismantling the "Ottoman Empire", as we shall see in the due chapter Inshallah. We can tally another fact that, this was the time when organisations like "East India Company", "East Africa Company" were establishing their rule in the continents by the famous slogan "divide and rule". These companies were; another veil used by Freemasons to generate their influence. Wherever these companies went, along went Freemasonry; rather, Freemasonry took these companies wherever she went, as we see in case of "Bengal Lodge".

Temple of Scottish Rite Freemasonry 2800 Sixteenth Street NW, Washington. From 1940 through the present time

CH-6 RIGHTS, SIGNS AND RITUALS

INITIATION

Like any other organisation, Freemasonry has got its grades; these grades or ranks are called **"Degrees"**. This organisation is designed in pyramid shape. This pyramid shape is carefully selected to be aware of lower degrees and hide the higher degrees from them. It has got two rites **"Scottish Rite"** and **"American Rite"**. Scottish Rite consists of three degrees, lowest degree is **"Entered Apprentice"**, this is the degree for new people, and from here, their ambitions and thoughts are observed and if they comply with masonic ideas, they are promoted. **"Fellow Craft "** is the promotion they get and the highest rank they can reach is **"Master Mason"**. This is the ultimate progress an outsider can achieve.

On the first two stages or degrees Masons are not revealed any "Secrets" of Fraternity. They are not even members of real masonry. To join into the Masonry, one has to be **initiated**, that is if one goes above the first two degrees and made a "Master Mason", which is very rare in case of a normal member other than special hierarchy (with a few exceptions). American rite has 33 degrees as compared to Scottish other rules are more or less the same. On the top of the pyramid is the **ALL-SEEING EYE! The eye of the Masonic Lord!**

The sign that our Prophet Mohammad (PBUH) told us of "Al-Masih Ad-DAJJAL (THE ANTICHRIST)" is that he will be One-eyed! This is how the "Top level Masonry" is always aware of their subordinate's actions. The "All-seeing-eye" is ever so watchful from the top of the **"Pyramid".** In fact this "Elite Freemasonry" is the actual masonry, the lower you are in degree, less is the awareness. These lower levels are only smoke screens to hide the "Elite's" strategy, only a mist! On lower levels, a lot of charity work is carried out to hide the evil in good.

"THE EYE"

A close look on the present events can reveal all that is happening. The sign of the **eye** is displayed everywhere, let it be bill posts, neon signs, Newspapers, films all TV (Including English and Asian) channels. On BBC1 a program called "A Tribute to Michael Caine" was shown, on 18-12-2000. "The Eye" was permanently displayed on the background screen for TV Clips. Even the shield of Knighthood, presented to Michael was a mask, with "One Eye", although Knighthood itself is actually an announcement of a Freemason's promotion to Master Mason. These things are not just a routine! This is a carefully monitored mass manipulation style to capture your sub-conscience. When the time comes and you see the actual "One-Eye", you will be familiar with it thus not resistant or repelled by it due to being "used to" it over the days.

Even the children's schools are being used as an introduction for "One-Eye". The "Computer Graphic Design" on their computer screen shows logo of "One-Eye".

If you start spotting "One-eye"---you will find it everywhere relevant or irrelevant to the advertisement's subject or topic even on the cotton-buds packets. All these advertisers are knowingly or unknowingly being used for Ad-Dajjal. Start spotting the eye---now---and you will know what I am talking about!

JEWISH INFLUENCE

Usually any Freemason will deny any Jewish influence on Freemasonry but there are enough evidences to strengthen this claim.

"Biblical reference can be given that there is strong Jewish influence in the traditional preparation of a masonic candidate. Mackey quotes the Talmudic Baracoth, which insists that 'no man shall go in the Temple with his staff, nor with his shoes on his feet, nor with his outer garment, nor with money tied up in his purse'". (1-266)

Further he quotes that:

"Slipshodness [bare-foot-ness] *is usually associated with two ancient Jewish traditions, the one providing the suggestion that the slipshod condition is a gesture of reverence and the other is the confirmation of a covenant". (1-268)*

Freemasonry is proud of its architecture and the buildings erected by their masons. Statue of Liberty, City of London, White House and whole cities built by them are taken as a credit to Freemasonry. Their slipshodness and architecture is described precisely in a Hadith as one of the signs of Qayamah:

"...The bare-footed and naked paupers will compete with one another in constructing high buildings..." (20-92)

Although bare-footed and naked paupers, making high buildings is not to be taken literally, but the exactness of the literal meanings cannot be ignored as well.

The covenant being talked about in the above-mentioned quote is the covenant between Moses (PBOH) and God (SWT), when according to Qur'an, Moses (PBUH) was told to take his shoes off on Kohe-Tur. From here we can detect the influence of the Jews on Freemasonry. With Jewish myths, traditions and rituals the fact cannot be ignored that Freemasonry, was, is and will remain a Jewish formation.

When Gabriel (AS) came to the Prophet (PBUH) in the guise of a Bedouin, and asked him about Islam, Iman and Ihsan; the Prophet (PBUH) answered his questions. But when he asked him about the Hour, he (PBUH) said:

"...The one questioned about it, knows no better than the questioner, but I will describe to you its portents. When the lady slave gives birth to her mistress, that will be of its portents; when the ***bare-footed*** *naked people become the chiefs of the people, that will be of its portents." (Sahih Al-Bukhari 6.300 narrated by Abu Hurayra)*

This thing is widely understood that "Jews own America" but who is using their title is not understood, and that understanding is our aim Inshallah.

OATHS OF SECRECY

With the time, ways to take an oath have been varied, sometimes the candidate had to hold his right hand up and sometimes his hand was on the book, which was different in case of different religions i.e., Bible, Torah, and Qur'an, whereas one object has been the same. The actual motive of **"Secrecy"** has never changed.

"The Grand Lodge MS. No. 2 (dated about 1650), contains the following oaths of secrecy:

'I, A.B, do in the presence of Almighty God and many fellows and brethren, here present, promise and declare, that I will not at any time hereafter by any act or circumstance, whatsoever, directly, or indirectly publish, discover or reveal or make known any of the secrets, privileges or counsels of the Fraternity or Fellowship of Freemasonry which at any time hereafter shall be made known to me. So help me God and the holy contents of this book'" (1-276) [To find out about their Almighty God please see "Jahbulon" Ch-7 "Solomon (PBUH) and Hiram Abif in Qur'an"]

Some times people deny the fact that Masonic society is surviving even after so many centuries and what is the explanation for their survival? Beside all these facts and proofs this seems very fictitious. Yes---that is true---no one can be so consistent and farsighted to plan for centuries to come. After all the secrecy he keeps and struggles for in his life, is not going to benefit him. Before all his efforts are rewarded and world becomes the way he want's it to be, he knows he is going to die, no one has lived enough to benefit from it. So, on what hope he carries on doing what he is. There are quite a few aspects to the answer; we will spotlight just a couple.

We all know that we can die any moment, yet we keep planing for years in a false hope, a hope to live and to achieve all targets in our lifetime. In the western countries when someone buys a house he borrows money from banks or building societies, in the form of a mortgage, which usually he has to repay over a time period of 25 years. He has no surety: that he will live long enough to live in a fully paid house, still he has hopes. In fact he has no assurity to live enough to pay the first monthly mortgage instalment or even be able to move into the house. This uncertainty does not stop him buying a house.

Secondly, how could Freemasonry survive generations after generations? Could it not be possible that one of their generations was not so determined to the cause of "New World Order" and Freemasonry would have dissolved? The finest example we can portray is banks. Take any bank, Barclays', Chase Manhattan or any bank of any country. Banks don't dissolve with generation change; they are there for good. They may have a different policy with a new generation but the main body remains the same. Another example is of governments. When a new President or Prime Minister comes, this change does not affect the actual existence of the country, though it can cause a little misbalance to the economy or policy but the civil servants and their institutions remain the same.

Likewise, is the case of Freemasonry, being a corporation and not an individual effort its policy varies with new "Elite group" but the actual goal is the same, "One World Government". This dogma has its own followers, like any other religion of the world. As a matter of fact, this religion is more attractive for secular people than any other, because all the benefits of the world are there. Once you are a Freemason, doors of success and fame are opened to you; there is no chance you want to go back to poverty and being no one.

Guidance is only in the hands of Allah. He knows the minute intentions and rewards or punishes accordingly. This greed of worldly benefits blindfolds the new comers and they drown deeper and deeper into the darkness of glittering evils, till there is no way back. Here is a little example of this darkness in these questions and answers:

Q. Why was you hoodwinked?

A. That my heart might conceal or conceive, before my eyes could discover.

Q. The second reason, Brother?

A. As I was in darkness at that time, I should keep all the world in the Darkness.

(1-268)

This is the darkness they have in their hearts and this is the darkness they want to spread in the world. This is the kind of oaths we are dealing with and this is the calibre of secrecy they have to keep, otherwise "Friday the 13th" could come again. Fraternity has no choice, other than concealing the truth from "Cowans" (non-masons).

"The Slone MS No 3329 (date about 1700): gives an oath containing what is now a very familiar phrase: (to the present Freemasonry)

'The mason word and every thing therein contained, you shall keep secret; you shall never put it in writing directly or indirectly; you shall keep all that we or your attenders shall bid you keep secret from man woman or child, stock or stone and never reveal it but, to a brother, or in a Lodge of Freemasons, and truly observe the charges in your constitutions; all this you promise and swear faithfully to keep and

observe without any manner of equivocation or mental reservation directly or indirectly so help you God and by the contents of this book (the candidate kisses the book)'". (1-277)

PUNISHMENT TO BREAK THE OATH (THE WORD)

Beside all the oaths there must have been some people who must had not been able to keep up with the secrecy. What happened to them, in other words, was there some punishment to break the oath? A dialogue between Simon and Philip, dating back to 1730, or perhaps many years earlier explains:

"...My heart plucked from my left breast, my tong plucked from the roof of my mouth, my throat cut, my body to be torn into pieces by wild horses, to be bury'd in the sands of the sea where the tide flows in 24 hours, taken up and burnt to ashes and sifted where the four winds blow, that there may be no more remembrance of me. SO HELP ME GOD". (1-229)

This is not fiction; this is reality, this has been happening, any one who breaks the oath was and is punished. This does not happen very often because the "Actual Secret" is not revealed to any Tom, Dick and Harry, the actual secret is only with the elite group, and they are not likely to slit their own throat. Yet, some lower grade Freemasons have betrayed Fraternity and they are punished severely:

"1- A thief was punished by mutilation, his body in which there was still life, Being 'cast to the beasts of prey and the fowls of heaven'.
2- a murderer in old German days was punished by having his 'flesh and body' thrown to the beasts in the forest, the birds in the air, and the fishes in the sea." (1-279)

To say, these were thieves and murderers but are they going to announce that, these people were Freemasons and punished for breaking the oath? Verily not! This does not leave any reason for killing them in the first place. But resemblance in the "case of breaking the oath" and the actual punishment speaks for itself, its credibility increases when these incidents are reported by their own writers. This is the way to pass the message secretly to the masons and to conceal from non-mason.

What can be more explicit than admittance of the whole conclusion from not only a mason but from a "Grand Master" and member of "British Royal Family"!

"News In Brief:
Mason's Oath

Freemason will no longer have to face having their tongs cut out and their throats slit if they break their oaths.
The United Grand Lodge, the Society's governing body, said yesterday that it would remove reference to physical penalties in candidates' obligation.
The "Grand Master", the "Duke of Kent", has said that such references contributed to the society's reputation for the secrecy and idolatry".
(The Independent, 13 June 1986)

Although, the word "reference" is used, it does not and cannot diminish the fact that; these punishments did take place and were not always only references.

"In New York, in 1821, William Morgan, a Freemason, who threatened to publish "Masonic Secrets" was kidnapped and abducted by Freemasons.
A general outcry followed for a decade and many Masonic Lodges had to be abandoned throughout the eastern and middle states.
In the northern states, the "Anti-Masonic Party" was formed. For a few years it was practically the only opponent to the Democratic Party. In 1832, the Anti-Masonic Party nominated a lawyer, "William Writ", as its candidate for the presidency, but he

was defeated by "Andrew Jackson", who supported Freemasonry. Ironically, "William Writ" himself was a Mason". (Encyclopaedia Encarta 96)

Interesting! Isn't it? This is the way they prey, capture both sides, and let people feel they are free. This is freedom of choice. This is Democracy!

SYMBOLS AND INTRODUCTIONS

Brotherhood's secrecy has been maintained through their symbols and way of introduction to another Mason. This minimises the chances of mistakes, among masons, not previously met. For example if you are stopped by a police officer and want to find out if he is a mason, so you can get away with the crime, following things will help you;

"Special Handshake": This is a half handshake, instead of your palms meeting each other, your inside fingers meet, as a half handshake, this brings your thumb automatically on other person's knuckles. Then you press appropriate knuckle of the finger to acknowledge your degree. If you are 1st degree Mason (Entered Apprentice), you press 'index finger' knuckle. If you are 2nd degree (Fellow Craft), you press 'middle finger' knuckle, if 3rd degrees (Master Mason), then you press 'ring finger' knuckle. Your **'Brother'** does the same to acknowledge his degree. Then the further information about lodge and membership is exchanged. If he were not a Mason, he wouldn't notice it and you are not exposed as well---Safe!

"Son of a Widow": If you are not in position of a handshake, then you can announce your Freemasonry by saying specific sentences, one of them is to include in your speech, 'I am son of a widow' or somehow mention this phrase, although this phrase is quite famous now and nearly abandoned. The other phrase is to mention the direction not the destination. Normally if someone is asked, 'where are you going?' He will mention the place, he is going i.e., New York or Lahore, a Freemason will say **'I am heading north'** or **'I am heading west'**. Other verses they mention are, **'My mother taught me to be cautious'**, **'I put my left foot in first',** the word **'Geometry'**, **'Lodge'**, **'On the Square'**, in fact these phrases and words vary when they are leaked or too open to nonmasons. You can actually see these phrase exchanges between Sean Connery and Michael Cane in the film **"The Man who would be a King"**, based on the novel written by 'Rudyard Kippling', a writer, poet and a Freemason. He was a great influence in Hindustan before partition. He was also the writer of a great Masonic poem called "Mother Lodge", which was made popular with the help of masonic media techniques.

These phrases are exchanged in case of verification, before these exchanges one can just look at a person and know if he is a Freemason. This is possible by **"Masonic Symbols",** such as a ring, stud, bracelet or any decoration piece in the premises, which are distinguished and instantly recognisable. Amongst these symbols are, **"Compass, Square, Triangle, Pyramid, Letter 'G', Star of David and beside many others, most important the sign of 'Eye'".** It is also reported that if a Freemason is applying for a job, to recognise his application among many others is made possible by a "**special fold of application"** or **"Capital A"**.

*"The Prophet (S) said: 'Before The Hour comes, there will be a **special greeting** for the people of distinction'..." (Narrated by Abd Allah ibn Mas'ud- Ahmad, Masnad, 1/407- Quote from 20-94)*

CH-7 HIRAM ABIF

In rituals, emblems, oaths and initiation of Freemasonry, among many others a particular name is used. This is a Biblical character and in Freemasonry, is idealised and adored. His name is "Hiram Abif".

"The central character of Freemasonry is named as 'Hiram Abif', who was murdered by three of his own men. The stylised death and resurrection of the candidate is the act that makes one a 'Master Mason'"...(9-23)

His actual character is again in the mist of countless legends to conceal the original identity. To save readers from confusion, we will adopt the only version of the story, which all masonic historians agree upon. That will give us a visible identity of Hiram Abif in the light of Qura'n and Hadith, Inshallah.

Hiram Abif's story is mentioned in the "Old Testament", we will check this first and then relate it to others.

"Solomon, then despatched this message to Huram (Hiram), King of Tyre,...I am now building a house for the name of Yahweh my God....So send me a man skilled in the use of gold, silver, bronze, iron, scarlet, crimson,violet, and the art of engraving too: he is to work with my skilled men....Huram King of Tyre replied...I am sending you a skilled craftsman, Huramabi, the son of a Danite woman by a Tyrian father. He is skilled in use of gold, silver, bronze, Iron, stone, wood...in engraving of all kinds, and in the execution of any design."... (2Choronicals 11:13-14)

"King Solomon sent for Hiram of Tyre; he was the son of a widow of the tribe of Naphtali, but his father had been a Tyrian, a bronze worker. He came to King Solomon and did all this work for him: He cast two bronze pillars...". (1Kings vii: 13-15)

There are some more references in the Old Testament as well, but these two are self-explanatory, we will concentrate on these two so we don't confuse readers. We learn two things from above references:

a) Hiram Abif was a skilled mason in building the "The Temple of Solomon", or in other words, we call him "Master Mason".
b) He was a son of a widow.

As we mention above, there are many contradictions in this story regarding different chapters in "The Bible". This does not mean that the original "Injeel" was contradictory, but this is the result of centuries of fabrications done by so-called "Christ—ians". So we will restrict ourselves to the adoptive version of "Hiram Abif", by Freemasonry. With different versions all Hiramic legends conform the following pattern of story.

HIRAM'S LEGEND

"When Hiram Abif nearly completed his Temple, one-day he was praying in the precincts. There, he was attacked by three villains who wanted to obtain the **"Secret Word".** Hiram had entered through the western door in the precinct. The villains blocked all the exits. Hiram, trying to escape, received the first blow, which wounded him, either at the north or south door. He staggered from door to door to escape, but received blow after blow at each blocked exit. Altogether he received three vital blows and finally died at the "East door". Eventually the villains proceeded to conceal the Master's body and buried it under a sprig of "acacia" (a Jewish sacred tree). Seven days after, nine of Hiram's subordinate masters, discovered his body. Realising that he was murdered, nine masters feared that Hiram might have given away the **"Secret Word"**, they agreed to change it, to whatever any of them utters as they disinter the corpse.

That word came when Hiram's hand clasped by the fingers and the wrist. One of the masters exclaimed, "Macbenae" or any variant, in some unspecified language, which meant, **"The corpse is rotten"** (the actual word you will find out at the end of this chapter). Subsequently the three murderers were found and punished." This story is not only a Hiramic legend, but also its references and incidents are in consistent use, in Masonic ceremonies, even today.

KING SOLOMON (PBUH)

Why is it, that Hiram Abif is a heroic figure in Freemasonry, instead of Solomon (PBUH)? Although that Solomon was a king and a prophet, yet Freemasonry mentions only his Temple and don't follow him. On the other hand Hiram Abif is referred as a deity even above Jesus Christ. Before we go further with actual Hiram, we need to have a look at King Solomon's biblical character.

"When Solomon grew old, his wives swayed his heart to other gods; and his heart was not wholly with Yahwah, his God as his father David's had been. Solomon became a follower of ***"Astrate, the goddess of the Sidonians"****. (1Kings; XI: 4-5)*

Astrate was known as the "Queen of Heaven" and "Star of the Sea". She was worshipped on the high places like hilltops and mountains and according to the Old Testament...

"Solomon loved Yahwah: he followed the precepts of David, his father, except that he offered sacrifices and incense on the high places". (1Kings III: 3)

So the Biblical version tells that, Solomon was a worshipper of Astrate, a goddess and he offered sacrifices to her on the high places like mountains and hilltops. In "Origin of Freemasonry", Thomas Paine claims that:

"Customs will often outlive the remembrance of their origin, and this is the case with respect to a custom still practised in Ireland, where the Druids flourished at the time they flourished in Britain. On the eve of St.John's day that is on the eve of midsummerday, the Irish light fires on the tops of the hills".

Further he writes:

"This can have no reference to St.John; but it has emblematic reference to the sun, which on that day is at his highest summer elevation, and might in common language be said to have arrived at the top of the hill".

This is an example of Freemasonry myths to spread confusion, they worship Astrate, Sun and Hiram Abif and these are their heroes. Astrate is the goddess that entered Christianity in the form of "Ashtaroth", a male Demon; even a Song of Solomon is a hymn to Astrate;

"Come from Lebanon, my promised bride,
come from Lebanon, come on your way.
Lower your gaze, from the heights of Amana,
From the crests of Senir and Hermon".

Keeping in mind that the present Bibles are those that were written after the "Decree of Nicea", the Roman Emperor Constantine: "the Sun worshipper". And the Bibles we hold today, is a result of countless "revisions" and "corrections".

Considering all these**Biblical Masonic Fabricated Stories,** we can establish the following facts.

1). Solomon was a demon worshipper (God forbid).

2). Hiram was the one, who actually built "The Temple of Solomon".

3). King Solomon's Temple is actually Hiram's Temple.
4). Hiram did the job, which Solomon couldn't.
5). Hiram knew the **"Secret Word"** or had the **"Sacred Knowledge"** or **"Sacred Geometry"** to build the Temple, through him, nine masters (in fact the "Nine unknown Men of Freemasonry"), through them, existing "Grand Master".

This **"Secret Word"**, is whispered in the ears of a mason when he is **"Raised"** as **"Grand Master"** or **"Master Mason".** Before this secret word, we will check another version of Astrate and Hiram's story, which we find in "Secret Societies of all ages", by Heckethorne:

*"There is a temple legend relating that through the jealousy of three workmen the casting of the brazen sea mentioned in 'Kings' and in 'Chronicles', was a failure, but 'Tubal Cain' appears to Hiram and confers on him, magical powers and the casting is then successful. Balkis falls in love with Hiram, who at the instigation of Solomon is murdered. The story then developing on lines familiar to Freemasons, and having reference to a **"Secret Vault"**. The story gains a little point, perhaps, when we realise that Balkis is Mohammaden name of the **"Queen of Sheba"**, who paid the historical visit to Jerusalem. The Koran knows her as Balkis, Queen of Sheba. (**Emphasis** added)*

With the help of above the story, we can add some more points to the previous conclusion.
6). Astrate was actually the "Balkis" in "Solomon's Song".
7). Hiram was killed at the instigation of Solomon.
8). Hiram was taken to a "Secret Vault".

W.W.Covey. Crumps in "The Hiramic Tradition (Masonic record, ltd 1934)", explains different possibilities and puts the question:

"Was this halting symbology, intended for us to see behind the traditional Hiram as a reference to another Master? As one of the brightest characters, recorded in the 'Volume of the Sacred Law', one who solemnly declared himself: 'I am the Resurrection and the Life?"

9). Hiram Abif claimed to be the "Resurrection and the Life".

Keeping in account these nine points, we shall see, upto what extent, Freemasonry is inspired by Hiram Abif? For this purpose we will go through some of their symbols and, questions and answers.

LETTER "G"

In masonic symbols letter "G" has a significant importance, often referred to as, "God", the "Grand Architect of the Universe" or "Geometry".

Letter "G" as **"Geometry":**

According to masonry, Geometry is the "Sacred knowledge of the Compass" or "Geometria", which according to the "Dictionary of Jewish Lore & Legends" is:

"In Hebrew, there is no separate number system. Each letter of the ALPHABET stands for a unique number, [which is the discipline of Numerology]. *Speculation on the date of the coming "Messiah", sometimes relied on hints found by means of Geometria". (P-83)*

Letter "G" as the **"Grand Architect":**

Usually understood as God, the one who made the universe! But is it what it actually means and is it what it merely means? In the following are the questions and answers of a Masonic candidate entering the Lodge from an expose of 1730:

Q- When you came in to the middle, what did you see?
A- The resemblance of the letter G.

Q- Who doth the G denote?
A- One, that is greater than you.
Q- Who is greater then I, that am a free and accepted mason, the Master of the Lodge?
A- The grand Architect and the Contriver of the Universe, or ***"He"*** *that was taken upto the top of the Pinnacle of the Holy Temple. (1-300)*

Here we find out that letter "G" does not stand merely for God, but also for **"HE"**, who was taken to the pinnacle and this is the actual deity they worship. Looking at Brotherhood's record [the allegations of idol worshipping], their secrecy and their oaths, we don't have to be a genius to conclude what they are concealing knowing that:

a)- Hiram was taken to a secret vault or pinnacle.

b)- Hiram claimed to be the "Resurrection and Life".

Now that we have established the fact that Hiram Abif is the "He", how do we find out his reality, who was actually "He"? With so many different versions and sky full of smoke hiding his origin, where do we go? Who do we consult? And what is the actual story of Solomon (PBUH)? Was he actually an Astrate worshipper?

The only way is, through some totally unfabricated, most guaranteed and the most truthful source. Which is always proved right in whatever way tested. Which is not only certified by The Most High, The Almighty God---Allah SWT, but also admitted by nonbeleivers to be authentic, Al-Qur'an!

SOLOMON (PBUH) AND HIRAM ABIF IN QUR'AN

"They followed what the Satans recited over Solomon's Kingdom. Solomon did not disbelieve. But Satans disbelieved...(Q: 2; 102)

We have no hesitation in admitting the fact that Solomon (PBUH) was a prophet and a pious slave of Allah SWT. Like any other prophet he was tested and tried by Allah, and he was successful in that trial, as we will see in the following verses of Qur'an:

"And we did try Solomon: We placed on his throne a body, but he did turn (to us in true devotion). He said O my Lord! Forgive me, and grant me a kingdom, which will not belong to another after me. For thou art the Granter of Bounties (without measure).

Then We, subjected the wind to his power, to flow gently to his order, withersoever he willed.

As also the Satans (jinns) every kind of builder and diver. As also others bound together in fetters. Such are Our Bounties: Whether though bestow them (on others) or will hold them, no account will be taken." (Q: 38; 34-39)

From above we understand that.

a)- Solomon (PBUH) was tested by Allah SWT, by throwing a body on his throne. [What was that body and what was the actual test, we are not told, the only Ahadith explaining this verse are taken from Ahle-Kitab (the People of the Book)].

"Remember all these legends are Jewish". (Q: 38; 34-40, Tafseer Ibn Kathir, Urdu translation Vol: 4, P-402)

b)- Then Solomon (PBUH) turned, (in his devotion) to Allah SWT.

c)- Then Solomon (PBUH) asked for forgiveness and supplicated for a kingdom, never given or to be given to anyone else.

d)- Then Allah SWT subjected the wind to his power and order. As also Satans every kind of **"Builder and Diver"**.

It is easy to establish that there is continuity in all these incidents. One happens after the other. So, Solomon (PBUH) was tested first and then granted the kingdom and power over wind and Satans.

Another point we notice that in Qur'an, word "Shayateen" is used only for the flock of "Iblis" [the Devil].

"And (remember) when We said unto the angels: Fall prostrate before Adam, and they fell prostrate, all save Iblis (Satan). He was of the Jinn..."(Q: 18; 50)

For other Jinns word "Jinn" is used as in Sura "Al Jinn" and "Al Rehman". So when in, d), Allah talks about Satans every kind of builder and diver, He is literally telling us about "Shayatin", and not ordinary "Jinns". And in the verse above:

"They followed what the Satans recited over Solomon's kingdom..." (Q: 2; 102)

Allah is telling us about the people who followed Satans, in modern language, "Satanists". So, a cult called **"Satanists"**, existed in Solomon's time. And the builder and diver were Satans. At the moment we will trace only the "Builder".

"Hazrat Qatadah" (RA), narrates this story, which according to "Ibn Kathir", is taken from Jews.

*"Solomon (PBUH) was ordered to build Baitul-Muqaddas, in a way, that no sound of iron should be heard. He tried many ways but succeeded not. Then he heard about, a jinn whose name was **'Sakhar'** or **'Asif'** that knows the technique. Solomon captured 'Asif', who showed him to cut stones with diamond. This way the condition was fulfilled. So was built 'The Temple of Solomon' or 'Baitul Muqaddas'.*

One day Solomon (PBUH) was going to bathe and handed his ring (a sacred ring, a seal of his kingdom) to Asif. (According to another version Solomon gave this ring to one of his wives and Asif took it off her) He threw that ring in the sea and guised himself as Solomon (PBUH), by changing his face and appearance. This way Asif snatched Solomon's throne and kingdom. Asif gained power over everything of Solomon except his wives. Now many things he started doing were against the good. There was a companion of Solomon (PBUH), like Umar (RA) in the time of Mohammad (PBUH).

This companion suspected Asif as an impostor of Solomon, thus he tested Asif. The companion asked Asif a question and Asif answered it against the writings of the 'Torah'. At this point every one realised that he was not Solomon the prophet".

Eventually, Solomon got his ring back from a fish, which had swallowed it and re-established his kingdom. Then he arrested Asif. (Urdu translation TIK. V- 4, P-400)

Jews, as not true believers and followers of Solomon (PBUH), have added blasphemous legends to this. According to them, Asif overpowered Solomon's wives as well.

"This is against chastity and nobility of a prophet's wives and Allah will never allow this". (Agreed upon) (Tafseer ibn Kathir Urdu translation, V-4, P-400)

Ibne- Kathir, tells us further that,

"One group of 'Ahle-Kitab' (Jews), did not believe in Solomon as a prophet, so it is more likely that these stories are originated by them". (Urdu translationV-4, 402)

Now that the things are a bit clear, we can compare "Freemasonry's" legends about "Hiram Abif" and Jewish legends about "Sakhra Asif".

	Masonic Legend	Jewish Legend
Name	Hiram Abif	Sakhra Asif
Time	King Solomon	King Solomon
Occupation	Mason	Mason
Special job	Building the 'Temple of Solomon'	Building the 'Temple of Solomon'
Punished	By Solomon	By Solomon
Powers	Magical powers	Jinn, or magical powers
Waiting for	A long awaited 'Master of Brightest Characters'	A 'Messiah'

As we can see that all facts are pointing towards the same direction, every thing is indicating the same personality. The only difference is between the first names. The second names "Abif" and "Asif" are still similar, except a little difference of the letters 'B' and 'S', which is not a significant difference in thousands of years, taking into account of all the changes in languages and writing styles.

It is well known to every Muslim and Christian that Jews are still waiting for the 'Last Messiah'. They did not believe in Isah and Mohammad (PBUTh). Now the situation is that.

Jews: Waiting for the 'Last Messiah'.
Christians: Claim Isah (PBUH), as 'Last Messiah'.
Muslims: Know that Mohammad (PBUH) was the 'Last Messiah'.

And:

Christians: Acknowledged by Isah (PBUH) about the 'Anti Christ'. (The Bible, Revelations)
Muslims: Acknowledged by Mohammad (PBUH), about "Dajjal".
Jews: Waiting for the 'Last Messiah'.

What does this show other than that Jews believe "Dajjal (The Anti Christ)" to be their 'Messiah'. But why and how did Jews come to be in this situation?

"The people of the Book (Jews and Christians) know this (Qur'an) as they know their own sons, but some of them conceal the truth, which they themselves know". (Qur'an, 2-146)

Of course they knew and still know that Qur'an is true, and Mohammad (PBUH) was the 'Last Messiah'. We still find so many evidences and signs in both 'Old' and 'New' Testament about the coming of the 'Last Messiah'. These conclusively fit no one, but Mohammad (PBUH). [Those, interested in this subject, please refer to "What did Jesus really say", by 'Mishal Ibne Abdullah'.]

As they know that Mohammad (PBUH) was the Last Prophet, they believe that, they have lost the right path because of their ignorance and insistence. Here are some reasons for their insistence for denying both Mohammad (SAW) and Jesus (Isa A.S):

1) Since almost, all the prophets and messengers came from the linage of Yaqoob (A.S) or Jacob (PBUH), who was from the linage of Abraham's (A.S) second son Isaac (Ishaq A.S), so surely Mohammad (SAW) should **not** have come from Abraham's first son Ishmael's (Ismail A.S) descendents. Isaac and Ishmael (A.S) had two different mothers, that's why even today, you cannot become a Jew, to be Jew you have to be born from a Jewish mother.
2) The objection they put on Jesus (Isa A.S) is that Jesus (A.S) did not come with a set of new laws, but as a reformer of Torah
3) Other objection on Jesus (AS) is because Jesus (AS) rebuffed the Jewish Rabbis' claim as the King of the Jews.

So in order to redress that last opportunity is to make Dajjal (The Anti Christ) as a Messiah.

"Jews claimed, "Dajjal" will be amongst them and when he comes, that day, they will have their kingdom and ***"Rule the World"****. (Urdu translation T.I.K, V-4, P-471)*

We will prove along the way Inshallah that how they are preparing themselves to welcome **'Him'** and establishing the grounds for **'His kingdom of the world'** or paving the way for **'One President of the Global Village'**.

Let us check these facts again with a different angle.

Hiram Abif or Sakharah Asif: Was the Grand Architect of the Universe.

: Was taken up to the top of the pinnacle of the Holy Temple.

Now we know that in Questions and Answers:

"The Grand Architect and the Contriver of the Universe".

Or

"He: that was taken up to the top of the Pinnacle".

Is the same Deity being referred to! In fact: where it says **'or'** is actually **'and'**. Their rituals and legends can help any one to understand their actual believes and dogmas. There is a never-ending series of these myths and legends, any one who criticises any ritual or thought, is made satisfied by alternatives. To prove their belief in all these 'legends', evidence is enough that, any other lodge with different belief is not out-casted. In fact this provides them with a good cover to maintain their secrecy. With all these facts we have proven, now the letter "G" of Freemasonry can be described in following terms.

1. God, as an Architect.
2. Geometry, as a sacred science.
3. Hiram Abif or Asif, as the main architect or Master Mason of Solomon's Temple.
4. Hiram Abif is Master of the brightest characters.
5. He (Hiram) solemnly declared: "I am the Resurrection and the Life". (An ironic coincidence that the same sentence refers to Jesus' claiming in today's Bibles)
6. Hiram is their Hero and awaited Messiah.

We, with our Qura'nic research can characterise Letter "G" through the known facts that it is referred to "Hiram Abif" and:

1. He (Hiram) was a Satan.
2. He was a mason in King Solomon's Temple.

Now we can clearly see whom Freemasons worship and why they call themselves Masons or "Freemasons". But is it the same one that is referred to as Dajjal in the Ahadith or is it some other personality Freemasons are waiting for? In other words, Does the description of Hiram Abif fit Ad-Dajjal (The Anti Christ) in Ahadith (The Narrations of the Prophet Mohammad SAW)? Ahadith not only describe many afflictions he will spread in the world, but also his appearance:

Allah's Apostle said:

"While I was sleeping, I saw myself performing the Tawaf of Ka'ba. Behold, there I saw a whitish-red lank-haired man)(holding himself) between two men with water dropping from his hair. I asked, 'who is this?' The people replied, 'He is the son of Mary'. Then I turned my face to see another man with red complexion, ***big body, curly hair, and blind in the right eye,*** *which looked like a protruding grape. I asked, 'Who is he?' They replied, 'He is Ad-Dajjal'..." (Sahih Al-Bukhari Hadith 9.153)*

To find out the description of Hiram Abif, (according to Freemasonry) we temporarily neglect the time factor, or simply overlook it because all the prophets have warned their nations against him, so his roots could be seeded anywhere since the history of good and evil.

"Once Allah's Apostle stood amongst the people, glorified and praised Allah as He deserved and then mentioned the Dajjal saying. 'I warn you against him (i. e. the Dajjal) and there was no prophet but warned his nation against him, but I tell you about him something of which, no prophet has told his nation before me. You should know that he is one-eyed, and Allah is not one-eyed' ". (Sahih Al-Bukhari Hadith 4.553)

The sign of the pyramid in the Masonic signs represents the reign of Pharaohs, going back to ancient Egyptian times. Keeping in mind that the Pharaoh himself claimed to be god. This claim was hierarchy, so adopted by all kings.

"When in 1881, Emil Brugsch discovered the mummy of Pharaoh Ramesses II, in the same cache was another royal corpse, some 300 years older than that of Ramesses, and distinguished by its putrid smell. According to the label this was the body of 'Seqenenre Tao, one of the native Egyptian rulers forced to live far to the south in Thebes during the Hyksos period, and as was obvious even to the ***'untreated eye',*** *Seqenenre had met a violent end...Although in life he had clearly been a* ***tall and handsome*** *young man with* ***black, curly hair****..."(Ian Wilson: The Exodus Enigma. Quote from 9-176,* ***emphases*** *added)*

Yes we recognise their **'Tall and handsome black, curly haired master with an untreated eye" as "Ad-Dajjal (The Anti Christ)".** [Please see "who is Ad-Dajjal and what does he look like?" Ch-19]

The writers further recognise and translate the secret words used in the "Third Degree Ceremony", which is the "Master Mason raising Ceremony"; "Ma'at-neb-men-aa, Ma'at-ba-aa", in pure ancient Egyptian language, meaning:

"Great is the established Master of Freemasonry, Great is the spirit of Freemasonry". (9-188)

That is why the Master Mason ceremony is called the "Raising" ceremony and not the "making" ceremony. They hope to raise the dead body of their Master and the Grand Architect of the Universe through **"CLONING"**.

The Great Architect of the Universe is denoted in the printed Masonic rituals as: ***TGAOTU*** *(22, p-234).* In Qur'anic version; false gods are referred as **TAGHOUT**

The other classification of the Masonic god is when the word**JAHBULON** is revealed in the ritual of exaltation (Master Mason). This word is in fact a combination of three words; **JAH-BUL-ON**

JAH: Jahweh, the God of the Hebrews.

BUL: Baal, the ancient Cannanite fertility god associated with "licentious rites of imitative magic".

ON: Osiris, the Ancient Egyptian god of the underworld. (22, p236)

Further, the author reveals *"Baal" as a devil (22' p-236).*

Some people might think how is it possible to really worship devil. The reason is very simple: If non-Christians can take an oath on Jesus (in lower degrees) as their lord then on a higher degree when you have all the success of the world why would you not the Devil as well. Can you afford to lose the wealth of this world?

In 1798, "Baron Dominique-Vivant Denon", the first director of the Lousvre Museum in Paris, and a close friend of Napoleon Bonaparte followed Napoleon to his Egypt's invasion. There he found "Irt-irw" a 2500 years old woman's mummy. The mummy's bandages were first unwrapped in 1830:

"A silver embalming plate, engraved with an ***eye*** *was also found in the bandages". (The Times, London 12-10-1999)*

This is not an evidence of Freemasonry being practiced by ancient Egyptians; the plate might have been put there rather to prove Masonry's practice in ancient Egypt. This is how they spread "confusion", the key factor to maintain secrecy.

Here are some rules or so-called "Land-marks" offered by the well-known American Mason 'Albert G Mackey', the original editor of "An Encyclopaedia of Freemasonry" (1858). For readers' interest we quote the last three out of a total number of 25.

23. Secrecy, "If divested of its secret character, it would loose its identity and would cease to be freemasonry".

24. The foundation of a speculative science upon an operative art, and the symbolic use and explanation of the terms of the art, for the purpose of religious or moral teaching, "The temple of Solomon was the symbolic cradle of the institution".

25. The crowning landmark (rule) is that these landmarks can never be changed".

Time to think, isn't it?

SOME SYMBOLS OF FREEMASONRY

Hand symbol for the Horned God. (Satanic)

Both Bill and George are confirmed Freemasons

CH-8 AMERICAN WAR OF INDEPENDENCE

Official history of the 'American War of Independence' tells us that: "Because of high taxation, enforced by the British Monarchy / Parliament, 'Benjamin Franklin', the 'father of America', fought for people's independence". Finally, Americans broke free from England. Just like in the "French Revolution". But why monarchs were enforcing high tax? Was it because they became greedy? Or, Was it because they were under debts? History sheets of all European monarchs show that they were under severe debts to bankers, formerly "Templars" and by now "Freemasons".

"American War of Independence", officially broke out in 1775 and on 3rd September 1783, "Treaty of Paris" was signed, which recognised the Colonies as independent republic, the United States. As these wars are 'Brotherhood's usual method to manipulate countries and in the smoke of independence or protectorate, bring them under permanent invasion. So let us approach this method from a little bit of different angle to understand it explicitly. This way we will be able to understand the future "Revolutions" and "Engineered Coups" easily.

Q. Why did the "War of Independence" brake out?

A. Because, England enforced heavy tax on people of colonies.

Q. Why did England have to enforce extra tax?

A. To meet the cost of "The Seven-year War" with France (British and French War).

Q. Why was there a war between Britain and France?

A. Because, George Washington, then a young military leader in British Colonial Army, had ordered to kill French troops in Ohio.

Q. Is this the same George Washington who became the first president of USA (1789-1796)?

A. Yes, indeed, he was not only the first President of the US but also a Freemason and is listed in the gallery of the Famous Freemasons (2-240).

"When George Washington was made First President of the United States of America he had been a member of the Craft for almost thirty-six years and was at the time a member of Alexandria Lodge, No.22". (9-463)

Q. Ok, I understand that the cause of the first problem was a Freemason, but what happened next?

A. The heavy taxation, because of "Seven Years War", caused a rebellion against the British Government.

Q. Excuse me, but who led this rebellion against the British Government?

A. Patrick Henry and Richard Henry Lee, both Freemasons (5-185) and Benjamin Franklin...

Q. Sorry to cut you off, but Benjamin Franklin? I don't believe that he had anything to do with this conspiracy and Freemasonry. He was the "Founding Father" of USA and very much against slavery, leave alone these brutal and bloodsheding incidents.

A. Ok, let us check slavery first. B Franklin owned slaves himself and sold them on his General Store. He placed an advertisement for a slave in 1733.

" *A likely wench about 15 years old, has had small pox, been in this country above a year and talkes English. Inquire the printer hereof".*

Not only B Franklin but also, George Washington and other big names in the "War of Independence", like "John Hancock" and "Patrick Henry", owned slaves too. Yet it was Patrick Henry who raised the slogan "Give me liberty or give me death". These are the heroes and models of generations to follow; all hypocrites and double faced. If we follow these people as history has portrayed them, no doubt we are following

"The people who followed Satans". Read this, Andrew Johnson (17th President, 1865-1869), placed an advertisement looking for a run-away slave and offering an extra ten dollars for every 100 lashes the captor gave to the slave (5-186).
Q. All right I admit as far as these other people are concerned, but nearly all the historians will disagree that a person like B Franklin had anything to do with this scam and what about Franklin as a Freemason?
A. We will check B Franklin's history and where abouts at the time of "A W I".
B Franklin was the first one to print an article about freemasonry in his newspaper "The Pennsylvania Gazette" on 8th December 1730. He printed the first Masonic book in 1734 in America. He founded the first "American Lodge" in his province Pennsylvania and that is where the so-called "American War of Independence" was organised, from! He was a member of Freemasonic network in France during French Revolution in 1789. He was an initiate of "Royal Lodge of Commanders".
He was a member of "Hellfire Club" with his close friend, the British Chancellor of the Exchequer, "Sir Francis Dashwood". There are countless evidences of their "Satanic Rituals" from anti- masonic writers, as we can easily draw from the name of the club, but we will leave them for some other time and consult Freemason's own book. After denying for centuries, at last they disclose about B Franklin that,

"He was initiated in 1731 in "St John's Lodge" Philadelphia, Pennsylvania, and was always an enthusiastic Mason". (2-32)

B Franklin's name is printed in "Famous Freemasons Gallery". (2-232)
Q. Who was incharge of British forces in America at that time and what were British forces doing to crush the rebellion?
A. In 1775, just as the war was getting into full swing, George Sackville was appointed Colonial Secretary, incharge of the American Colonies. He became "Grand Master" of the "Irish Grand Lodge" in 1751 and was a close friend of "King George III", who was himself a member of "Black Nobility", which is another offshoot of Freemasonry.
As far as the resistance by British forces is concerned, historians write; "The British Military and Naval operation during the 'War of Independence' was incredibly inept. It wasn't that the colonies won the war, it was that the British chose to loose it".
Q. With this clear evidence I understand that the "War of Independence" was a stage play only, but why did Freemasonry have to do it? Why couldn't they leave it like that? After all they were the ones, who were ruling behind the monarchy and colonial system too.
A. Monarchy is a hierarchical throne, any king during his reign could turn against them and if the king is clever enough, history could repeat itself like King Phillipe of France and Friday the 13th could come again. Monarchy system gives the main power of decision in one person's hand for an unlimited time, depending on his life. Yet the biggest power in any civilisation is the power of the people, if people turn against any thing the future of that thing is unstable, let it be monarchy, inheritance or any other form. To establish a long lasting system, Freemasonry had to control this biggest power of the people; so turn from an **"overt control"** to a **"covert control".** A control that makes people believe, that they are free, yet they are mentally captives, slaves of an unknown magical power. The power that illustrates nothing but phantoms and false promises, the power; that makes people run after the shadows of dreams, blindfolded. What power could be better than "Democracy", let people think they are free and keep ruling them with Parliamentary system.
Q. Just a last question before we go. Earlier you mentioned about "Treaty of Paris", what exactly did you mean by this and who signed this Treaty?

A. Good question! It was called "Treaty of Paris", because Benjamin Franklin was very active in French Masonry and that is where he monitored all this play from, during the "American Revolution" he was based in France where the revolutionary strings were ending. From France it was easy to keep in touch with British and French Brotherhood as compared to America, keeping in mind the lack of communication and travelling conditions of that time. Treaty could not be named better than Treaty of "Paris" with B Franklin in Paris, although these were British and Americans who fought the war.

Freemasonic historian, Manly P Hall points out that out of 56 signatories of the "American Declaration of Independence" almost 50 were known Freemasons and only one was definitely known "not to be"!

What other can be more evident than the first Masonic American flag? (Please see photo No-1)

AMERICAN MASONIC PRESIDENTS

For your interest I quote the names of Presidents of America who are so far announced Freemasons, not including the names of un-announced or in simple words those who Freemasonry did not think appropriate to disclose yet as Freemasons.

1. George Washington (1732-1799)
First President, (1789- 1796) initiated on November 4, 1752 in the lodge at Frederickburg, Virginia.

2. **James Monroe (1758-1831)**
Fifth President, 1817-1825. Initiated in Williamsburge Lodge No.6, at Williamsburge, Virginia, at the age of 18.

3. **Andrew Jackson (1767-1845)**
Seventh President1829-1837. Initiated in Lodge No.1 at Nashville, Tennessee. Became Grand Master of the Grand Lodge of Tennessee in October 1822-Oct 1824, also a member of "Royal Arch". (Another sub society of Freemasonry)

4. **James Knox Polk (1795-1849)**
Eleventh President, 1845-1849. Initiated in 1820 in Columbia Lodge No.21, Columbia, also a member of "Mark" and "Royal Arch".

5. **James Buchanan (1791-1868)**
Fifteenth President, (1857- 1861). Initiated on Dec 11, 1816 in Lancaster Lodge No. 43, at Lancaster, Pennsylvania. Worshipful Master in 1825, he was also "Deputy Grand Master" of the Grand Lodge of Pennsylvania.

6. **Andrew Johnson (1808-1875)**
Seventeenth President, 1865-1869. Who succeeded Lincoln. Initiated in Greenvillr Lodge No. 19, at Greenville, Tennessee, in 1851. He was a "Knight Templar" who, according to "Scottish Rite" received 32 degree in June 1867.

7. **James Abraham Garfield (1831-1881)**
Twentieth President, 1881. Initiated on November 19, 1864, in Columbus Lodge No.246 at Garrettsville, Ohio also a "Knight Templar" and of Scottish Rite.

8. **William Mc Kindy (1843-1901)**
Twenty-fifth President, 1897-1901. Initiated in Hiram Lodge No. 21 at Winchester, Virginia on May 1, 1865, also a Knight Templar and a member of Mark and Royal Arch.

9. **Theodore Roosevelt (1858-1919)**
Twenty-sixth President, 1901-1909. Initiated on January 2, 1901 in Matinecock Lodge No.806 at Oyster Bay, New York State.

10. **William H Taft (1857-1930)**
Twenty-seventh President, 1909-1913. He was made a mason "at sight" on June 18, 1909. He was also "President of Supreme Court of Justice" in 1921.
11. **Warren G Harding (1865-1923)**
Twenty-ninth President, 1921-1923. Initiated on June 18, 1920. Also a Knight Templar 33 degree and member of Mark and Royal Arch.
12. **Franklin Delano Roosevelt (1882-1945)**
Thirty-second President, 1933-1945. Initiated on October 11, 1911 in Holland Lodge No.8, New York City. He was present when his three sons were "**raised**". Elliott on February17, 1933. James and Franklin D Jr in November 1935, all of them in Architect Lodge No.519 New York City. He was also a member of Scottish Rite.
13. **Harry S Truman (1884-1972)**
Thirty-third President, 1945-1953. Initiated on February 9, 1909 in Belton Lodge No. 450 at Balten, Missouri. Also a Knight Templar of Scottish Rite and a 33 degree "Grand Master" of the Grand Lodge of Missouri.
14. **Lyndon B Johnson (Born 1908)**
Thirty-sixth President, 1963-1969. Initiated on October 30, 1937, IN Johnson City Lodge No. 561 at Johnson City Texas.
15. **Gerald R Ford (Born 1913)**
Thirty-eighth President, (1974-1977). Initiated on September 30, 1949 in Malta Lodge, at Grand Rapids, Michigan.
16. **Ronald Reagan**
Freemasons did not portray him in the Famous Freemasons Gallery but the evidence comes from the late Stephen Knight. He also claims:

Seventeen Vice-Presidents including Hubert Humphrey and Adlai Stevenson have also been brethren". (22-34)

Again keeping in mind, these are the only ones that Freemasonry felt safe to announce. Even today, the present President "Bill Clinton" is a 33rd degree Freemason and a member of "Skull & Bone Society". Formerly a high class drug dealer and a murderer. (Refer to Book 4)

OPPOSITION TO FREEMASONRY IN AMERICA

William Morgan was a Freemason; he got tired of their satanic rituals, and threatened to publish Masonic secrets. William was kidnapped, a general outcry followed for a decade. Eventually:

"Many Masonic Lodges had to be abandoned throughout the eastern and middle states. In the northern states the Anti-Masonic party was formed, for a few years it was practically the only opponent to the Democratic Party. In 1832 the Anti-Masonic Party nominated a lawyer, [Liar, he should be called] *' William Writ', as its candidate for presidency, but he was defeated by 'Andrew Jackson' who supported Freemasonry* [in fact a Grand Master, Ibid.].

Ironically, Writ himself was a Freemason. After that date Freemasons encountered Little political opposition in the US or elsewhere, until the rise of the 'National Socialists' in Germany".

(Encarta 98 Encyclopaedia) [Emphases Added]

STATUE OF LIBERTY

America was discovered merely for Masonic purposes. Columbus was no one else but a Templar himself! So how could Freemasons let it go! It is still not free. Statue of Liberty is not a memorial of freedom from British but this freedom is from God.

When they shout freedom, do you ever think which freedom they are talking about? Are we chained or enslaved? From whom are they going to liberate us? What does this slogan of democratic Freedom stand for if we are not imprisoned? The only conclusion is that they are liberating us from the laws of God! Look at America now, where is the law of God? The statue of liberty is in fact a symbol of freedom from God's Law! To practice Satanism! To raise the flag of darkness!

William A. Brodie, then Grand Master of Freemasons in New York, laid the cornerstone of the pedestal of Statue of Liberty with "full Masonic ceremony" on August 5 1884. The Statue was created by "Fredric Auguste Bartholdi", a Freemason too!

In 1886, when the statue was formally dedicated, thousands of Freemasons paraded in New York City.

In 1984, on the exact day that the corner stone had been laid, one hundred years before, several thousand Freemasons gathered beneath the statue to re-dedicate and to commemorate the earlier ceremony. They also pledged to raise a substantial sum for the restoration project. Every Grand Lodge in United States took part in fund raising and eventually amounted to $2 million.

Today, the large plaque of the "Statue of Liberty" with the "Square and Compass", the well known Masonic sign tells millions of visitors of Freemasonry's role in the creation and erection of the world-renowned symbol of Freemasonry. The plaque clearly mentions the names Grand Master, Deputy Grand Master and Grand Lodge.

$

This sign, every one in the world recognises.*Let him be literate or illiterate.* This sign is the base of world commerce. This is the sign of Dollar, one Dollar! The United States' Dollar! This dollar contains "The Great Seal of the United States". At reverse of the bill the front of the seal is on the right hand side as you hold the dollar in your hands, it has main picture of an eagle on it. The rear side of the seal is on the left-hand side with a visible shape of a pyramid, on top of that is the sign of the **EYE!** This sign of the eye is readable by every one, literate or illiterate. (Please see Photo)

The great seal of the United States, which appears on the dollar bill, exhibits many principles familiar to Freemasons.

13 stars: as **herald** of the Deity representing his glory.
Eagle is the symbol of the spirit.
13 leaves laurel is of peace.
13 arrows are of war.
13 steps of pyramid; represent the diverse base of United States, with the cap-stone not set fit on the top yet, till "He" arrives.
The sign of the eye represents the single divine centre, which is the source of a "New Secular Order" the "Novus Ordo Seclorum"! All these Masonic symbols make "The Great Seal of the United States".

The Prophet said, "Allah did not send any prophet but that he warned his nation of the one-eyed liar (Ad-Dajjal). He is one-eyed while your Lord is not one-eyed. The word 'Kafir' (unbeliever) is written between his two eyes." (Sahih Al-Bukhari 9.505 Narrated by Anas)

The dollar is not Al-Masih Ad-Dajjal (The Anti Christ), but merely a part of a Dajjalic system. When Dajjal comes, he is not going to rule by virtue of magic; rather he will have means, i.e., science, commerce and followers!

CH-9 ROTHSCHILDS

Mayer Amschel was born in Frankfurt, Germany in (1743-1812). He was trained to become a Rabbi but after his parents death he was apprenticed to a banking firm. Later he established his own banking house in the Jewish quarter of the city. Around 1770,1780s he developed a friendship and relationship with "Karl Friedrich Buderus", Prince "William's" principal financial agent. With Friedrich's help and intercession, Mayer became a banker to the court of "Hanan" and in due time to the court of "Hesse Kassel". Mayer Amschel had five sons and five daughters. His daughters did not play any active part in the family business, as was the custom of the Jewish families. So we concentrate on his sons.

Mayer Amschel
(1743-1812)

Amschel Mayer Rothschild (1773-1855)	Salomon Rothschild (1774-1855)	Nathan Mayer Rothschild (1777-1836)	Karl Rothschild (1788-1855)	James Rothschild (1792-1868)

The family got the title of "Rothschild" after they gained some financial stability in banking business. This word "Rothschild" is actually a combination of two words, "Roth" and "Schild", literally meaning "Red" and "Shield". This red shield was there to rule the world's banking system for next two hundred years and still is one of the independent, privately owned banking systems of the world. Rothschilds played a vital part in political affairs of Europe first, and then the Globe. At one time they became "Absolute Masters" of the world's economy.

In October 1785, Landgrave of Hesse Kassel died, succeeded by "Prince William IX, who made Mayer Amschel his financial adviser. It did not take too long for the trained "Rabbi Amschel" to open additional four branches of his bank in four major cities of Europe. These branches of "House of Rothschild" were established in Berlin, Paris, Vienna and Naples. Each branch run by one of his sons except his eldest son "Amschel Mayer Rothschild", who stayed behind with his father in Frankfurt to supervise their growing banking interests and later became head of the family.

William gave Amschel £3 million for transaction to England. This £3 million played an integral role to change the world's economy. This money was handed down to "Nathan Mayer Rothschild", his third son. Nathan was the founder of "Bank of England" and a "Grand Master" Freemason (2-236). Nathan used this money to help "Arthur, Duke of Wellington" to gather and train an army to fight the future war, "Battle of Waterloo" with Napoleon. Arthur, Duke of Wellington (1769-1852) also called "Iron Duke" was initiated in the "Family Lodge" No.494 at Trim on December 7th 1790. His father was "Grand Master" of the "Grand Lodge of Ireland" in 1776.

BATTLE OF WATERLOO

Before we look into the regular version of this battle (rather shouldn't it be called a "War"?), it is better to check a "Masonic Napoleon". Because **'war'** could not happen if Napoleon wasn't there and Napoleon couldn't wage **'war'** if he didn't have his "Marshals" with him. But first, just a glance, on the activities of "Brotherhood", prior to war!

"By 1760 all brotherhood orders were brought together under an organised Masonic rite, the "Grand Lodge of France". (2-41)

Those who understand wars know that, these things don't just happen. Heroes and villains, danger to public safety, fear of a strong enemy, threat of survival, are the elements, mixing in background to form a compound of war. The most important of all these is propaganda, to create an atmosphere so fearful for public that they are ready to sacrifice every thing they posses, even their lives to overcome the fear. Napoleon was propagated by masonic channels as a threat to rest of the Europe, just like Sadam Hussain was a threat to rest of the world, with nowadays media and technology it was made possible within two weeks. Whereas in those days it took them a long time to achieve their target. Napoleon had to travel and invade several countries before he could be considered a serious threat.

All Masonic historians agree*"Napoleon was surrounded by brotherhood as advisers"*. Napoleon himself didn't have to be a Freemason as long as he was dancing to their tunes and achieving their targets, believing them to be his own. Still he is quoted as:

"Although he was described as an 'Illustrious Brother' by contemporary French Freemasons, it has never been proved that Napoleon was a Mason. But what is certain is that the 'Craft' in France recovered from the disastrous effects of the 'Revolution' and firmly re-established itself under his regime. Equally certain is the Masonic membership of the majority of his marshals". (2-108)

Do they have to be more open to make us believe that Napoleon was a Mason; still we don't claim what they don't accept! So we just leave it to them.

Along with male Freemasonry, female Freemasonry was very active too, though not considered and trusted as males, yet women were used as tools to achieve the targets that Freemasons as men could not. If you have read the actual history of the "Crusades" you will know what I am talking about, where specially trained women were sent into Muslim army to spy. These women used the weapons of artificial innocence and beauty to capture the minds of Muslim soldiers. In 1774 the "Grand Orient of France" (A women masonic branch), had formally adopted the "Rite-de Adoption". Each of these "Orders" or "Chapters" (as those were called), were attached to regular Masonic Lodges, whose Master also presided over the female lodge, assisted by a female "President" or "Mistress". One of these orders was called "Adoptive Rite".

"Empress Josephine (Napoleon's wife) *was an active member of 'Adoptive Rite' and during the 'French Revolution' when Freemasonry was closed down* [which was never the case. In fact they went underground for not to be spotted as the cause behind the so-called 'Revolution'], *along with 'Adoptive Rite', she helped to revive it". (2-212)*

What do you expect from a Napoleon, surrounded by masonic marshals and masonic wife? What will you do if your weapons are in control of your enemy? Under these circumstances was fought the Battle of "Water-Loo" on June 18, 1815, near Waterloo, what is now Belgium. In his reminiscences about the "Water-Loo Campaign", Napoleon severely criticised his Marshals 'General Grouchy' and 'Ney', whose strategies caused him to loose the war. What else could he do? Leaving aside the details of the war we go straight to casualties as a result of the War, so we can understand the ruthlessness of "Brotherhood". They don't feel mercy; they have no sympathy for any race, any creed, any nation or any religion. Any hazard in their way is simply to be removed, by hook or crook.

"The Battle of Waterloo was one of the bloodiest in modern history. During the fighting of June 18, French casualties totalled about 40,000, British and Dutch about 15,000. And Prussian about 7000; at one point about 45,000 men lay dead or wounded within an area of 8 sq. km (3sq m). Additional thousands of casualties were suffered by both sides during the three-day campaign, that preceded the final battle. (Encyclopaedia Encarta)

Allied forces needed a great regular supply of cash during their manoeuvres in Europe. They needed francs, pounds, gold and in some places local currency. This was a difficult job and how could they get someone reliable and yet so wealthy that money supply should not be cut off. It was impossible to carry enormous amount of gold and then cash it or exchange it at every new camp. It was also impossible to deal with different banks or companies on every new place. Rothschilds with their offices all over Europe could come out with a steady supply everywhere required in Europe.

Now we know the reason for branches of 'House of Rothschild' in every big capital of Europe. On the other hand their Paris office was responsible for Napoleon's funding. Nathan got permission to smuggle the gold out of England to supply to the British forces. This permission was granted by the 'Iron Duke' (Duke of Wellington and a Freemason). What the Iron Duke did not know was that the same gold was being smuggled back to England and sold in the black market! Rothschilds had every thing going the way they could possibly dream of.

Considering Freemasonry active on both sides in form of 'Duke of Wellington' a Grand Master himself and 'Napoleon' surrounded by masonic marshals and masonic wife, if not a Freemason himself, whom would you blame for this bloodshed? Who is responsible for the loss of so many lives? ---**Think**---!

Battle of "Water-Loo" was organised for two reasons.

a) To re-instate Louis XVIII, who lived in exile in England since1807 and now was "ready" to bring more disasters to the remaining economic freedom of France.
b) To get absolute control over British Stock & Exchange and French economy.

For a), Louis's return to a war battered country it would have been better if he entered with a motif of savings. Instead what does he do? He splashes £200,000 for his stylish triumphant entry to Paris. Not mentioning the lender, who could he be other than 'Nathan Mayer Rothscild', the third son of Amschel, the "Grand Master", as a result: 1). 25 million Francs indemnity was levied on the French Government. 2). Future funds were required to re-build the war-battered economies. Rothschild bankers in Frankfurt and London enjoyed giving them loans. Other branches in Berlin Vienna and Naples became regular lenders to governments with their hold on Stock & Exchange.

For b), Nathan Mayer played his part with masonic responsibility, he was first one to get the news of the result of war, or we should say he already knew the result. On the day when every one was impatiently waiting for the news, he came into the "London Stock & Exchange Market" down faced and with shattered voice announced that 'England has lost the war'. This would not have mattered a lot to the stockholders, but to complete the venture he said 'Napoleon is coming to invade England' and sold all his shares at whatever price he could get. This gave the other stockholders assurity that the news is true. After all Nathan was a renowned businessman. Panic struck the Market and shares de-valued, people sold them at whatever price they could grab. This was the time Nathan waited for. He bought all those cheap shares with fake names of real relatives. This was the last nail in "London Stock & Exchange's" coffin. Bragging about this occasion he claimed that he increased his capital 2,500%.

To hide their enormous wealth from these branches of "House of Rothschild" came, under various names, different companies. In America, "Kuhn Loeb and Co", "J P Morgan", "Speyer" and "Lehman". In 1875, Lionel Nathan (son of Nathan) lent £4 million to the British Government to buy a controlling stake in "Suez Canal", which "Ismail Pasha", the "Khedive (Viceroy) of Egypt", personally owned. (We will discuss that in "Suez Canal" chapter Inshallah). Benjamin Disraeli the Conservative Prime Minister of England and a "close friend" of Rothschild family describes Nathan as "Sidonia" in his novel "Coningsby", based actually on his family story;

"He arrived here [London] *after the peace of Paris with his large capital. He staked all that he was worth on the "Waterloo loan" and the event made him one of the greatest capitalist in the Europe...*[This is where he is talking about the London Stock & Exchange Market fiddle]. *He reaped the due reward of his sagacity. Europe did require money and Sidonia* [Nathan] *was ready to lend it to Europe. France wanted some, Austria more, Prussia a little, Russia a few million: Sidonia could furnish them all. The only country he avoided was Spain. He was too well acquainted with its reasons. He established a brother* [James] *or near relative in whom he could confide, in most of the principal capitals. He was lord and the master of the money markets of the world and of course virtually, lord and master of everything else. He literally held the revenues of Southern Italy in pawn and monarchs and ministers in all countries courted his advice and were guided by his 'suggestions'".*

Nathan's presence in the London Stock & Exchange was regular and his masonic dedication to his duty was consistent. He was always found in the S.E corner of the market, keeping in mind the Hiram Abif's legend and the corner in which he received his final blows. In fact he was so regular that he was named "A pillar of the Exchange".

RICHEST PEOPLE IN EUROPE

Then came the time when "Rothschilds" were known as the**"Richest people in Europe".** They owned thrones in real meanings, monarchs had to beg them, number of kings and countries were under their debts! On one occasion Nathan talks about Napoleon:

"Born in cognito in Ajaccio, made all the thrones of the earth, quake! I, then thought of avalanche. Which launches itself under the claw of a starling and five minutes later buries a village- and of Rothschild, whose father sold ribbons, and without whom no power in Europe today seems able to make war. (6-69)

This was not a mad man talking, they [Rothscilds] were known as "King Makers". In true meanings they were the war masters. What does a war require? Money! Where does the money come from? Banks or in simple words 'bankers'! When two war-battered countries need to rebuild themselves, where do they borrow money from? Banks or in simple words 'bankers'! Again, who benefit's from all this process? Banks or in simple words 'bankers'! Who were the bankers at times of these costly battles? 'Rothschilds' or in simple words, "Freemasons". No wonder, in 1816, just after the 'Water-Loo', Paris bank was re-founded as "Rothschild Fre'res".

Sep 1818, the leaders of Europe met in congress at Aix-la-Chaplle (Aachen), for re-habilitation of France, the removal of foreign troops from her land and most importantly, a second instalment of a French loan, designed to 'help' the re-stored government to pay off its war indemnity. Other businessmen and bankers were determined to cast Rothschilds out of this second loan. This was not acceptable by Rothschilds, so they bought the shares [parcel of loan]; this raised the value of shares. At this point, they sold all their shares, this created a severe panic in the market and shares value went down. Market and other businessmen bowed down to give them their share in loan.

In 1818, the Prussian government urgently needed a loan. They had to make an application to Rothschilds, as there was no alternative. No other bank could arrange loans on high levels except Rothschilds. To apply for a loan from Rothschilds, this is what 'Humbolt' the Ambassador points, N.M. only transacted deals on his own terms.

"I must add that if business is given to him to carry out, it will be necessary to fall in with his ideas. For he has acquired the independent habit of mind, developed by riches and a fairly long sojourn in this country, and he is now engaged in such a constant number of financial transactions, that it will not greatly affect him if one of them fails to come his way. He wants to take over the whole loan himself, on this point he is likely to be exceedingly firm, and he has asked in advance that the Prussian Consul here, against whom he is prejudiced, shall not be allowed to interfere in the matter in any way". (6-74)

This is the kind of power we are talking about. If one person is holding all the financial resources of a country: think how destructive it can be, this is what is called a 'Dictator'!

In Sep 1827 J C. Herries, a close friend of Nathan, was appointed 'Chancellor of Exchequer' by George IV [a member of Black Nobility and Freemasonry. *Initiated in 1787 with his brother William, the future William IV (22-p26)*]. This gave Nathan enormous power over the finance of England. Brotherhood started manipulating Britain's economy the way they wanted. Bells started ringing and people suspected a conspiracy. Corruption charges were brought against Herries and the following January, he got dismissed only to be appointed as 'Master of Mint'.

In July 1830, the French king suspended the constitution to re-store the autocracy. This caused a coup and several thousand people were killed and wounded. As a result, Charles X became the king; he was given enormous welcome by the media, portrayed as in favour of people. He was named 'Citizen King'. This 'Citizen King' was no one else but 'Louis Philippe' an old friend and client of James Rothschild (The fifth son). Another engineered coup! James wasted no time and donated fifteen thousand Francs for wounded and the widows of those who died in this experiment. In result; James got accepted by people; as a "political leader".

James helped and campaigned on behalf of 'Casimir Perrier', to get him appointed Premier, in March 1831. Perrier was a fellow banker and friend with whom James had worked 'closely' for many years. Perrier suddenly died in 1832. The wife of Russian Foreign Minister, Count Nessel Rode; who wrote to Moscow:

"Do you know who is Viceroy or even king of France? It is Rothschild". (6-98)

From the outcomes of all these revolutions we can observe that these were created to lead the countries in a certain direction. Rothschilds or 'Fraternity' were holding power in Europe from behind the curtains. There were some other revolutions, which were genuine and not engineered, independent from Masonic influence. Such was the case when public of Belgian were oppressed by their 'Dutch Masters' and they stood-up to fight and gain their freedom. Their leader asked Salomon Rothschild for financial support, in answer Salomon Rothschild quotes:

"These gentlemen should not count on us unless they decide to follow a line of prudence and moderation...". (6-100)

What moderation is he talking about? The moderation of French revolution? Which caused thousands of people's lives, or moderation in 'Water-Loo', which is the bloodiest war of the modern history. This is a little example of their intention to gain political power in every revolutionary government, which meant 'Democracy'.

Simply what Salomon means is that if we don't cause the coup, we don't finance it! If we don't finance, it is a failure. Their objective is clearer in the following, when after many engineered coups, Nathan writes to his branch office in Belgium:

"Now is the moment of which we should take advantage to make ourselves ***'ABSOLUTE MASTERS'*** *of the country's finance. The first step will be to establish ourselves on an intimate footing with Belgium's new Finance Minister, to gain his confidence... and to take all the treasury bonds he may offer us". (6-100)*

They did gain this mastership. Rothschids' historian Derek Wilson dedicates a whole chapter to their unchallenged power, named "Absolute Masters" in his book, "Rothschild, A Story of Wealth & Power".

In 1835, the Spanish government, affected by civil war abrogated the terms of loan. Rothschilds decided to teach her a lesson. They allocated eighteen hundred thousand pounds to buy Spanish Government's Stocks and thus engineered a dramatic fall in the value. One of the journalists watched all this tremendous show of enormous financial power, and said:

"Wouldn't the world be happier if all the kings were deposed and the Rothschild family placed on their thrones"? (6-101)

On 28 July 1836, Nathan Rothscild died, with him went nothing, only his deeds, all wealth, fame, villas, banks and Freemasonry could not help him to escape **"The Hour"**.

After Nathan's death, the family tree grew further, new brains, new blood and new thoughts captured more fields of different businesses. Freemasons were gaining power in different countries. Countries were being colonised rapidly; new industries were introduced. Rothschilds did not hesitate to explore these new lands and their resources. Salomon Rothschild took-over Austria, "Austrian Nordbahn" was opened by him on July 7th 1839. Then he went to take over the ironworks at Wittkowitz [modern Vikovice in Czechoslovakia], for one and a half million gudden.

In Britain and other European countries, this responsibility was handled by other Rothschild brothers. British venture was capitalised by a state loan of a hundred and fifty million francs. Bank of "N.M.Rothschild and Sons" received the major stake to provide that loan.

The French Railways' 25% capital was held by London and Paris Rothschild houses. James and Lionel were the members of the board. Media was another industry, they owned. Brotherhood had already realised the importance of the media. Tell people only what you want them to know. **"No news is good news"**. Rothschilds and Freemasonry had this vital tool in their hands, by using this they could turn 'black into white' and 'white into black'. Along with Freemasonry and Rothschilds went all the revolutions, coups and destruction of monarchs. Media turned public opinion against the kings and Rothschilds provided the rebels with finance. This corroboration created storms of revolutions and financiers or Freemasonry got the desired governments in return. This is how Democracy is enforced, not by will, but by cheek!

Crises broke out in Paris in Feb 1848. On the 24th of the February, elderly king had to flee to England with his family. In mid-March the revolution spread to Austria and Germany. Metternich [the king] fled to England in disguise. Salomon was very generous to lend him money for his flight. This is the type of control they had on both sides. If revolution is successful, their job is done, if revolution fails they are the only ones who helped the disgraced king. If the king is re-stored they have all the sympathies and favours of the good old friend in hard times. A friend in need is a friend in deed. Very true!

In Prussia the character of the press in revolution was sensed and a ban was put on it. When the petition was signed against this ban, its demands included:

1. Freedom of press.
2. Pardon of all political prisoners.
3. Trial by Jury.
4. Civil and religious liberties.
5. Open Courts of Law.
6. Permission to carry arms.

Another army mutiny broke out in Vienna on the 6th of Oct, resulting; a financial burst in all major cities. This was a different experiment done by 'Brotherhood', to destroy a peaceful nation. This time, Rothschilds played at the front to show their stability, to break the other small bankers' trust on public.

"In Paris everyone is ruined. The bankers are tumbling one after the other. Rothschild alone stands erect, albeit bled white". (6-140/141)

How would the public feel if the banks collapsed and collapsed with them their money, the very money they gathered penny by penny? The answer is in **BCCI's situation.**

"Throughout the upheavals of 1848, few public figures had stood so outwardly calm and resolute as the Great Baron- James de Rothschild". (6-141)

They had all the reasons! Editor of the "Tocsin des Travailleurs", writes with sarcasm:

"You (James) are a wonder, sir, Louis Philippe has fallen, Guizot has disappeared, the constitutional monarchy and parliamentary methods have gone by the board; you, however, are unmoved! ...Where are Arago and Lamartine? They are finished, but you have survived. The banking princes are going into liquidation and their offices are closed. The great captains of industry and the railway companies totter. Shareholders, merchants, manufacturers and bankers are ruined en masse; big men and little men are alike overwhelmed; you alone amongst all these ruins remain unaffected. Although your House felt the first violence of the shock in Paris, although the effects of revolution pursue you from Naples to Vienna and Berlin, you remain unmoved in the face of movement that has affected the whole of the Europe. (E Corti, op. Cit, 11, pp-270-1)

After Nathan died, "Lionel Nathan" became head of the family on the British side. Lionel Nathan Rothschild extended loans to British, American and Egyptian governments. He was very active in Masonic formations and:

"Lionel also acted as agent to Russian government for twenty-five years". (Jewish Encyclopaedia, vol-10, p-501/502)

With Rothschilds' influence, grew influence of the Jews. In 1835, David Salomons another Jew, Founder Governor of the London and Westminster Bank, was elected Sheriff of London. Being a Jew, he could not take a Christian oath. A declaration was quickly passed through parliament to change the oath. After this, many Jews were elected on many provincial corporations and the Christian oath, which was the basic factor to take over the responsibilities, was simply ignored. Finally, a legislation; was passed in 1845 to change the oath on the Jews' insistence. Salomons became an alderman in 1847 and Lord Mayor in 1855.

"Lionel Nathan also became the first Jewish member of the British Parliament". (Encyclopaedia Encarta)

N Mayer's brother in law Moses Montefiore was chosen Sheriff of London. He went personally to St Petersburg in order to persuade Tsar Nicholas to revoke some of the Russian's harsh anti-Semitic laws. After Lionel, his eldest son, Nathan Mayer Rothschild took over. N M Rothschild took his seat in the 'House of Lords' in 1885, appointed as 'Governor of Bank of England' titled as 'Sir', 1st 'Baron Rothschild' and in 1855 he was already made the first Jewish peer in Great Britain.

By 1870 these "Jewish-Masonic Brotherhood" were so strong that they were holding assets everywhere in Europe and America.

"There is not a people or government in Christendom in which the paws of the Rothschilds are not plunged to the very heart of the treasury". (6-175)

Not only business, politics was also on their plate. At that time, the chief manager of 'American Democratic Party', August Belmont, was an agent of the Rothschilds. They had big stakes in every government's big projects.

"London Rothschilds had five and a half million pounds tied up in the 'Ottoman State' loans". (6-238)

In 1867, diamonds were discovered in South Africa. "Rhodes" came to "Natty Rothschild" in July 1887 looking for financial backup. Natty offered him one million pounds. Rhodes was a Colonialist and eager to enforce British Imperialism. By 1892 Rothschild Bank had floated a loan for "Boer Government" of the Transvaal, and had investments in **"South Africa Mines"**, railways and general developments. Rothschilds received 4 million gulden worth of **"Royal Dutch"** shares and £240,000 worth of **"Shell"** shares.

AFTER 2ND WORLD WAR

Around 1941, Rothschilds gathered in New York and started a new office at a rented place on 5th Avenue. They were surrounded by all their family members and friends. In 1950 this office was reformed as an investment bank, under the name of "New Court Securities". Soon, Rothschilds were given the projects such as, "Churchill Falls". Another subsidiary company of Rothschilds is "American Commercial Transocean".

Edmond Rothschild, a friend of Henry Kissinger and the only direct descendent of the "Father of Israel", paid his first visit to Israel in 1958, after his uncle Jimmy, died in 1957. Over the next few years he built the first pipeline from the "Red Sea" to the Mediterranean to bring Iranian oil into Israel. Then he constructed a chemical plant and founded the "Israel General Bank".

Meanwhile in America, they were progressing under RITN. In August 1983, they moved into Wall Street with a 50% share in a New York merchant bank. Two months later, RITN merged with "Charterhouse Banking Group". By the end of 1983 they became "Charterhouse J Rothschild", with a £400,000,000 capitalisation. It was one of the largest banks in the City. In March 1986, it became "J Rothschild Holdings", with £603,500,000 assets. An English Socialist, writing in 1891 castigated the Rothschilds as a "blood sucking crew".

"Wherever there is a trouble in Europe, wherever the rumours of war circulate, and men's minds are distraught with fear of change and calamity, you may be sure that a hook-nosed Rothschild is at his game". (6-284)

In France when all the banks were going public by law, Rothschilds changed from a pure merchant bank to a "Financial Commercial Conglomerate". Thus could not be made public by law and skipped the clause. Big names---Big games. For these people law is not a problem, rather law is made to protect them. This is still going on, poor getting poorer, rich getting richer. This role of the financial commercial conglomerate went on in oil, mining, cold storage, shipping, hotels, etc.

Again in 1967, bank changed its identity to a corporation under the name of "Banque Rothschild". The mining company "Rio Trinto" allocated two seats to its major shareholders they were both De-Rothschilds. From 1962 to 1968, Georges Pompidou was Prime Minister of France and from 1969 to 1974, he was President. What people don't know is that Pompidou was a life long friend of the Rothschilds and ex manager of the Paris Bank of Rothschilds. Baron Guy Rtothschild and Pompidou used to meet at lunch once a month.

In 1982 the "Banking House" [Paris House], was nationalised by the government [to show that Rothschilds are not above the law]. The new "Paris House" known as "P.O.Banque" [Paris Orleaw Banque] was opened in 1984.

N.M.Rothschilds is still the only pure family bank with Evelyn its chairman and the Chairman of the "Accepting Houses Committee", the elite of City of London, representing 16 banks, which have a special relationship with the "Old Lady of Thread needle Street". This relationship gives them a very privileged credit status. This position means that the Chairman of "N.M.Rothschild and Sons" is second only to the "Governor of Bank of England" in the unofficial hierarchy of the City. In fact N.M.Rothschilds is more active internationally than ever before. The group's banking division plays a key role in global precious metal trading and stake's a few billion bars in its vaults.

The Evelyn family resisted any suggestions of going public and affirmed strongly that "Rothschilds" can still raise private capital whenever necessary, as they could in the past.

The Grand Lodge of the State of Israel

Freemasons Temple, 5 Weizman St., POB 33206, Tel Aviv 61331, ISRAEL
Tel. +972-3-6954218/9
Fax. +972-3-6960271

CH-10 FOUNDING OF ISRAEL

In 1840, there were only 6000 Jews in Jerusalem. Silently, in 1880, within 40 years their number increased to 20,000. In 1914 they were 35,000.

In 1880, there were about 5 million Jews in the world. Around 75% were spread throughout Russia, Poland and the Balkans. Only 15% lived in Europe.

In autumn, 1882, 'Joseph Feinberg' of "Rishon Le Zion" (First in Zion), approached 'Edmond de Rothschild', then head of the family and Rothschild banks.

Around 1882, Jews started migrating into Europe. Natty Rothschild wrote shocking stories in a series of articles for "The Times" in January, describing the injustice and killings they faced and sufferings they went through in their lands. These articles and other media support justified and reasoned their migration. Not only people sympathised with them but also protested prejudice against them. Help poured from all corners of Europe, only one meeting held at the 'Mansion House'; raised one hundred thousand pounds. This was done to introduce people with 'Jewish problem' and to prepare them to welcome the immigrants with open hearts and arms. Rothschilds could afford to settle all those immigrants at their own cost, which they did. Multitudes of men, women and children made their way to Germany, Austria, France, England and the USA.

If we look at the above dates and figures, we don't have to work hard to sense the planning of a 'Jewish State' in the continuity of the incidents. With 'Rothscilds' the "Absolute Masters", supporting Jews, and Jews themselves! Their forefather, 'Mayer Amschel', never used the Christian calendar throughout his life in all his correspondence he stuck to 'Jewish' instead. This immigration was the middle episode of a long serial.

Among the immigrants were the group of "Zionists", those, determined to create a "Jewish State" and whose leader "Joseph Feinberg" [relevant or irrelevant to Zionists], had already had a meeting with 'Edmond de Rothschild'. In that meeting of 1882, Edmond Rothschild put a practical sketch, instead of financial help, to whom Joseph Feinberg apparently opposed. Edmond Rothschild put the following conditions to help Jews.

The immigrants were to work on the land.
Not to set up as trades and craftsmen.
Not to sub-let or sell their holdings.
Not to hire labour.
Not even allowed to pay their children wages.
Above that, Jews were to be constantly supervised by Rothschild's agent. Any one not acting accordingly was to be expelled.

Beside these strict conditions, new settlers had to sign an agreement for 'Rothschild Administration'. In that was:

"To submit my self totally to the orders which the administration shall think necessary in the name of M.Le.Baron in anything concerning the cultivation of the land and its service, and if any action should be taken against me, I have no right to oppose it".
(Quoted in S.Schama, op. Cit. P-71)

Rothschild Administration started buying land in Jerusalem through their agents. While Muslims were too busy fighting with each other, this work was being done discreetly. It was planned in such a way that inhabitants of Jerusalem did not realise the actual game till the last moment---and when they realised, it was too late. Nowadays, if any Muslim Arab sells his land or property to a non-Muslim other

Muslims humiliate him so no one dares to do it. At that time a while later, locals started getting suspicious about the increasing number of Jewish colonies, so Rothschilds got careful and used their Masonic secrecy.

"We must postpone the founding of any new colonies and put all emphasis on those that are already in existence. There must be unity especially in buying land, for if each one acts separately the price of land will rise greatly. In general it is necessary to avoid publicity in such matters. Only if we proceed quietly and 'cautiously' will our work be crowned with success". (S Schana, op. cit, p-75)

All this was being supervised by Edmond, closely, but quietly. He used to travel to Jerusalem in secrecy. At one point him and his wife journeyed in their yacht as far as 'Port Saeed', then made their way to 'Jaffa' and then fifty miles to 'Jerusalem' in a carriage with the blinds down. Edmond says:

"I am not a philanthropist, I have set out this enterprise to see whether it is possible to establish Jews on Palestine soil". (6-293)

No doubt, Edmond was not a philanthropist; rather he was a cannibal, as we shall see in 2nd World War, the way Brotherhood planned to get 6 million Jews slaughtered by Hitler. This is not surprising at all when "David Ben-Gurion", the first Prime Minister of Israel spoke of Edmond as the "Founding Father" of Israel, he said:

"It is doubtful whether throughout the entire period of close on two thousand years, which the Jews have spent in exile, any person is to be found who equals or who can compare with the remarkable figure of Baron Edmond de-Rothschild".

In 1900, Edmond founded the "Jewish Colonisation Association" and remained its president for life. He could not see how a Jewish political state could be a reality as long as the "Ottoman Sultans" ruled Palestine. The details of conspiracies they did along with Freemasonry, against "Ottoman Sultans", we will disclose in "Ottoman Empire" chapter Inshallah.

ISRAEL, PRE-DECIDED

A Zionist, named Theodor Herzl, who founded the "Zionist Movement" at Bazel in Switzerland, published a pamphlet in Vienna in 1896 called "The Jewish State", prophesising that a Jewish state would come into existence in 50 years. He also described how it is going to be possible, he:

"Regarded assimilation as most desirable but, in view of anti-Semitism, impossible to realise. Thus, he argued: *if Jews were forced by external pressure to form a nation, they could lead a normal existence only through concentration in one territory". (16)*

As we shall see further this is exactly how it was done after the 2nd World War. Jews were forced by or because of Nazis to form a nation. In 1897 Herzl convened the first Zionist Congress at Basel, Switzerland, which stated their target as:

"Zionism strives to create for the Jewish people a home in Palestine secured by public law". (16)

At one point Herzl met with German Emperor William II and Sultan Abdul-Hamit II of Turkey to convince them for the establishment of a Jewish State. Abdul Hamit II was the last Sultan who could hold on to his throne with a powerful grip, unaffected by any Masonic conspiracies. In his diaries, Herzl gave free reign to an imagination racing with him:

"Jews would create initiation of Paris and France; they would have a style of their own; language would pose no difficulty; Switzerland would be the model for federation; women would not work in factories; here would be a nation of thinkers and artists". (The Closed Circle. p-187)

BALFOUR & ROTHSCHILD

Dear Mr Balfour

There was one point I forgot to mention on Friday and I think you might draw the Prime Minister's attention to this; during the last few weeks the official and semi-official German newspapers have been making many statements, all to the effect that in the peace negotiations the "Central Powers" must make a condition for Palestine to be a Jewish settlement under German protection. I therefore think it important that the British declaration should forestall any such move. If you, as you promised, can arrange the interview as I suggested please let Dr Weizmann know...

Yours sincerely
Rothschild

Foreign Office,
Nov 2nd, 1917

Dear Lord Rothschild,

I have much pleasure in conveying to you, on behalf of His Majesty's Government, that following declaration of sympathy with Jewish Zionist aspirations which has been submitted to, and approved by the cabinet.

> **"His Majesty's Government view with favour the establishment of a national home for the Jewish people, and will use their best endeavours to facilitate the achievement of this object, it being clearly understood that nothing shall be done which may prejudice the civil and religious rights of existing non-Jewish communities in Palestine, or the rights and political status enjoyed by Jews in any other country".**

I should be grateful if you would bring this declaration to the knowledge of the Zionist Federation.

Yours Sincerely
Arthur James Balfour
(The above two letters quoted from, 6-341/342)

BALFOUR DECLARATION

On November the 2nd 1917, British Foreign Secretary 'Arthur (Lord) Balfour officially recognised Palestine as a homeland for the Jews. This recognition was named "Balfour Declaration". This was the same year when USA entered the 1st World War, keeping in mind that this entrance was pre-decided. Stating this declaration **Encyclopaedia Encarta' 96 states**:

"The declaration, contained in, a letter from Foreign Secretary Arthur J. Balfour to a British Zionist leader, approved the establishment in Palestine of a 'national home for Jewish people'".

This not only verifies the above stated letter but also proves Rothschild as a British Zionist leader. Hope it clears the background of "Balfour Declaration". This was a terrible blow to Arabs, who under the leadership of T E Lawrence [Lawrence of Arabia] fought their own brothers---Turks---! T E Lawrence was responsible to give Arabs the concept of "nationalism", to pour hatred in Arabs hearts against Turks. This hatred is still taught in British schools and colleges, teaching students "Turks were racist to attack Christians" not mentioning that racism is derived from the colour of skin, not religion. But when it comes to protect Muslims in Europe, they understand this difference. By virtue of this, attacks on Muslims cannot be dealt as racial attacks, but prejudice. Any attack on other religions like Judaism, Hinduism and Sikhism, is considered as prejudice as well as racial.

T. E. Lawrence, full name, Thomas Edward Lawrence, known as Lawrence of Arabia (1888-1935), other names adopted, "J. H. Ross" and "T. E. Shaw", was born in Tremadoc, Wales, in England. Educated in Oxford, learned Arabic in Sinai, in 1914, joined British Military Intelligence Service in Cairo. Later went to Hijaz to the Arab Prince Faisal [later King Faisal 1 of Iraq], worked for him as military adviser, activated Arabs against Turks, promoted nationalism and inaugurated hatred. Lawrence promised Arabs a free country with full sovereignty after the 1st World War, provided Arabs helped British, to fight Turks. Allied forces could not defeat Ottomans unless Arabs helped them, which they did. Arabs actually fought the war for the British just like Afghan Mujahideen did for America [the Afghan Russian war]. In return, Arabs were deprived for their own land. Lawrence is not named as a famous Freemason, but looking at his role this fact cannot be denied. Particularly when he was a cousin of the Queen, a "close friend" of Churchill [a Freemason, whom we shall discuss in 2nd World War] and the role he played was, no doubt Freemasonic. Some years later, Lawrence said:

"I risked the fraud on my conviction that Arabs help was necessary to our cheap and speedy victory in the East, and that better we win and break our word, than lose...The Arab inspiration was our main tool for winning the eastern war. So I assured them that England kept her word in letter and in spirit. In this comfort they performed their fine things: but, of course, instead of being proud of what we did together, I was continually bitter and ashamed". (Documents on British Foreign Policy, 1919-1939, first series. Vol-IV: p 245-247. Quote from 4-79)

Lawrence knew all the way that Britain is deceiving Arabs but he kept his mouth shut. The first clause of Freemasonry is secrecy. When he opened his mouth, he was killed in a motorcycle accident in Dorset. No wonder he is not listed in the gallery of Famous Freemasons.

Today, the Bank of England is still the fiefdom of the global elite. Gertrude Elias says that the Bank collaborated with the leading Zionist, Lord Beansted of Royal Dutch Shell, to arrange the transfer of the assets of the wealthy German Zionists to Palestine. It was these transfers she says, that helped to build up the economy of the embryonic Zionist State.

"In 1903 the British government offered 6,000 square miles of uninhabited Uganda for settlement, but the Zionists held out for Palestine". (16)

Hitler's large-scale extermination of European Jews led many Jews to seek refuge in Palestine. Palestine problem was submitted to United Nations, which on Nov. 29, 1947, proposed partition of the country into separate Arab and Jewish states and the internationalization of Jerusalem. The creation of the State of Israel on May 14, 1948 brought about the Arab-Israeli war of 1948-49, in result Israel obtained more land than had been provided by the UN resolution, and drove out 800,000 Arabs who became displaced persons known as Palestinians.

Thus: 50 years after the first Zionist congress, Zionism achieved its target of establishing a Jewish State in Palestine.

Still feel that Jews were looted and killed unjustly in 2nd World War? Of course they were, but only poor, this killing was used to invoke the general sympathy for a Jewish homeland. This homeland is not founded for Jews, for Christians or for Muslims. This homeland is founded for Freemasons, for Hiram Abif and for Satanism.

הלשכה הגדולה למדינת ישראל
של בונים חופשים קדמונים ומקובלים

The Grand Lodge of the State of Israel
of Ancient Free and Accepted Masons

CH-11 FIRST WORLD WAR

The reasons for the First World War are usually summarised in four, Nationalism, Imperialism, Militarism and Alliance system. None of this is true. There was only one reason for this global-bloodshed: "Global-ism"! With various factors instigating all the other Isms, people always forget the actual factor, "Media" or in those days, "Press". Kent Cooper, the president of 'Associated Press', wrote in the 13th Nov 1944 issue of "Life":

"Before and during the 1st World War, the great German news agency, 'Wolff' was owned by European banking house of Rothschilds, [in simple words, "Zionists" or "Freemasons", both, different sides of the same coin] *which had its central headquarters in Berlin. A leading member of the firm was also Kaiser Wilhelm's* [William II] *personal banker (Max Warburg). What actually happened in Imperial Germany was that Kaiser used 'Wolff' to blind and excite his people to such a degree that they were eager for World War One. Twenty years under Hitler the pattern was repeated and enormously magnified by 'D.NB', Wolff's successors". (4-69)*

On November 23 1908, "Field Marshal Earl Roberts", who was Commander-in-Chief of the British during "Boer War" made a public speech In his speech he stated that:

"A German invasion of Britain was "possible", and calling for a much larger army in order to meet such an attack". (14, vol 1, 175)

This was the same Field Marshal, under whose command, in the "Boer Concentration Camps" the folks and rebels were being imprisoned in South Africa. Barbaric conditions, inhuman oppression and no medical facilities, caused a high death rate:

"Where a funeral was an event...Here some twenty or twenty-five were carried away daily..." (14,vol 1, 38)

The same Field Marshal'sspeech was widely published to create the feeling of insecurity in public. He only mentioned the "possibility", and never said that it is going to "happen". This was a calculated political statement, which still works, "expert critics" complete rest of the job---guided---or unguided. Background of the war, was formed by elite's statements from either side!

Finally, the war was sparked off by the assassination of "Archduke Ferdinand", heir to the Austro Hungarian throne, on 28th June 1914. Ferdinand had already told his friend, Count Czerin that Freemasons have years before decided to kill him. This assassination was carried out in Serbia, by a Serbian secret society called "Black Hand", a sub-society of Freemasonry working in Serbia. The place where he was supposed to be murdered, six assassins failed to complete the job and he escaped alive. After escaping, the "driver" took the wrong turning and stopped right in front of the, 'would be killer', "Garrilo Princip", who completed the job. Sounds like J F K murder, doesn't it?

While this was happening in Serbia, in Russia, same day and nearly same time "Rasputin", [who opposed the war] was being attacked. This was a failed attempt. Rasputin was the most influential adviser to the Tsar of Russia. Auther Colin Wilson, in his book "Rasputin" says:

"There are fifty degrees of longitude between Sarajevo and Pokrovskoe, which means that 11.00 hrs in Sarajevo is about 2.15 PM in Pokrovskoe. It is a strange coincidence that two assassins struck at almost exactly the same moment- a coincidence that makes one inclined to doubt the 'blindness of history'. Ferdinand's death made war

possible; Rasputin's injury made certain, for he was the only man in Russia capable of overturning it". (4-69)

It seems appropriate to give a brief introduction of **"Kaiser Wilhelm"** here, to find out that who was actually fighting who? Full name: "Friedrich Wilhelm Viktor Albert" (1859-1941). He was emperor of Germany and King of Prussia from 1888-1918. He was born in Berlin and educated at the University of Bonn. He was the son of Prince Frederick William, later German emperor as Frederick III and Victoria Adelaide Mary Louise, the eldest daughter of Queen Victoria of Great Britain. That means---he was grandson of Queen Victoria.

Edward VII (1901-1910) was the eldest son of Queen Victoria and Prince Albert, born on November 9 1841, in Buckingham Palace. George V (1910-1936) was born in London on June 3 1865, the second son of Edward VII. So the two rivals in WW1, Britain and Germany, were ruled by "Cousins", (family business) no wonder that:

"He (Wilhelm) ignored the 1917 peace resolutions submitted by the Reichstag and urged continuation of the war." (E/Encarta)

Kaiser Wilhelm, urged on by his advisors (though he didn't need their advise), supported Austria and declared war on Russia and France. Britain joined war, (family war) against Germany. US followed in 1917. Kaiser Wilhelm already surrounded by "Brotherhood" advisors in administration; Masonic press completed rest of the job. Slogans of Nationalism, uncertainty of future, and fear of the enemy were grounded in everybody's mind through daily newspapers. They couldn't smell the minutest of the conspiracies.

It was thought that within a few weeks, the war would end. It lasted four years, with 5509 losses per day, 10 million men were killed in direct action, the economic losses alone were $180 billion, Ottoman Empire was broken into pieces, all defeated countries were ruined and the victors were half bankrupt, apart from the USA. Britain owed US, $4.7 billion; British national debts had increased by 924%. In 1914, British taxation in £1 was only 6p; in 1922 it was 30p. Who did they borrow this money from? Of course from banks or in simple words bankers!

RISE OF HITLER

The allies decided that Germany was responsible for starting the war and should pay $12 billion in reparations. For a staggering German economy, this was a severe punishment. To ensure economic disability, the financial committee decided to return to the gold standard, which made it impossible for Germany to comply with the payments. Gold standard caused such chaos and suffering that it had to be abandoned, but the damage was done. All these factors ensured the rise of a messiah-----Hitler!

After World War 1, "Ludendroff", published a book called "The Protocols of the Elders of Zion", which revealed a Judeo-Masonic plot for world domination. In 1933 Hitler came to power and:

"In that year Hitler charged the Masons with responsibility for various subversive activities, including all the incidents leading to World War 1, and decreed the dissolution of all Masonic bodies in Germany". (Encarta 98 Encyclopaedia, Freemasonry-Opposition)

The German Grand Lodges were closed down, Freemasons were removed from the army and civil services, and many being transported to concentration camps, Masonic records, regalia, and artefacts were seized. This did not affect the elite of Freemasons; they were prepared like Friday the 13th. Only the poor were affected again, this time, Jews.

Another step towards "globalisation" was taken by founding the "League of Nations". This league was founded to introduce people with the global concept; with very limited powers it held, people did not object, rather supported it. This was made a necessity of the time; every one agreed that such organisation would help humanity and prevent wars. No body realised that this "League of Nations" was already decided to be followed by a very powerful constitutional organisation, the "UNO", United Nations Organisation, a full fledge "World Government". To give League of Nations more power, more devastation was required: more blood, more lives, more destruction and more manipulation, was essential. This target was achieved by "World War Two"!

If you look in this picture at the Nazi soldier you will see that he has the whole set - the Maltese Cross, the reversed swastika, the skull and bones and the eagle!

CH-12 2ND WORLD WAR

Thousands of books have been written on this war, few have reached the depth of the conspiracy. So many questions are unanswered, so many blanks in the history that it takes days and numbers of books to find out and to tally the contradictions within one event described by various historians. Rather than going into the usual details of the repeated story, it is better to analyse it. We have already explained the cause of the First World War, that it sparked after the murder of Archduke Ferdinand, heir to the Austro Hungarian throne. If someone was to be blamed for it, it was Austria or Serbia. If someone was genuinely to be blamed, it was Freemasonry who arranged the murder, who got Rasputine attacked, who instigated Kaiser Wilhelm to declare the war against his uncle. The misfortune was that those who had the power of decision were the culprits themselves. They did not decide justly, they decided in corroboration to their agenda, the "2nd World War".

After the 1st World War Germany was brought under severe debts, other decisions at "Versailles" had cost Germany 75% of her iron-ore, 68% of her Zinc and 26% of her coal. Soon France announced that Germany had defaulted on reparation payments and French troops occupied "Ruhr". This "defaulting turned out to be a small short-fall in deliveries of coal and telegraph poles. France's occupation prolonged and it sent the German 'Mark' into a free fall; it plunged to 7'592 to the dollar. The "one eyed dollar". This free fall was hardly surprising, considering the fact that 'Ruhr' produced 80% of Germany's iron', steel and coal and it was occupied by France. By November 1923, the mark had plummeted to "4,200 Billion" to the dollar... yes Billion.

The price in Marks of a loaf of bread in Berlin:

December	1918	0.54
December	1921	3.90
December	1922	163.50
January	1923	250.00
March	1923	463.00
June	1923	1,465.00
July	1923	3,465.00
August	1923	69,000.00
September	1923	1,512,000.00
October	1923	1,743,000,000.00
November	1923	201,000,000,000.00

DAWES PLAN AND YOUNG PLAN

After the devaluation of the German Mark, more oppression was required for the strongest rebellion. This was made possible by two plans, called "Dawes Plan" and "Young Plan", a double strike from Wall Street and British banking cartel. These banking cartels first financed German re-armament and then collapsed the German economy again to bring Adolph Hitler to power.

"General C. Dawes" was appointed by the U.S government to propose a solution to the German reparations fiasco. He introduced a series of short-term loans from Wall Street banks to bail Germans out (basically these banks are different subsidiaries of the same cartel). All these short-term loans did; was to add the debts and delayed the moment, when the German economy would collapse. A collapse, that was to be timed to bring Adolf Hitler into power. What made it even easier is the fact that German bankers and the Allies were on the same side! The Brotherhood side! The all-seeing eye!

The banking system has got its own rules, its own government and its own President. It was N.M. Rothschild who claimed that "give me the control on the currency of a country and I don't care who rules". It would not have mattered if Hitler was not there, someone else would do the same... you would do the same!

"Behind the scene, the U.S was supporting Germany's re-armament, through subsidiaries of American corporations". [Edgar B. Dixon (editor), Franklin D. Roosevelt and Foreign Affairs, (Belknap Press, Cambridge, 1969) Vol. III, p-456] (Quote from 4-93)

Still the stage was not set, something more needed to be done, then came the "Young Plan", which made Hitler's rise to power, certain! After 1929 when the Dawes Plan of short-term loans came to an end with Germany owing an extra "$16 Billion"...yes extra 16 Billion in debt, came one of the Franklin D. Roosevelt's main financial banker Owen D. Young. This gentleman was appointed to propose the "solution" to Germany's inability to pay. This gentleman; "Young", was a "Morgan" executive (a subsidiary of Brotherhood) and the head of the Morgan controlled General electric.

This gentleman indeed found a solution for German problem and demanded payment in "cash" instead of goods. The little prestige and credibility Germany had, wiped out, the economy collapsed overnight. A major financial supporter of Hitler, Dr Fritz Thyssen said under interrogation in 1945:

"The acceptance of 'Young plan' and its financial principles increased unemployment more and more until about a million were unemployed. People were desperate, Hitler said he would do away with the unemployment. The government in power was very bad and the situation of the people was getting worse. That really was the reason of Hitler's enormous success, Hitler had in the election. When the last election came, he got about 40%". [U.S Group Control Council (Germany), Office of the Director of Intelligence, Intelligence Report No. EF/ME/1, September 4th 1945] (Quote from 4-94)

Once Hitler was elected the attitude of the Bank of England and the Federal Reserve to Germany was transformed. The same Germany, which was a defaulter, was offered credit and that also to a Nazi regime! Even after Germany successfully invaded Czechoslovakia, Norman the Head of Bank of England, released £6 million of Czechoslovakian government's gold to Hitler, which was deposited in London. This release was done with the agreement of the then Prime Minister, Neville Chamberlain. Norman was a close associate of Rothschilds and spent a period of time in the U.S, at the offices of the Rothschild funded "Brown Brothers" (later Brown Brothers-Harriman) and was a yes man to Rothschilds.

BROTHERHOOD MEETINGS PRIOR TO WAR

Jimmy Rothschild sat as "Liberal M.P" for the 'Isle of Ely' from 1928-1945, his place 'Baron Ferdinand's Mansion' was the meeting place for the elite of Freemasonry/Zionists. Jimmy's widow, 'Wryly' recalls:

"I like to think our friends, including even such dominant personalities as Mr. Asquith and Mr. Churchill, regarded Waddesdon as a place where they could relax from their labours and indulge in such pastimes as golf, bezique, bridge and Mah-jong, the most popular games at that time. Any political discussion was largely confined to the period at the end of the dinner when, in English fashion, [Masonic compulsion] *the ladies retired from the dining room and the men remained, unencumbered by femininity, to settle down, may be to serious talk. However useful*

these masculine exchanges of view may have been to the participants, I chiefly remember them for the unconscionable length of time they seemed to go on". (Mrs James de Rothschild op. cit. p-110)

While this was happening on the British side, Jimmy's younger brother, Maurice looked after the French border of the, 'would be war'. Maurice entered politics and until 1925, he served as Deputy for the Hantes Pyre'nees. He was extremely popular and after 1926 he represented the Hantes Alpes in the upper house.

During these years the "League of Nations" headquarters was established in Geneva and:

"Maurice frequently entertained the leading statesmen of the age at nearby Pregny. In the late 1930s the chateau became a meeting place for the politicians, like Churchill, Paul Reynaud, and Leon Blum, to organise international opposition to Hitler". (6-365)

LORD HALIFAX (FREERMASON), MEETS HITLER

In fact, Britain did not want to go into war with Germany, at least this was assured to Hitler, when Lord Halifax (The Foreign Secretary to Churchill, both illustrated in Famous Freemason Gallery), met him in Berchtesgaden on 19th November 1937. "The Anglo-American Establishment", a research done by Carroll Quigley reveals, Halifax convinced Hitler that:

1- *Britain saw Germany as the main defence against "Communism" in Europe.*
2- *That Britain was prepared to be part of a four-power agreement with France, Germany and Italy.*
3- *That Britain would allow Germany to liquidate Austria, Czechoslovakia and Poland,* ***"if it could be achieved without British public opinion demanding a war with Germany".*** *(Carroll Quigley, The Anglo American Establishment,p-275)* ***Emphasis*** *added.*

The most important was; "if it could be achieved without British public opinion..." This 'if' was to be used as an excuse to declare war against Germany. Britain waited patiently when Hitler invaded Austria and even released the Czechoslovakian gold to assure the British impartiality. But in March 1938, Lord Halifax---the same Lord Halifax who assured Hitler, Britain's impartiality, and others launched a propaganda campaign known as "War Scare". They told exaggerating stories about Hitler, just like those of Napoleon and Saddam Hussain. Some of the tricks they used were so stupid and childish that amateur critics can show their hollowness. Government dug trenches in the parks to generate fear in the public. Who in their right mind will be having a walk in the park when bombs are blasting everywhere? The appropriate places for these bunkers are in the back gardens of the houses. To top up the fear, government distributed gas masks in the public, with a warning of Hitler's capability of "Chemical Warfare". Remember "Gulf War"? These are the little techniques, which cause big wars, world wars! This is a small example how the mass mind manipulation is done, through the media; it is still being done today, now even sophisticatedly. Britain waited again, till Germany occupied the whole of Czechoslovakia, which gave Hitler all the resources like, Skoda works, the biggest munitions factory in Central Europe, the biggest steel works owned by Rothschilds like the "Czech Explosives".

"Round Table" was another sub-committee formed to mislead people, first acting in favour of the general public and when the time of decision comes, making people believe the only way out is to accept the elite decision. Its name is very charming gesturing equality of the members but there is a "Corner of the Round Table" where "Freemasonry" sits, surrounding every decision.

"The Round Table's driving philosophy was to have Round Tablers in positions to formulate and carry out special policies through social institutions ...called, 'the masses' could be manipulated". (10-155)

First the Round Table kept on opposing war, so won the people's confidence and when the public generally accepted them as their voice, they blew Masonic trumpet; "war is inevitable"! After Hitler occupied Czechoslovakia, "War Scare" propaganda succeeded the majority of its objectives. Round Table turned around and started favouring the war.

THE FIFTH MAN

Lord Victor Rothschild, a Zionist, a Freemason and an agent for MI5 (Military Intelligence Section-5) was a close friend to "Anthony Blunt" from Cambridge days. Anthony Blunt and "Guy Burgess" were both MI5 agents and part of a cell organised by Blunt to pass secrets to the Russians. "Donald Maclean" another fresh face from University joined Burgess in the Foreign Office in 1940. In 1951, the great spy scandal broke and Maclean came under suspicion. Blunt organised his escape and Maclean fled to Moscow along with Burgess. Several members of MI5 came under suspicion but never, Blunt.

Lord Rothschild and Blunt were still friends, till in 1950 they apparently drifted apart. "Kim Philby" another member of Blunt's network, working for MI6, was under suspicion as well but cleared. The following year, Kim Philby took up a career in Jerusalem. Philby's cover blew up and he fled to Moscow as well in 1962.

One year after Philby's defection, "Michael Straight" a U.S citizen, confessed being sucked into "Soviet Spying Network" while at Cambridge by a recruiting officer called "Anthony Blunt". The whole matter was hushed up; it was too dangerous to be investigated, too dangerous for Lord Victor Rothschild. The same Lord Rothschild was made a head of "Think Tank" in 1971 by the then Prime Minister Edward Heath.

Lord Rothschild gathered a team of "young" enthusiastic members and had an approach to all; secret documents, leaders and experts. He was responsible only to the Prime Minister and answerable neither to the electorate nor the civil service chiefs.

In 1973 the "Labour Party" under Harold Wilson returned to power and Victor resigned. Later, he became head of the "Biotechnology Investments Limited" (re-named as N. M. Rothschild Asset Management Limited"), a separate company, which channelled money into a wide variety of scientific and technological projects.

The "Anthony Blunt" story was only revealed after his death in 1980. Then arose the question of the fifth man. But the fifth man was never disclosed, Lord Victor Rothschild, the fifth man, was safe.

OPPOSITION TO WAR

Beside all the tactics used to manipulate the majority of the peoples, still there were a minority who knew; this is wrong! They opposed it, among them was the British Prime Minister "Neville Chamberlain". He did not oppose a defence (in fact Britain had declared war on Germany in Sep 1939), but an offence! This was against the "Lord Halifax Settlement". As a result: he got shouted at, in the "House of Commons" by, "Leopold Amery":

"You have sat too long for any good you have been doing. Depart, I say and let us have done with you. In the name of God, Go!" (House of Commons May 8th 1940)
Chamberlain (1869-1940) was forced to resign in May 1940, just after 3 years since he became the Prime Minister. Chamberlain was succeeded by Sir Winston Churchill. Chamberlain served in Churchill's cabinet as lord president of the council until October 1940, when "illness" forced his resignation. Chamberlain died the following month. Do you smell something? It was not a motorbike accident! He is also not listed in Gallery of Famous Freemasons.

Other opposition to war came from some intellectual people. A "Regulation 18b" was enforced, particularly for:

"Anyone opposes the war or pointed out that it was being engineered by a secret force". (4- 110)

Hundreds of people were imprisoned, without even trial. Guess who was in-charge of the prosecution under "Regulation 18b"? The fifth man! Lord Victor Rothschild!

CHURCHILL

Churchill (1874-1965) Half American himself became Prime Minister of England on May 10th, 1940. His father, Lord Randolph Churchill was "Chancellor of the Exchequer" in mid 1800s, during this time, was constantly funded by the "House of Rothschild".

"When Randolph died he was in debt to the Rothschilds to the tune of some £65,000". (The Churchills, Independent T.V May, 1995)

Soon as Churchill became Prime Minister he took over the Ministry of Defence too, which enabled him to keep an eye on the war, on day-to-day basis, without any interference. And guess who was "Under Secretary to the Ministry of Supply of Britain"? You are right! James de-Rothschild, the old friend of Churchill, "Jimmy"! Now when the set was complete, Churchill promptly ordered to attack the Germans. The combination, was not overlooked by some opposition, and in March1945 they gave Jimmy such a hard ride that Churchill commented:

"If the Commons were ever as rude to the Rothschild again, he would make him [Jimmy] *a privy councillor". (6-392)*

That is a good friend indeed.

On the other side Maurice de-Rothschild, Jimmy's younger brother arranged the meeting of P.M Churchill and French P.M Paul Reynaud, along with Paul's Minister of War, "Georges Mandel", in May 1940. It was the same month as Churchill had taken the oath of office. Derek Wilson, Rothschild's historian quotes the occasion:

"He [Maurice Rothschild] *arranged a private dinner party for the four Statesmen at the Ritz. He* [Maurice] *presided at the table while others talked". (6-392)*

What they talked and discussed we will discover later on in the chapter.

Churchill corresponded with American President, Roosevelt (Freemason) on daily basis. Within his 17 days in the office, British forces were on the verge of retreating. When panic broke out in public, Churchill was very confident in winning the war. 10 Downing Street were packing up to move the valuables because Hitler forces were due any time, at the time when they were hiding some antique photos, his secretary recalls:

"He stopped them by saying 'don't hide these photos, we are going to win the war". (Finest hour, BBC1, 24-11-99)

No doubt this was a very encouraging statement for a nearly defeated nation but what was the real confidence about? Let me tell you! It was the assurance of Freemasonry, the pre-planned American indulgence in the war. Think carefully,

Churchill, a Freemason, Roosevelt, a Freemason, French P.M a close friend of Maurice. All resources of Hitler were depending on Freemasonry. And on the top, the only way to occupy England was through the English Tunnel/Channel Tunnel, which was heavily guarded by French ships. War was engineered any way, but the plan was a little bit different at this point. To create a real horror, it was necessary to provide Hitler's forces an access through the "Channel Tunnel". This was not possible if French ships were present there. The answer was very simple, remove the French ships, this was done, exactly:

"Churchill ordered the British forces to open fire on the French ships. Within minutes1300 French sailors were dead, warships drowned and German way was clear". (Finest hour, BBC1, 24-11-99)

French, and British were allies, French could not---and---did not expect this from Britain and died defenceless. Now you know what was decided in the secret meeting at "Ritz"? Yes these are the war heroes and icons of patriotism! What about the poor French sailors who were sacrificed for this Masonic, Satanic ritual?

Churchill statue in paint attack

From Susan Bell in Paris

"VANDALS have attacked a statue in Paris of Sir Winston Churchill, painting the hands red as if to denote culpability for bloodshed and daubing the effigy with the words 'Mers el Kebir, 1300 killed'. This recalls the wartime leader's controversial order to fire on French ships in the Algerian port on July 3 and 6 1940. Police said the vandals struck on Monday, All Saints day, which is devoted to remembrance of the dead. (Times, London 3-11-99)

What would you call them? VANDALS OR PATRIOTS?

"We must not surrender, we will fight in the hills, in the houses and on the beaches" was the famous speech from a brave P.M of England, but it is easy to sense the drunken tone in the recording, yes Churchill was a regular drinker, according to his secretary Marian Holmes:

"He would prefer Brandy in stead of water with sardines sandwich. He used to drink regularly day and night, a proper party man, even on the eve of Sep the 7th, when Hitler was bombing London Docks, Churchill was holding a dinner party in 10 Downing Street". (Finest hour, BBC1, 24-11-99)

Churchill is listed in the Gallery of Famous Freemasons. What they did not list is, his other activities for Freemasonry. He was one of the founders of the 'National Reconnaissance Office' (NRO), another organisation set under "Committee of 300" (see ch-17), which is an elite organisation working for Freemasonry. NRO has a strict control on America. NRO is one of the most top-secret organisations in America.

"Churchill had a hand in setting up the NRO...Even today NRO's annual is not known to 'The Congress' of the United States, and it is responsible to only a selected few in Congress. But it is a creature of the Committee of 300 to whom its reports are routinely sent every few hours". (10-177)

OPERATION FULLER

After the French ships were removed from Channel Tunnel, on July 3 and 6 1940, Hitler could attack Britain at any time. A war strategy was planned to defend Britain, this was named "Operation Fuller". Germany's ship had to travel altogether 160 miles to reach the British coast. This was a long and dangerous journey. RAF deputed 3 Aircrafts to patrol the English Channel regularly, alongside British Naval Ships' presence in the Channel. On the night when Germans decided to come through the Channel, All three patrol Aircrafts came back with a technical problem. Germans kept advancing and every British Naval Ship failed to spot them. Hours later, it was an Airforce Base officer, who checked German advance on the radar.

Panic broke out in the RAF, first thing they tried was to contact the Royal Navy, they failed; telephone lines were busy---all-lines---so were the all-ies---! No one knew that the British had a pre-planned strategy for this situation. Finally when some high ranked officer informed about "Operation Fuller" plan, duty officers went looking for it. Unfortunately no one knew the "Fuller Officers". Eventually, when they found out who the officers were, they tried to find them, only to know that the "Fuller Officers" are on holidays. At least they could get hold of the files once they knew where those files were, they did find out where the files were but they could not get them. The files were locked and officer had taken the keys on holidays---have a nice holiday---!

11 hrs had gone past, before the British army came to realise what was going on. 15 hours, later RAF came into action whereas the Germans had travelled all 160 miles safely.

(Source of information, "Great Military Blunders" BBC, 9-3-2000)

This was mid July when the Germans took control of the English Channel, when RAF realised what had happened, they retaliated and lost 110 fighter planes. More damage, more debts, more interest. More money for banks in simple words---for **bankers**.

THE AMERICAN FRONT

George Washington
Worshipful Master
and proposed for
General
Grand Master
of the
United States

Image and Text from:
Mackey's Encyclopedia
of FREEMASONRY

On 16th June 1941, Churchill requested again to USA for "help", it was turned down saying: "people won't allow it". How could people allow it? Why will someone jump into someone else's fire? There was a need for "mass mind manipulation", people need to get hurt to cry out; "some thing should be done". This mass manipulation was done on 7th Dec 1941 when Pearl Harbour, was bombed by Japan. How Japan fell into this trap is another story, the American fact is that Japanese messages were de-coded 4 days before. Like "Operation Fuller" the messages went missing from navy files.

If the Americans did not know about the bombing then how come the cream of U. S. Navy was out of Pearl Harbour? 3,000 people who got killed were ordinary sailors and civilians.

The story will not be complete if "General Douglas Mac Arthur (1880-1964) is not mentioned. He worked as an aide to President Roosevelt (Freemason), was Chief of Staff of 42nd Division in W.W.1, retired in 1937, but was brought back at the age of 61 to fight the war with Korea. He tried his best to pursue China into the war but was defeated and retreated to 300 miles.

It was General Douglas Mac Arthur on whose will "Atom Bombs" were dropped on Japan and it was him who accepted the surrender of Japan in August 1945. Amazingly, the surrender was accepted on the same terms, to which the Japanese had already agreed to previous summer. The sole purpose of signing a year later was to create a terrible atmosphere of atomic destruction. [How this bomb was created, see "Project Paper Clip" in UFOs, Ch-23]

After Roosevelt's death (perhaps he did not agree on mass atomic destruction), Harry S. Truman (F.M) authorised the use of new weapon on Hiroshima and Nagasaki, on August 6th and 9th 1945. Eighty thousand men women and children were killed at Hiroshima alone only by explosion.

"Japanese had agreed to surrender the previous spring on the same terms that were accepted after the bombs were dropped". (4-118)

So why did America throw atom bombs?

"The psychological spin behind the explosion of the bombs was to create such a world wide fear of the power of nuclear energy that countries would give up their sovereignty, turn all their weapons and armed forces over to a world government and surrender their freedom". (Colonel Donn Grand Pre, The Spotlight 12 Sep 1994) (Quoted from 4-119)

This was General Mac Arthur Douglas, and guess---who was he? Yes---you are right---a Freemason!

"He was made a mason 'at sight' by Samuel Hawthrone, Grand Master of Philippines on January 17 1936 and he affiliated with Manila Lodge No.1 Manila. He received 32nd degree of the Scottish Rite at Manila the same year and was a life member of the Nile Shrine Temple, Washington". (1-237)

In General Douglas' case, it was an exception that is why he was made a "Freemason on sight". But a General alone could not take such powerful decisions i.e., using a bomb. To match him perfectly was Harry S. Truman also a Freemason. To put true colours to the picture of a peaceful cause of war, Truman, ousted Gen. Mac Arthur Douglas from military, but let him command the occupational forces in Japan until 1951. When Mac Arthur returned to America after 15 years (when the dust had settled down) of withdrawal from army, he received a heroic welcome, by seven and a half million American citizens-----we love peace-------!

More than 20 years after the 1st W.W, on April 25th 1939, U.S Senator Gerald P. Nye of North Dakota revealed to the Senate some of the background to Britain's recognition of a Jewish homeland and the 1st W.W in general. He said; he had been given some documents called "The Next War". The title referred to the 2nd World War, which the writers of the documents already knew, was going to happen. One volume was called "Propaganda in the Next War".

Indeed this is the success of the propaganda that the 2nd W.W is remembered for the killing of 6 million Jews and every one forgets to mention about Hiroshima and Nagasaki. **Only 6 million are remembered, what about the rest of 42 million?** It is mentioned nowhere, not in the general history books, not in the "Microsoft

Encarta Encyclopaedia", like it never happened. And who was responsible for the war on the first place? Hitler is a villain! What about Gen. Arthur! What about Churchill! Roosevelt! Truman! What about Freemasons!

Six million Jews were sacrificed merely for Propaganda, and that is being done! But who were the killers? No one mentions. Jewish sacrifice was to create worldwide sympathy for Israel, for the illegitimate first born of Zionism and Freemasonry. Still on "V-Day" the film called "Schindler's List" is shown free in schools to memorise Masonic propaganda to the next generation.

"Templars felt no loss"; the Elite of Jews already escaped with their treasures and holdings, this was the actual "Schindler's list", list of rich Jews, the Freemasons, to be let gone! Those who were looted; were poor and those who looted, were Americans.

Nazi gold looted by US generals

From Damian Whitworth

In Washington

Towards the end of the Second World War, Adolf Eichmann ordered that a train leave Budapest for Germany crammed with gold, silver, paintings and fur seized from the 600,000 Hungarian Jews he had exterminated. Months later American troops found the train hidden in a tunnel. Then according to a new investigation by a presidential commission, they proceeded to help themselves. According to the report... US officials allowed the Nazi loot to be pilfered by American generals, sold to soldiers at auction and turned over to Austria, instead of trying to return it to the survivors of the holocaust. (Times, London 16-10-99)

With the end of the 2nd World War, Brotherhood got closer to their target of "One-World-Government". "League of Nations" was re-formed into "United Nations", a fully empowered world government. Debts increased through out the world. Bankers had more material to manipulate masses. America proved her supremacy by killing millions of innocent Japanese and the horror of Communism was spread world over. This was the beginning of another era, "The Cold War"! To understand this "Cold War", is essential to understand Russia, to understand Russia, is essential to understand Freemasonry in Russia. If Freemasonry is active in Russia that means: "Cold War" was another illusion designed by the Brotherhood. Controlling both sides and mass manipulating!

RUSSIAN FRONT

The main competitors of "Democracy" in the 2nd World War were "Communism" and "Socialism". As we have described Democracy (richer getting richer) already, that it is a form of "Capitalism". We will analyse the rest two and then proceed.

The Karl Marx Plan:
From capitalism to socialism

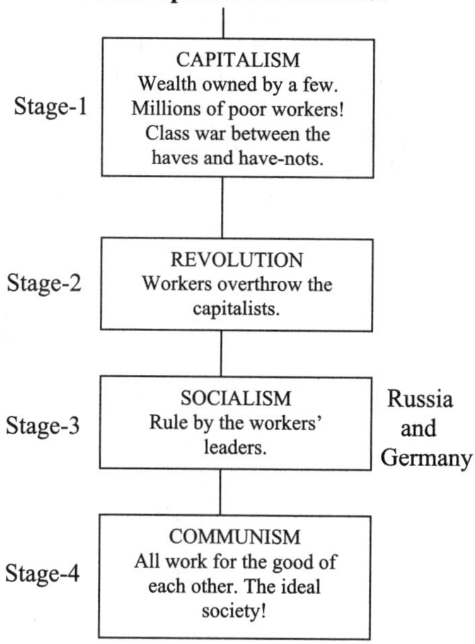

(11-93)

As we can see "Socialism" is coming from the same roots, but only one step behind the actual "Communism". After the revolution, Russia was transformed into "USSR", which stands for "United Soviet Socialist Republic". It puts Russia on exactly the same place as Germany. Then how come the "USSR" was acceptable and not "NSGW", the "National Socialist German Workers", famous as "Nazi", which exactly matches stage-3, as does "USSR". The only difference is "NG", National German or subsequently "German Nationals". Of course one had to be a German National to join the ruling party, "imported rulers" would seem funny. Can one be a British MP if not a British National? Or American Congress Rep: being an illegal immigrant?

One can give hundreds of reasons for WW2 and write pages and pages arguing different circumstances that sparked WW2, but in simple words, there were only two:

1-Globalism.
2-Zionism.

FREEMASONS IN RUSSIA

In 1731, "Captain John Phillips" was appointed "Provincial Grand Master" of Russia and Prussia. His successor was "General James Keith", a Russian army general. James was appointed a Grand Master in 1740 by the "Grand Lodge of England".

In 1772, "Ivan Yelagin" became Grand Master; he was responsible for establishing the "Scottish Rite" of three degrees in St Petersburg and Moscow.

Masonry flourished in Russia under the regime of "Catherine the Great", till Catherine realised what exactly Freemasonry was doing behind the face of a harmless society. Later he arrested some of them for "Revolutionary" activities.

"Paul I" was more alert about Freemasonry, but could not clean up totally, although he banned them. The reason of his leniency was his own son, "Alexander I" who was "possessed" by Masonry and was a Freemason himself. Alexander I permitted "Lodges" again in 1803, he did not understand its dangers, the result was "Napoleon's" invasion of Russia. It took him another 19 years to realise that the invisible hand, behind all troubles was of Freemasons. Alexander banned all "secret societies" in 1822. Freemasonry changed shape; they adopted the name "Decembrists" and became re-formers. Finally in 1825, when he crushed the "Decembrists", he forbid Masonry in "all varieties".

Masonry did not finish with the ban; all Russian Masons became members of Foreign Lodges and carried on their mission till the end of the 19th century. One of these "foreign masons" was "Maxim Kovalevsky", who initiated their second episode in 1906, by establishing the first of several Lodges under the jurisdiction of the "Grand Orient". By 1910, all old Russian Lodges were inaugurated. According to "Freemasonry in Russia" and " The Modern Encyclopaedia of Russian and Soviet History",

"These Lodges were more oriented 'socially and 'politically'.

In fact after the First World War, it was the elite who financed the "Russian Revolution". Lenin and Trotsky were both puppets in Masonic hands. "Lieutenant Colonel John Bayne Mac Lean", the founder and president of "Mac Lean Publishing" was known for his close contacts with "Canadian Intelligence". In 1918, in "Mac Lean Magazine", he writes,

"Originally the Brits found through Russian associates that Kerensky, Lenin and some other lesser leaders were practically in German pay, as early as 1915 and they uncovered in 1916 the connections with Trotsky, then living in New York. From that time he was closely watched by the 'Bomb Squad'. In the early part of 1916, a German official sailed into N Y 'British Intelligence Officials' accompanied him. He was held up at Halifax, but on their (B. Intelligence) instruction, he was passed on with profuse apologies for the unnecessary delay.

After much manoeuvring he arrived in a dirty little newspaper office in the slums and there he found Trotsky, from whom he bore important instructions. From June 1916, until they passed him onto the British, the N.Y Bomb Squad never lost touch with Trotsky. They discovered that his name was "Braunstein", and that he was a German, not a Russian".

Kerensky finally settled in US where he lectured political and social science. "Russian Social Democratic Labour Party" was founded in 1898. It was a small party whose members were largely exiled. This party wanted to bring a revolution through class conflict, the "Marxism".

"Vladimir Ulyanov, known by his underground name "Lenin", was chief contender of the party leadership". (14, vol-1, p-34)

Lenin left Russia in 1900, when he was 30. From there he moved down to Western Europe. This is where he started his campaign against the Tsar. "Iskra" (The Spark), was the newspaper founded in December 1900, which in fact "Sparked" the revolution. This newspaper had its publishing centres in London Munich and Geneva.

"From his [Lenin] *base of exile in Switzerland, Lenin used 'Iskra' to urge and to forge a centralised party structure"... (14, Vol-1, p-34)*

Wherever you go, wherever you see you will find the same invisible hand behind all revolutions in the world, call it Democracy, Socialism, Fascism or Communism.

In 1848, "Karl Marx" (a Jew), wrote the Communist Manifesto, under the direction of "Illuminati", a sub branch society of Freemasonry. "Professor Karl Ritter" of "Frankfurt University" wrote the anti-thesis, under the direction of Illuminati as well. The idea of two thesis was that any one opposes "Karl Marx" would join "Karl Ritter". Thus: divide the world into two ideologies, while controlling both sides. Use the differences to engage the two camps into wars, and dividing them further into larger and larger number of enemies. As the world history tells us, the conspiracy was and is successful.

The work "Karl Ritter" started was continued after his death and completed by "Friedrich Wilhelm Nietzsche"! This is the same "Nietzsche", who wrote the book called "The Gay Science" in 1887 and claimed "god is dead".

"Mao Tse Tung", was the founder of Chinese Communism, he started studying "Karl Marx", while working in the University Library of Peking. There he met a "group" of professors and students, looking for "new ways" to solve China's problems.

"In 1920, a Russian agent arrived in Peking to help found a "Chinese Communist Party". The following year, Mao and 12 others formed the "Chinese Communist Party" in Shanghai. (11-168)

The organizer of the Chinese revolution was Dr Sun Yat-Sen. A Christian by religion, and a graduate of an American University. He had never held any political office in China, from where he was in exile for the last fourteen years. Yet he was chosen to lead China and hailed by all moderates and reformers. How did he become a leader of the most populated part of the globe? Propaganda, of course! Media, indeed! This is freedom! This is democracy! A person totally inactive previously in his country, living in exile is the leader of the nation.

Dr Sun Yat-Sen raised the slogans for women freedom, democracy and, a China free from all the "economic strangleholds" of European powers and United States, yet:

"Sun Yat-Sen was fundraising in the United States when the news of the uprising reached him". (14, vol 1, p-240)

But he did not rush back to his country, as a responsible leader would. Instead he went to a European tour for more "fund Raising" from United States, where he had been living in exile. He waited patiently till all struggles were over and republicans had crushed Manchu and loyalist troops in Nanking. Brotherhood found this time suitable to ship him back to his native country. He sailed from France and reached Shanghai on Christmas day and on 31st December 1911 he was "elected" president of the new "Chinese Republic" by "Chinese Republicans". Dr Sun took-up office in Nanking on the following day and marked it by introducing the "Pagan Calendar" normally called the "Solar Calendar", by abolishing the ancient Chinese calendar of 10-day period, based on lunar calculations.

"Before the 2nd World War there were Lodges in China under Massachusetts jurisdiction". (22-33)

To celebrate their wickedness and the world's madness, Stalin, Roosevelt and Churchill met in Tehran (Iran) in 1943 and again in Yalta, in 1945. The famous: "big three".

This was the 2nd World War and this was the "The Cold War".

---Judge for yourself---

CH-13 OTTOMAN EMPIRE

While "Templars" were gaining power in Europe, they never forgot the humility and defeat they faced by Muslims, their actual enemy. They continued their "Crusades", but in a different battlefield, with different weapons. The "Army" they deployed this time was invisible, also because of leisure and greed of the Muslim Sultans, invincible! This army consisted of different groups formed on humanitarian basis as well as religious. Among them were "Daughters of Nile", "The Free Thinkers", "Christian Missionary", and besides several others, most important, the "Jesuits".

JESUITS

Although all the societies and groups mentioned above had different names and approaches but the main purpose of them all was the same: to induce others specially the "Muslim World". Muslims were unaware of this warfare so were easily mislead. For verification of their mottos and skipping minute details we quote only "Jesuits". Readers are requested to go through this quote thoroughly and patiently.

"Ceremony of induction and 'Extreme' oath of the Jesuits"

{Given to a Jesuit of minor rank when he is to be elevated to a position of command}

Superior speaks:

"My son, heretofore you have been taught to act the 'Dissembler' (a phoney who acts like he is on your side, but he really is not) among the 'Roman Catholics' to be a 'Roman Catholic', and to be a Spy even among your own brethren, to believe no man, to trust no man..

Among the 'Reformers' to be a 'Reformer' among the 'Hugenots' (French Protestants) to be a 'Hugenot', among the 'Calvinists' to be a 'Calvinist', among the 'Protestants', generally to be a 'Protestant', and obtaining their confidence to seek even to reach from their pulpits, and to denounce with all the vehemence in your nature our 'Holy Religion' and the 'Pope'; and even to descend so low as to become a Jew among Jews, that you might be enable to gather together all information for the benefit of your order as a faithful soldier of the Pope..

You have been taught to insidiously plant the seeds of jealousy and hatred between states that were at peace; and incite them to deeds of blood; involving them in war with each other; and to create revolutions and civil wars in communities, provinces and countries that were independent and prosperous, cultivating the arts and the sciences and enjoy the blessings of peace, to take sides with the combatants and to act secretly in concert with your brother Jesuit who might be engaged on the other side, but openly opposed to that with which you might be connected, only that the Church might be the gainer in the end, in the conditions fixed in the treaties for peace, and that the end Justifies the means.

You have been taught your duty as a Spy, to gather all statistics, facts and information in your power form every source, to ingratiate yourself into the confidence of the family circle of 'Protestants' and heretics of every class and character, as well as that of the merchant, the banker, the lawyer, among the schools and universities, in Parliament and Legislatures, and in the Judiciaries and Councils of State, and to 'be all things to all men' for the peoples sake, whose servants we are unto death.

You have received all your instructions heretofore as a 'Novice', a 'Neophyte' (a newly ordained priest), and have served as a Coadjutor, Confessor and Priest, but you have not yet been invested with all that is necessary to command in the army of 'Loyola' in the service of the Pope.

You must serve the proper time as the instrument and executioner as directed by your superiors, for none can command here who has not consecrated his labours with the blood of the Heretic, for without shedding blood no man can be saved. Therefore, to fit yourself for your work and make your own Salvation sure, you will, in addition to your former 'Oath of Obedience', to your Order and allegiance to the Pope, repeat after me:

"I,....now, in the presence of Almighty God, the blessed virgin Mary, the blessed Michael, the Archangel, the blessed St John the Baptist, the holy Apostles, St Peter and St Paul and all the Saints and sacred hosts of heaven...I furthermore promise and declare that I will, when opportunity presents, make and wage relentless war, secretly or openly, against all heretics, Protestants and Liberals, as I am directed to do, to extirpate (to pull out by roots) and exterminate them from the face of the whole earth, and that I will spare neither age, sex or condition, and that I will hang, burn, waste, boil, flay, strangle and bury alive these infamous heretics, rip up the stomachs and wombs of their women and crush their infants' heads against the walls, in order to annihilate forever their execrable race (cursed race). That when the same cannot be done openly, I will secretly use the poisoned cup, the strangulating cord, the steel of the poniard (a dagger) or the leaden bullet, regardless of the honour, rank, dignity or authority of the person or persons, whatever may be their condition in life, either public or private, as I at any time may be directed so to do by any agent of the Pope or superior of the 'Brotherhood' of the 'Holy Faith' of the 'Society of Jesus'".

["The Engineer Corps of Hell", c-1883, by Edwin A Sherman, p118, "Library of Congress", Catalogue Card No 66-43354,]

(Special thanks to Eddie)

For those who haven't read the above, I insist to go through it, so you get an exact picture of what kind of people, the Muslim World had to deal with.

"Jesuits", were founded by "Saint Ignatius" of "Loyola" in 1534, and confirmed by "Pope Paul III" in 1540. To promote their activities in corroboration with the "Missionary", they used the veil of "Education" and "Secular disciplines". The order is governed nowadays by a superior general, residing in Rome, elected for life. The general congregation of the order, consisting of representatives of various provinces elect's the Governor. World is divided into 65 regional provinces, each under its own father province.

"The aim of Ignatius of Loyola in forming his band was to make a pilgrimage to the Holy Land to convert the Muslims". (Encyclopaedia Encarta 96)

Jesuits members took a leading role in the "Counter Reformation", by establishing schools and colleges throughout Europe.

"For 150 years they were the leaders in European education, by 1640 they had more than 500 colleges throughout Europe". (Encyclopaedia Encarta 96)

Another century later their colleges increased to more than 650 and 24 universities. "St Francis Xavier" took Jesuits to India and Japan; others expanded it to interior China and the coast of Africa. They were responsible for oppressing and killing millions of native South Americans. In Paraguay they almost ruled for 200 years. At one time or another "Jesuits" have been expelled from every European country. They carried on their activities under local "Brotherhood Orders". When this army discreetly entered Muslim World with their mischief, Muslims did not even realise, the slight but rapid change this entrance caused, and eventually completed the

Muslim destruction. "Jesuits" kept their oath with the Pope; Muslims forgot theirs with Allah.

WARNING TO OTTOMANS

"We have sent thee with the truth, a bearer of glad tidings and a warner; and there is not a nation but a warner hath passed among them". (Qur'an, 35-24)

"If We willed, We could raise up a warner in every village". (Qur'an, 25-52)

"Ibrahim Muteferrika", a Hungarian revert to Islam, published a book in 1731, called "Rational Bases for the Politics of Nations". In that book he offered the European perspective to his Turkish brothers. He pointed out the Ottoman's laziness and corruption, which he contrasted with European energy in opening the world, for example, the colonising of America. If the Ottomans would also acquire the useful sciences, military science especially, they would defeat their enemies.

Merely for this he had to import a printing press into Turkey to produce the book. His message was gone unheeded; the printing press was folded, to start again after a lapse of half a century.

Light of Freemasonry

GENIOLOGY OF TURKISH SULTANS

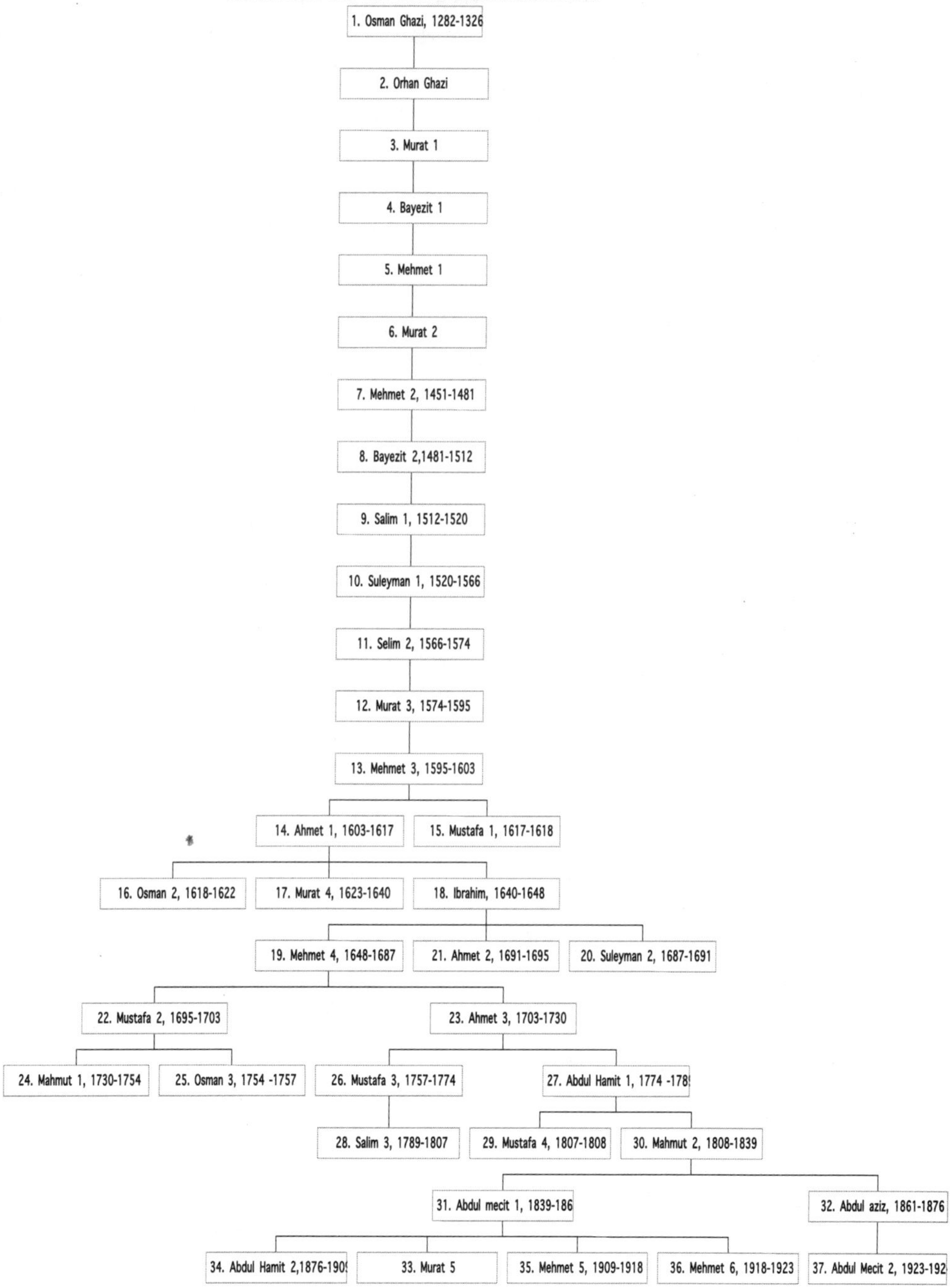

DECLINE OF THE OTTOMANS (BIG GAME, 1ST HALF)

When the Ottoman Empire fell, the West declared: "The Big Game has Finished" a strange phrase. Was this just a sarcastic remark or really there was a "Big Game" going on? We shall find out in this chapter Inshallah.

The only Kingdom, eternal is His, to Whom belong Worlds. Every other kingdom is momentary and nothing but an allusion. We, human beings are His vicegerents (Khalifah), given authority to enforce Allah's law on earth by Allah's command. When we mix our own ideology with Allah's commands we assume that we know better and adopt such a way that slowly leads us astray. That is why we are commanded to recite in every prayer:

"Ihdenas siratal mustaqim"

'*(O' Allah), Guide us, to the straight path'*

"Straight path", is truly obeying Allah (SWT), not differing to the minute extent. In this chapter we shall see, how our ancestor rulers slightly left "Sirat Al Mustaqim" and slowly drifted away completely from the "Right Path".

Although Muslim history has witnessed glorious Muslim kings and rulers, still we all know that prophet Mohammad (PBUH), never established his kingdom, but Allah's, neither did the "guided Caliphs". When monarchy came into Islam, it infiltrated the purity of "striving in the path of Allah"(Jihad), with elements of "personal greed". Even "Khilafah" became essential hierarchy, which was never practiced by our "Khulafa-e-Rashedin". Only "Ottoman dynasty" lasted 642 years excluding prior monarchies, this is enough time Allah (SWT) gave us to mend our ways but we collectively proved ourselves guilty of our own destruction.

"On that account: We ordained for the children of Israel that, if anyone slew a person unless it be for murder or for spreading mischief in the land it would be as if he slew the whole people". (Q, 5-32)

Although 'Jews' are addressed in this verse, but this is a general command applying to every Muslim. "Mehmet I" (5th Sultan) was the first Ottoman, who killed his own brothers for throne. I am not in authority to insinuate or defend him; I am just stating a fact of history, which did happen! Centuries, that followed saw this greed of throne changing into a permanent conflict amongst all descendants. Then came a time when a Sultan would imprison his brothers or children into a cage permanently, fearing their claim to the throne. An even darker act was children's and infants' killing just for the cause of saving one's throne. Hundreds of infants died in the Harems (Sultan's palaces), many were executed in their youth for the sake of the throne.

"Mehmet", brother of "Abdul hamit I" who became "Mustafa III", was the last in the chain of 78 princes, executed in fear of mutiny in 400 years. This was a separate occasion other than their mysterious deaths in infancy. Abdul Mecit I (1839-1861) alone fathered eighteen sons and twenty-five daughters, including two sets of twins. Twenty-five of his children died as infants. Amongst his own brothers and sisters, he was one of six children survived out of thirty-six.

Whenever these cage-grown, death-fearing claimants got the chance to rule; these isolated sultans became nothing but puppets in the hands of conspirators. Leaders of the nations were people, who had not seen the outside world. They had not experienced day-to-day life or gone through ups and downs of worldly affairs, but they were "Kings". On their decision, depended millions of Muslims' lives and future.

NAQSHE-DIL

In 1502, Christopher Columbus discovered and explored an island in East of 'West Indies'. In 1635 the island was settled by French Government and now after many years of struggle between Britain and France, constituted an overseas department of France. This little island is called "Martinique". In middle of 18th century this island was a centre of "brotherhood" activities. In Martinique were born two girls, who changed the world and were a test for humankind. One of them was Josephine, born in 1763 the wife of Napoleon:

"Martinique... Birth place of Empress Josephine". (Encyclopaedia Encurta 96)

Josephine's part we have described in the Battle of Waterloo, how she manipulated Napoleon, (the Illustrious Brother) along his marshals. The other, however, not mentioned in history books as from Martinique particularly but her name reveals it all. She was a cousin of Josephine, born around 1770s and her name in the Western history is "Marie Martha Aimee Dubuc de Rivery of Martinique". Muslim historians know her by her 'Adoptive Name', "Naqshe-Dil". Both of these girls were extremely beautiful and specially trained by "Adoptive Rite" of 'Freemasonry', 'Jesuits' or 'Brotherhood', whatever you want to call them. When their trainers were confident on the years of training they received from their childhood and the power of their femininity, they shot these poisonous arrows to their due targets.

Josephine was easy to log in because she only had to reach France and Napoleon was easy to approach with western cultural values. The cousin of Josephine, "Marie Martha", rather had a difficult task. Somehow she had to be implanted in the "Harem" of Turkish Sultan without any suspicion. For this, Brotherhood needed some statistics, which were provided by their surveyors. Such a survey is quoted in the book called "Constantinople, Ancient and Modern" by 'Dallaway'. In this survey, "Avret Bazar" (Women Market), is described in detail. It tells what kinds of women are sold here and amongst them what kind of women can reach the "Harem". The surveyor notes the ordinary women's deals and quotes about pretty ones as "others":

"The exquisite beauty of the others is enhanced by every art of dress and orient accomplishments, and they are usually sold for several thousand piastres. Many are reserved for Seraglio [Sultan's Harem], *where though they are considered as most fortunate".*

He goes on to describe the even safe upbringing root of these girls to the Harem by teaching of dance and tambourine, *conducted "solely by elderly women"*. Then he writes the strict guard, four, five miles around the Harem by fierce Bostandjis (special guards for Harem), and declines any chances of a direct approach to Harem, suggesting:

"Greek and Frank ladies occasionally visit them, whose husbands are connected with the Porte as merchants and interpreters, under pretence of showing them curiosities from Europe. From such opportunities all the accurate information of the palace must be collected, and to such I am, at present, indebted".

Around 1784, a beautiful, 14 years old young girl is brought in "Avret Bazar", her beauty refrained anyone to bid for her. The seller told everyone that she is a descendant of early French or Spanish settlers of the New Land (America), and was kidnapped by pirates, later captured from them (he never mentioned, who captured her from pirates). This was the reign of Sultan Abdul Hamit I (1774-1789). The girl was taken to the Harem of "Topkapi". The girl was quick in learning Turkish (probably she already knew), and did not take long to reach the Sultan's heart. On 20th August 1785, she bore a child; this child was named "Mahmut", later on to become

"Mehmut II", the 30th Sultan (1808-1839). This 14 years old girl was given the Harem name "Naqshe-Dil", a name that would be known throughout the Ottoman Empire.

Once Naqshe-Dil was in the Harem, the "Big Game" was kicked off. The problem was now, how to get the information from inside the Harem. In the light of above quoted statistics it seemed impossible. But "Brotherhood" is not familiar with impossible.

It took them another 7,8 years but they waited patiently. In 1792 a gardener named "Jacob Ensle" was brought to the "Summer Harem" of Sultan, to give a "New Look" to the gardens around the Harem. Jacob was an Austrian and brother of Austrian imperial gardener at 'Schonburn'. Jacob was brought by the 31st Sultan Salim III (1789-1807) and remained there for a whole 10 years. Jacob had a **"Lodge"** in the palace gardens and often invited **"Guests"** to visit him there.

"One of his guests, "Edward Daniel Clarke", describes the Valide Sultan [mother of Sultan] *and Sultan's four wives, which he caught a glimpse through two small gimlet holes, bored for the purpose, in a small scullery window of the gardener's* [Jacob's] *"Lodge". (12-222)*

It seems very strange; that a gardener's friend's words are quoted in the history books. What kind of a gardener was Jacob that had "*two small gimlet holes, bored for the purpose"?* What kind of guests did Jacob have, that only visited him to peep through the holes, to see women! What do they call these people in British English?

Clarke not only went once but he tried again, and this time with another friend:

"Clarke and a 'friend' made another lengthy visit to 'Topkapi Sarayi' during the holy month of Ramadan, when as Jacob Ensle assured him... the guards, being up all night would be stupefied during the day with sleep and intoxication". (12-222)

Now we know who this gardener was and why did he build there, a special "Lodge". This time, however Clarke and his friend succeeded to reach inside the heart of the Harem. Where he found some belongings of Sultanas (Sultan's wives), and "*went through them for any clues"*. What clues was he looking for, after all what was it that he was searching there? We find out when "*he found an English writing box of black varnished wood"*.

He found the clue he was looking for; "Marie Martha Aimee Dubuc de Rivery" of Martinique was there. With Martha there was another prince who was of her age group. In fact he was two years older to her, he was Salim III, the nephew of her husband. To check the progress in Martha's mission we will check the changes in Ottomans. How much everyone was in her control; direction of circumstances will tell us! After Abdul Hamit I's death on April 6th 1789, Salim III (1789-1807) became Sultan. He was the first Ottoman Sultan, who employed the first Frenchman, "Jacques Le Brun" to construct forty-five naval ships of "Modern design". From 1793-1804, Jacques Le Brun, "supervised" ships construction. History tells us that in 1798, Napoleon (Naqshe-Dil's cousin's husband) successfully invaded Egypt, then under Ottomans.

Salim III was dethroned and imprisoned, on 28 May 1807 by Janissaries, an influential Ottoman regiment (we will explain Janissaries later). In 1808 Naqshe-Dil (apparently) met Ali Efendi, a Jenissary, son of Albanian horse merchant and a Venetian Christian, from Corfu. She was already "Walide-Sultan" (Sultan's mother) and Efendi was her son Mahmut II's Lieutenant. Naqshe-Dil had an open affair with Ali Efendi. After Naqshe-Dil announced Ali as her lover, Mahmut promoted him to a rank of Pasha equivalent to today's rank of "Major General". Below is a quote from letter LXXXVII, written by "La Comtesse de La Ferte-Meun", in Constantinople on

August 15, 1818, and published anonymously in Paris in 1820. After describing life history of Naqshe-Dil and then her death, the letter quotes:

"The Sultan Valide [Naqshe-Dil] *openly favoured second only to her son, Ali Efendi. The Sultan* [Mahmut II] *continues to lavish upon him his devotion. 'It is in memory of my mother', he said, 'that he deserves my beneficence'. Certainly there is a French soul in such touching goodness". (Turcoman International, Bridging East &West, Vol-1, Issue V & VI, 1999, p-19)*

This French soul died soon, after his mother died in 1837 Mahmut II, executed his long time favourite and his mother's lover Ali Efendi.

A British film called "Two Englishmen went up the Hill and came down the Mountain", tells the story of a village in 'Wales', who are very proud of their big mountain. When two Englishmen come to survey and measure the height of the mountain, they announce it only to be a hill. To be a mountain it had to be another 20 feet higher. This becomes a challenge for Welsh pride; they want to convert it into a mountain overnight by carrying another 20 feet earth from the valley, high up the hill. Each man, woman and child gets busy struggling miles up and down the hill. The problem they faced was that two Englishmen had to leave earliest as possible in the morning, and a re-survey was not possible. To keep them another day, they use a bartender girl to "engage" the young surveyor till late night. This delay's their departure in the morning and subsequently they agree for a re-survey. In the morning they go up the hill for survey and when they measure it they announce it a "Mountain", so they come down the mountain. This film is a fine example of prestige kept by a small village people, however the ethical message shows the difference, when the bartender girl, who "engages" the young surveyor late night, becomes the heroin of the village.

Here lies the difference; what they call pride, we call it shamelessness. What we call chastity and nobility, they call it unnecessary "shame and honour".

Naqshe-Dil did every thing for the "Crown" with "Jesuistic" pride of performance.

MAHMUT II (1808-1839), SON OF NAQSHE-DIL

Janissarieswere a regiment of Ottoman Empire, formed long ago as Sultan's guards. Mainly Janissaries were the orphan children, regardless of religion, brought up under Sultan's care. They would be taught Islam as their religion, at the age of puberty, trained for army and then appointed as Sultan's guards. These guards were under Sultan's direct command and answerable to him only.

Their devotion to Sultan and their unbelievable bravery ascended them as a symbol of prestige and honour. This not only placed them high in the forces but also increased their power and influence enormously. A time came that they became a threat to every Sultan himself. They had become the "King makers".

Salim III (who employed the first Frenchman) was very concerned about Janissaries power. To weaken their monopoly, he developed a new infantry force, known as "Nizami cedits" or "New Order" (probably this name was also recommended by Naqshe-Dil). Janissaries found this a threat to their existence. On 28 may 1807, the Janissaries in Istanbul known as the "Yamaks" revolted under the leadership of "Kabakci Mustafa Agha", in favour of "Sultan Mustafa IV". Salim, powerlessly agreed and summoned his cousin Mustafa, handed him the throne and went to live in prison with Prince Mahmut II.

On 29 May 1807, Mustafa IV was enthroned at that time he was 28 years old. Opposition to, Mustafa's regime, was led by Bayraktar Mustafa Pasha. On 18th July 1808 (the year Naqshe-Dil met Ali Efendi), Bayraktar reached outside Istanbul with his army. When he reached the palace, Mustafa IV ordered to kill Salim and Mahmut, the two candidates for the throne. Salim got killed while Mahmut was rescued while hiding and trembling with fear. Mahmut II was imposed on July 28 1808, in return, Mustafa IV was sent to prison.

Now Napoleon and Josephine's distant nephew was the most powerful king of the Muslim world. The **"Big Game"** was approaching towards the end of its first half.

"Marie Martha Aimee Dubuc de Rivery" of Martinique, had another 29 years to live as Valide Sultan, the most influential French mother of Muslims' king.

"Mahmut II's reign opened seriously the period of westernization, in Turkey". (13-602)

A little bit intellectual sight can see through Mahmut's orders and actions, that this is a "French soul with touching goodness" working for Muslims' benefit:

1- Mahmut II himself discarded the "turban" and adopted the "fez" and European costume, and ordered all the officials to do the same.
2- He appointed "Helmuth von Moltke" as a general of his army, among the large number of French and Prussian instructors. This General Moltke was the future Prussian Field Marshal.
3- A medical school opened by the experts from Europe.
4- Civil service set upon the same footing as European. A number of students were sent to Europe for the first time.
5- A newspaper and first official printing press established.
6- Compulsory elementary education laid down by a royal proclamation, which forbade children, with no elementary education to take up any craft.

Newspaper and printing press itself was not a bad step, but the motive behind was the actual mischief. So was the elementary education, and students sent abroad. At that time "Jesuits" or "Brotherhood" owned 640 colleges and nearly 24 universities in Europe...almost dominated the modern education to *cultivate the arts and the sciences* (Ibid.).

Once the door to the West opened, it never closed. Although now and then oppositional rebellion from the Ulama (Muslim Scholars) arose, but was strictly crushed. Reformation in Islam or in the name of Islam was found necessary.

The Europe-returned students brought with them all but Western ideology. Amongst these European returned was "Mustafa Rashid", the Turkish Foreign Minister who returned in Abdul Mejit I's (31st Sultan) time. He never slowed down the efforts to enforce his European lords' ideology.

Islamic schools were running on private donations, whereas for "Modern Education" the centralised council of education was founded. Both primary and secondary schools were run by the state.

Civil courts were opened with European law, separating Commercial Courts from Civil and Penal Courts, latter under "Shariah". A school of judges was opened and attached to the Sheikh ul Islam's office.

Christians shared all the offices in the administration even up to the rank of cabinet minister.

Mahmut II's military organisation was extended, by engaging more foreign instructors and opening more military schools.

The Christians were exempted from military service up on payment of a little tax: And guess who was responsible for collecting these taxes? Same Europe returned "Mustafa Rashid", or shall we call Freemason?

Mahmut II died on 1st July 1839 succumbing to the combined effects of Tuberculosis and Cirrhosis of the liver. His addiction to fortified wine hastened his death.

His successor and son Abdul Mecit I (31st) 1839-1861 spent most of his time in his palace on the Bosphorus at Besiktas where his preferred entertainment was Western Music.

Sultans became icons, nothing else. Along with this another side of monarchy was exposed to the general public---the bad side. Any decision against public's benefit was summoned through Sultan, the puppet Sultan. Freemasonry was at its best working for the destruction of Muslims once and for all. Mustafa Rashid was the tool they were using to bore through the foundations of Ottoman Empire. Mustafa Rashid made all this possible by preparing a "Tanzimat", which he "personally" formed and made Sultan (Abdul Mecit I), sign it. This decree was issued under the name of "Gulhan'e-hatti- humayouni" (Royal decree of Gulhan'e). This decree also emphasised that all these reforms are in accordance with Islam. Encyclopaedia Britannica describes Mustafa Rashid as:

"The greatest statesman and westernizer of the re-form period...Mustafa Rashid with a few 'convinced' and 'westernised' men around him made gigantic efforts to enforce new principles in every department". (13-603)

Now 'Brotherhood' took a step forward in the **"Big Game"**. They formed local secret societies and committees to propagate their dogma. If we look at the changes they introduced in a short time limit, this is not the work of a few individuals. Reforms and their rhythmic speed clearly show, a whole big organised congregation of expertise in action. Mustafa Rashid could not do it all alone, not without the help of "Freemasons".

"Towards the end of Abdul Mecit I's reign a secret committee was formed in Constantinople which propagated the idea of a constitutional regime for Turkey". (13-604)

This presence was felt by some aware Muslims of the time, but no one paid attention to them. However the Greeks of Turkish Macedonia have been recorded feeling and declaring the presence of this alien force of **"Antichrist":**

"The Greek Patriarch declaring that the Greek regions of Turkey-in-Europe were being ruled by 'an invisible power, the aim of which is annihilation of all religion and the national existence'" (14, vol 1, 210)

Scottish Rite Fez, 33° Inspectors General Honorary

FALL OF THE OTTOMAN EMPIRE (BIG GAME, 2ND HALF)

"Abdul Aziz" (1861-1876) the 32nd Sultan and son of Mahmut II was the first Muslim Caliph to tour Europe in 1867. With him were his son "Yusuf Izzuddin" and his two elder nephews, "Murat" and "Abdul Hamit". This tour was arranged on Louis Napoleon's invitation, to see the "Great Universal Exhibition".

"Murat" was famous for his seriousness; he never smiled in his life. While on his European tour, he was presented, wine and chocolate, which he thanked with a smile to the Queen of France, the first ever smile any one saw on his face. This was a positive sign for Europeans, especially when they saw that this young prince is taking back the taste of European wine and brandy along with chocolate. Another positive sign of assurance was **"Dr Capoleone"**, the **"Royal Physician"**; appointed in by **"Mahmut II, son of Naqshe-Dil"** and since then he stayed in this position. **Mahmut II** also appointed **"Julius Millingem"** as **"Sultans' personal Physician"**, who also worked in corroboration with Dr Capoleone. Dr Capoleone was a Greek and apparently "cured" 7,8 Sultans. Dr Capleone was an influence on Murat from his teenage; when Murat met a group of "Yeni Osmanlilar" (Young Ottomans), who influenced him in European culture. Later Dr Capoleone was the one who:

"Initiated young Murat into Freemasonry". (12-279)

What do you expect from a Freemason Muslim Caliph? On their tour to Europe they were given a new ride, the "train ride". This engine was a new invention at that time and this ride became a dream ride for both Ottomans and for "Rothschilds"! Yes, Rothschilds are back in the scene. The Sultan instantly ordered locomotives. Rothschilds got a contract to build a rail track in Turkey in early twentieth century.

"Sultan Abdul Aziz" did not live long enough to see his dream come true. First he became mentally unstable and was dethroned by his Vizier and Head of Army, "Midhat Pasha" on May 29 1876 and then after spending few years expelled, committed suicide. He apparently cut his wrist with a pair of scissors.

Guess: who announced his death? Dr "Julius Millingem"! Along with another nine doctors. A bag full of "Masonic Medicine"! Before his death he cries out to his mother: "Mother! Mother! They are going to kill me!" Rumours of a murder were strictly rejected and crushed. Son of Sultan Abdul Aziz, "Yusuf Izzuddin" was alive. Brotherhood "cured" him too, not only him but his wife as well. They both committed suicide in 1916.

After Abdul Aziz, **Murat V, the Freemason**" became next Sultan. Taste of European brandy and wine that he brought back from his European tour, soon became a necessity, he turned into an alcoholic. Not only an alcoholic, but mentally ill too. His mother Valide "Sevkefza" tried to cure him with charms and spells. When this did not work, Dr Capoleone was called to cure him. The fact worth noticing is that after Dr Capoleone's appointment, most of the Sultans or their children were either mentally ill or suffering from "Tuberculosis" (TB) or physically so weak that they could not take any responsibilities leave alone governing. Western doctors still blame these diseases on Muslims inter-family-marriages, i.e. cousins marrying each other. Anyhow Dr Capoleone tried his methods like, bloodletting, applying leeches, cupping glasses, and prescriptions of tonics. All "Kabalistic" treatments could not cure him.

"Dr Leidesdrof", a renowned Viennese physician was called for Murat's treatment. When he saw Murat, surrounded by all Kabalistic wizards, he instantly analysed his disease and like any other honest doctor he proposed to take Murat to his clinic in Vienna. He also suggested him to stay there for three months. He knew that Murat does not need any cure but prevention, prevention from Kabalistic tonics. He was refused as such, although it will cure Murat but weaken Freemasonry.

Meanwhile, Midhat Pasha was trying to depose "Murat V" with constitutional monarchy, mainly modelled on the French constitution. On August 30 1876, Midhat Pasha deposed "Murat V" and offered "Abdul Hamit II", the throne on condition of the French constitution. Abdul Hamit II agreed seeing the power held by Midhat Pasha. The conference for the French constitution was held on 23-12-1876, dragged on for four weeks and then Abdul Hamit II, disbanded the constitution. Two weeks later on 5-2-1877, the Sultan dismissed and banished Midhat Pasha.

"London Rothschilds had five and a half million pounds tied up in Ottoman State loans. A close confident of Midhat Pasha, the Turkish Grand Vizier was reporter to Berlin prominent politician 'Ludwig Bamberger', who was a dispatcher to Lionel Rothschild". (6-238)

We don't have any grounds to reject the possibility that these reports were being sent either by Midhat Pasha's consent or by him-self. "Abdul Hamit II" was thought to be a liberal and easily lead, but what this man was proving, was entirely opposite. This rang bells in the Freemasonry and they started their usual propaganda. Later on in 1878, Sultan Abdul Hamit had to give Midhat Pasha a free pardon and appoint him Governor of Smyrna (present Izmir). On May 17 1881, Midhat pasha was arrested again; this time he was charged with the death of Abdul Aziz (the one who cut his wrist), condemned, reprieved and exiled. European Brotherhood could not swallow this trial easily and "Sir Henry Elliot" called it a "disgraceful mockery". Midhat Pasha was finally executed in prison.

The trial of Midhat Pasha and dismissal of the constitution was a terrible blow to the Fraternity; they could not easily digest it. But Abdul Hamit's grip was too strong and within the courtiers they couldn't do much. They decided to attack from out side.

TREATY OF SAN STEFANO

Two and a half months after the dismissal of the constitution, on April 24 1877, Russia declared war on Turkey. By January 31 1878, Russian forces had reached Istanbul and "Treaty of San Stefano" is signed. This is exactly what brotherhood does, even now! Any country abolishes Democracy; they block the aid, stop loans and even wage war. Their constitution is very sacred to them. Look at Afghanistan, the people that were once American aides, soon as Afghanistan announced Shari'ah law they became "New World Order's" worst enemies, they are backward, their women are oppressed, they are terrorists, they don't allow their women, education; you name it. Look at Sudan, tried to enforce Shari'ah and got cut from outside world for 10 years. No one even knows about it, because "Fraternity" own all the news outlets. **You only hear what "they let you"!**

Russia attacked Turkey because Russia was ordered to. To understand their moves, don't see who did what, but see who got what! Keep in mind that it was Russia who declared war on Turkey; it was Russia who reached Istanbul. On July 13 1878 the "Congress of Berlin" is held and Turkey is held responsible for war. An indemnity of 300 million Roubles is imposed on Turkey. As a result, Turkey had to hand over the Island of "Cyprus" to "England". Why to England? There must be 101 political reasons for that, but who benefit's at the end? "Brotherhood"! Cyprus provided a base for Britain that enabled her to occupy Egypt in 1882. (Encyclopaedia Encarta does not mention about indemnity)

THE YOUNG OTTOMANS

Very first known "secret Society" in the heart of a Muslim state, was formed in the regime of "Sultan Abdul Aziz" (1861-1876). This society; was formed by his grand vizier, "Aali Pasha" (Ayeli Pasha). This society the "Young Ottomans" had Aali Pasha and Fuad Pasha as essential parts of the machinery. They had an influence on other courtiers as well. This was the same society that had "Murat V-the Freemason" as a member. So what does this society represent? ---Freemasonry---this is a proof and we will prove more Inshallah.

Although the fall of Ottomans happened in Turkey, but it was seeded in Egypt, at that time a province under Khilafah. In 1863, Ismail Pasha became the "Khedive" (viceroy) of Egypt. "Suez Canal" idea (see "Egypt and Suez Canal") served him as an excuse and a free hand to borrow money from his "Masonic Brethren". Rothschilds, in guise of French and English loans provided him money with interest. He not only took these loans to build Suez Canal, but:

"To bribe a large number of influential men in the Porte". (13-604)

This bribery served him two causes; first, to increase the number of "brotherhood", second, to get the permission of succession from father to son in the establishment of Egypt. Sultan Abdul Aziz not only agreed to this because of the influence of his courtiers, but also because it served his causes to pass his throne to his son, Yusuf Izzuddin. Which never happened, brotherhood let him live as a mentally unstable person till he and his wife committed suicide (or whatever). This permission for succession was granted on May 27 1866, by the name of "Firman".

We will explain the details of the Suez Canal loans, and how it caused crises in next chapter. Suffice is to say that artificial financial crises were propagated. In mid artificial crises another way to panic was introduced, by the name of "Budget".

Budget was not introduced to show the actual loss or income, but to create an uncertainty among public---It still works! Turks had no experience on budget or "Stock and Exchange", we can imagine "who" made and let this dragon out on the public. With centuries of experience and domination of European market, it was an easy job for Masonic Rothschilds to create a suitable budget in 1866,67.

Mahmud Nadeem Pasha was obliged to announce that the government could only pay a 50% annuity on her debts (war indemnity, Suez Canal and Hijaz railway loans), where upon Europeans considered Turkey bankrupt, and she began to lose prestige. To pay the debts, government had to enforce heavy taxes on public. This was a way to create disliking to Sultan amongst public. The budget revealed a deplorable state of treasury. More loans to pay the previous loans and who could be the sympathiser other than Rothschilds or Brotherhood or France and England? They gave more loans!

Sudden deaths of Aali Pasha and Fuad Pasha (I wonder why they died! Had they completed their jobs?), brought Midhat Pasha to succeed Aali Pasha, a Mason and father of Turkish constitution. In 1873:

"Bankers stopped lending more loans". (13-604)

This caused another panic in general public, with the help of Masonic media, this issue was enlarged, hatred to Sultan increased and people started demanding Freedom---What freedom---Is Turkey Free today---?

"The great Turkish poet and patriot, Namik Kemal Bey and Zia Pasha, another poet and Satirist, fled to Paris and published pamphlets inciting the people to demand a constitutional government and succeeded in smuggling them into every part of Turkey. Midhat Pasha, who shared the opinions of the Young Ottomans, succeeded in wining over other members of the cabinet for constitutional change and obtained

a fatwa for the deposition of Abdul Aziz. Who was accordingly dethroned on May 30 1876 with the purpose of establishing a constitutional regime". (13-604)

It is amazing when they write about Zia Pasha, Namik Kemal Bey, pamphlets, and *"succeeded in smuggling them into every part of Turkey"*. How is this possible? Did these two men have so much influence or means? No not at all! This is how it was done, these pamphlets:

"Were sent into the empire through the foreign post offices, which protected by the 'Capitulation' were free of Ottoman Government control". (Encyclopaedia Encarta, Turkey-European sabotage)

Isn't it amazing? Every step they take is calculated. They had already decided these pamphlets were going to be distributed so they put a condition in the treaty, which spared "post offices", established---in Ottoman kingdom---free from their---own charge! Do we have any "Modern Post Offices", like these in modern countries? Yes---and nowadays we call them---"Embassies".

Now the job of "Young Ottomans" was complete, another change was needed. If one person or one party is opposing any regime, it can be taken as a biased opinion, if every man and all the parties are opposing, this makes the opinion genuine. Brotherhood knows this very well. They make a net of parties, every one blowing their trumpet. That's how they create mass-opinions. Which is called---"voice of people"---! The-moc-racy---!

THE YOUNG TURKS

After Young Ottomans made a background "Young Turks" took it further. In a way we can call them the successors of Young Ottomans. They had worked after the closing of first parliament in secret for the restoration of the constitution, by means of "publications" and "secret societies". This society's main members were young students in military and medical schools.

When Namik Kemal Bey and Zia Pasha (Ahmed Riza, nicknamed as Riza the dreamer), fled to Paris, they took over this society in 1889. Ahmed Riza was son of an Austrian woman "converted" to Islam and a Western educated father. An English writer explains the scene of initiation of a man into "Young Turks":

"The form of initiation crystallised into a definite ritual. The man was blindfolded, and led to a secret place whose whereabouts were entirely conceded from him. The bandage was then removed from his eyes, and he found himself, perhaps in a darkened room, perhaps in a lonely hollow of the hills, in the presence of three strangers wearing black masks. These administered to him the oath, which was to become the rule of his life. Swearing on the sword and on the sacred book (Qur'an) [which Mustafa Kamal Pasha later replaced with revolver]. *He bound himself to devote his whole energies to the redemption of his country, to obey every order given to him through the channels of society, never to reveal its secrets, and to kill every person, however near and dear to him, whom it might condemn to suffer death. His eyes were again covered, and he was led back to the place from where he had started on the mysterious journey". (The Closed Circle-105)*

Does it sound familiar? Isn't it the initiation of Freemasonry? What does this tell us...? It tells us that any one joining "Young Ottomans", was actually joining "Freemasonry". It also tells us that all the leaders given to Turkey through "Young Ottomans" were actually "Freemasons", this is a proof, we will prove more, later Inshallah.

This is how Brotherhood was preparing the background of new secular Turkey. Their propaganda and pamphlets played a vital part in the mantel reformation of youngsters. "New" pamphlets were printed to humiliate the "old" Islamic ways, showing the Caliph with wild beard and moustache, wearing ancient Islamic dress, holding a rusty sword in his hand, in the background a neatly dressed Frenchman holding a rifle. This was all being done to inspire the young generation and for mass manipulation. So they can stand up to fight their own brothers, so called backward Mullahs, all this in the name of Freemasonry, all in the name of Satanism. The harvest of these seeds were:

1- Talat Bey, a chief clerk of Salonik "Post Office" and a law student.
2- Rahimi Bey, a local influential man of Salonik.
3- Dr Nazim, the leader of the Turkish revolutionary societies in Europe (Europe, the heart of Masonry).

CUP (COMMITTEE OF UNION AND PROGRESS)

The first two (Talat and Rahimi), mentioned above, with their other comrades formed "The Secret Society of Union and Progress", usually known as CUP, on the model of Freemasons Lodges (actually Freemasonic Lodges under a different name). Third one, Dr. Nazim already working for Freemasons in guise of revolutionary societies joined them later. Together they started gaining power; it became even stronger when army leaders started joining them. Amongst these army leaders and so called intellectuals were:

1- Major Niazi, a Macedonian Army Officer.
2- Enver Pasha, The statesman and soldier. He led the military revolt in 1908, which resulted in the "Young Turks" revolution. Responsible to take Turkey into 1st World War. In 1913 Enver Pasha became the War Minister, and in 1914, took Turkey into war.
3- Jamal Bey.
4- Mustafa Kemal Pasha, the founder of modern Turkey. The hero of young and old Turks. It is worth dedicating, a separate heading to him... We will.

(All above names are mentioned likewise in 13. Vol, 22. P-605)

Together, this Masonic force gained a lot of power. Youngsters were already under French influence rest of the job was completed by media and pamphlets. This propaganda became so bad that in 1882, Sultan Abdul Hamit II had to put the press under a strict censorship and by an elaborate network of spies. He abolished freedom of speech.

While this was happening, war with Russia had weaken Turkish economy. Indemnity of 300 million Roubles played another part to crush the surviving prestige. "Decree of Muharram" was signed in Dec 1881, which gave the control of payments of the debts to European delegates. These European delegates had a weighty influence in Turkish finance until 1914. This was made possible through Sait Pasha, the Grand Vizier after Midhat Pasha.

"You give me the control of the currency, and I don't care who rules the country".
(Nathan Rothschild)

Abdul Hamit II ('Abdul the Damned' to his European critics---No wonder why), carried on ruling despite assassination attempts. Opposition to Abdul Hamit was led by, Mahmut Sevket Pasha, the commander of the third army in Salonica. Along with his Macedonian troops he put Istanbul under siege in mid April 1909.

On April 22 1909 most of the dispersed deputies and cabinet ministers met secretly in San Stefano and under the chairmanship of Sait Pasha, decided to depose Abdul Hamit. His reign finished on April 27 1909. After two days he was exiled to Salonica, where he lived for rest of his life.

YOUNG TURKS RULE

After deposition of Abdul Hamit II, Young Turks officially ruled Turkey. To see their efficiency we look at the following facts.

"Army was put under intensive German instruction. Navy was put under instructions led by Admiral Sir Douglas Gambles. A French expert, Charles Laurent was engaged for the financial department. European companies were given concessions to bring foreign capital into the country. (13-606)

Once Europe had a total control on Turkey, a series of wars followed.

September 28 1911, Italy gave an ultimatum for 24 hours. Having been assured of the neutrality of the "powers" took over Tripoli and Cyrenaica.

Montenegro and Bulgaria made an alliance against Turkey and declared war on Oct 8 1912.

On October 17 Turkey declared war on Serbia and Bulgaria, Greece declared war on Turkey next day (Balkans war). **Turkey lost all these wars.**

Before the "Balkans War" broke, "powers" had decided that whatever the result of the war would be but territorial "status quo" would be maintained in Balkans (i.e., the land map prior to war wouldn't change). This promise---was never kept---! Lame excuse of a new Turkish cabinet was used, beside the "cabi-net" was suggested by them anyway.

A month later, Greece and Serbia started fighting Bulgaria over the division of conquered territory. Turkey availed this chance, marched to Adrianople. At this point, different peace treaties were signed with European consent, with Greece, Serbia and Bulgaria, which resulted as Turkey's loss of all the possessions to the west of the Maritza river. Same Turkey played an igniting part in W.W.1, for Allies.

"Young Turks Revolution" could not succeed if a religious backing was not there. So:

"Even the head of the Muslim religious hierarchy in the Ottoman Empire, the Shaikh-ul-Islam, took an oath to the constitution, and declared that there was nothing wrong in the demands of Young Turk revolutionaries that conflicted with Islamic Law". (14, vol 1, 160)

NATIONALIST MOVEMENT

The successors of "Young Ottomans" were "Young Turks". The name they used to create anarchy in Turkey was, "CUP" (Committee of Union and Progress). The Union they created was, to dismantle the Khilafah into pieces and progress they made was that, in May 1919, Allied forces had their fleet and armies in the Straits, Istanbul and even places like armistice line.

We have proved that behind all these organisations were "Freemasons", overtly or covertly. Now the time had reached to take over the whole Turkey. That was not difficult at all now. Turkish army, navy, finance under their control and Sultan, just a name to be used and abused.

But to control a country you need a constant surveillance and all-seeing eye. Time and energy is permanently engaged. Military, Police and other daily headaches...Too much. Best thing is to put their own men those who are faithful to you and let them carry on your dirty work. This is exactly what "Brotherhood" did.

It was time for a re-birth, old names had to die and new organisations and new heroes should appear on the horizon. The previous defeats and loss of land was put on "CUP" and few leaders were made scapegoats, but poor leaders took "refuge" in Germany. Just like today, did you ever think why Europe or America provides "political asylum" to refugees? Humanitarian grounds---! I am sure---! To finish the investigations, rather suspicions, "CUP" was dissolved. Mustafa Kemal Ataturk, although a member of CUP, was spared to be used in the future as a hero.

The presence of Allied forces finally started waking Muslims up, they held meetings in Istanbul and other provinces. This was the beginning of "Nationalist Movement". Time for sacrifice was approaching and some blood was needed. This task was given to Greek Army, when they landed in Smyrna on May 15 1919, under the protection of British, French and American fleets. Greeks slaughtered thousands of unarmed, civilian Muslims. **In full view of Allied Forces!**

These massacres were the final stroke by Allies or Freemasons before their permanent control. But this blow brought Muslims back to their senses and aroused general indignation in Turkey. Time for "Jihad" had arrived! Muslims took oaths on Qur'an to fight till death. The only thing a non-believer fears about "Muslim Ummah" is their passion for Jihad. This is why even today they try to deface and ridicule Jihad by terrorist activities, which in fact they do themselves.

This "Jihad" activity; was led by "Nationalist Movement". At this point we look at the actual targets of Freemasonry, once again.

a) To disintegrate Khilafah (beside it was not a Khilafa any more, with Sultan in their captivity and actual power held by "Young Ottomans").
b) To appoint such a permanent system, that can never revert to Islam or Shari'ah.
c) To humiliate and kill as many Muslims as possible, and leave the country under mighty debts.

Last of these, was already achieved via Greece and constant engagement of wars, 'a' and 'b' were very near to success.

ATATURK (FATHER TURK)

Rather than going into his biography (you can find hundreds of books on that), we just start where he appears in **"BIG GAME"** on a **"BIG SCREEN"**. Having fighting for Allies ad formerly being a member of the infamous "CUP" and "Young Ottomans" and "Young Turks", now he suddenly switches over to "Nationalist Movement's" side. Now he is against Allies and Sultan. Against Allies, because they let Greeks carry-on the Muslim massacres and against Sultan, because Sultan is in alliance with Allies. What a joke! No Sultan, after "Abdul Hamit II", had any power, they were all captives to "Young Turks" through them to "Allies" and through them to "Ataturk".

"In April 1909, units stationed in Istanbul mounted a counter part. 'We want the Holy Law'. Concealing their purposes for fear that they would be disobeyed, the officers rallied the soldiers, marched on Istanbul and brought Caliph ' Mehmet V' to Salonika, where he remained, deposed, under house arrest, returning to the capital only to die in 1918. (The Closed Circle-139)

For mass manipulation, all ruinous orders were carried out on Sultan's behalf. This broadcasting was very important to restrict public from reverting to Shari'ah. How long can you govern some one with stick in your hand, better make the stick look like carrot. Don't chain people's wrists and fetter their ankles, control their thoughts and minds, they will do what you order them to, yet thinking---they are free!

To control the "Nationalist Movement" and disperse if necessary, Ataturk as "Military Inspector General", made his journey to Eastern Anatolia. On the way to Erzurum he met, Rauf Bey, Ali Fuad Pasha and Colonel Rifat (Nationalist Movement's leaders). This meeting "changed Ataturk's thoughts" (how dramatic) and at Amasia on June 19 1919, they signed the "Amasia Protocol", which declared the national determination to "resist, both Allies and Sultan". Now Freemasons had covered "both sides". On July 23 1919 a National Congress assembled in Erzurum and having resigned from the army, Ataturk presided. No president was chosen but Ataturk's leadership was generally recognised. Now Ataturk was leading opposition to Allies as well, the set was complete, just like American War of Independence; both sides were completely in Masonic control.

In January 1920 a new parliament assembled in Istanbul containing a Nationalist majority. Through the "eye" of Ataturk, Allies were watching all the actual, and to them unwanted members, and means of ammunition transport. When Ataturk had had the leadership and stronghold on the only existing threat to Freemasonry in Turkey, Allies decided to wipe off the rest of the genuine members and could-be members of the Nationalist Movement.

On March 16 1920, just two months later Allies stroke on Istanbul, at that time Ataturk was in Anatolia. Allied Forces walked in the Parliament House itself and seized a large number of Nationalists, including Rauf Bey, the leader of Nationalists in Istanbul. That was the end of "Nationalist Movement" and it was all done in the name of Sultan (in the name of Satan, more appropriately).

Afterwards the Government of Istanbul (Allies) issued a Fatwah (decree) denouncing all Nationalists as "out laws" and condemned them to death.

Ataturk issued a proclamation inviting Anatolia to elect its deputies for a new assembly, which was opened in Ankara on April 23 1920. Ataturk was elected President to both, Assembly and Government.

Still there were people who wanted to restore Sultan; little flame was still there. *"Ataturk kept saying* [deceiving, lying] *to public that Sultan is a prisoner in hands of Allies and will be restored after the realisation of the national ideal", (13-608)*
The same prisoner Sultan was free when it came to misuse his name.

The following three and a half years were fantastic example of Masonic engineered wars. Ataturk had to be a hero of the nation to forget Sultan. Muslims wanted a leadership Masons provided them.

1- War with Allies, with French army in Cillicia and Aintab.
2- War with Russia in which Ataturk captured Kars and Alexandropol.
3- War with Georgia, Ataturk occupies Ardahan, Artvin and Batum.
4- War with Greece from January-April 1921 at Inonu.
5- Another war with Greece July 10 1921, the "Battle of Sakariyee", by now he was a General and after the 20 days war, given the title of "Ghazi".
6- Another war with Greece from August 26 1922, in which he captured Smyrna on Sep 9 1922.

All these wars: won by Ataturk!

Don't you wonder how? I do as well! But that is how Freemasonry could put Turkey under heavy debts, and create a hero, a hero that will fade the Sultan's charm away. Sultanic icon was overridden by Masonic. Ataturk, the father of Turks, was elected President on Oct 29 1923.

Mustafa Kemal Ataturk. (1881-1938)

Leader of "Young Turks" and the father of the modern Turkish state, he was President from 1923 until his death. Ataturk was a member of an Italian Lodge, "Macedonia Resorta e Veritas". A Freemason and "Grand Master" of "Turkish Lodge". (2-226)

I am sure you will be disappointed, but you can't deny the fact. He is listed in "Gallery of Famous Freemasons". His comrades weren't famous they are not listed!

Is Ataturk still your Hero?
Anyone joining "Young Ottomans" was actually joining "Freemasonry".

OTTOMANS FALL (BIG GAME ENDS)

After "Abdul Hamit II", Turkey throned three more Sultans, "MahmutV", "Mehmet VI" and "Abdul MecitII", but none of them was really a Sultan. Only Freemasons were watching the last drowning pulses of "Ottoman Empire". Officially all the power was held by GNA (Grand National Assembly) and through them "Freemasons".

On March 3 1924, GNA passed a law, abolishing the "Khilaphah" and deposing "Abdul Mecit II" The 37th Ottoman Sultan. This law also stated that he and all of his descendants were forbidden to reside within the boundaries of the "Turkish Republic".

Same night a special carriage had been prepared for the royal family on the "Simplon Express", due to leave at mid-night, from Sirkeci station in Istanbul. Abdul Mecit and his family had to leave before dawn, within five hours: otherwise they would have to leave everything behind. An American journalist "Constantine Brown", describes the scene:

"Crying and shouting with despair, all the servants, well over two hundred men and women, began to bring out old-fashioned Turkish carpet bags and luxurious silver and gold dressing-cases and to fill them with most unbelievable things, which might have done for a bric-a brac shop but not for the journey of a large family. They were piling up all kinds of Persian and Arabic silks and velvets, antique coffee-cups in gilded holders, rosewood-framed band-mirrors inlaid with mother-of-pearl, court dresses and gold-braided uniforms. No one thought of packing some practical every day cloths or linen.

At half past two in the morning nothing had been done. The Commissioner of Police: who together with the other four representatives, was all the time in the palace. Keeping a close watch over the crown jewels, decided to intervene, and in a business-like manor, assisted by a few other men, brought the Caliph's personal belongings, together with other things the family might need in exile, and packed everything in seventy-two trunks and bags". (12-321/22)

With them, was packed history of "642 years" and Khilafah of 1400 years!

CONCLUSION

What did Turkey get?
Freedom!
Freedom from whom!
Freedom from dictators, the Sultans!
What bad did Sultans?
They killed their opponents!
What did Ataturk do in Republican Turkey?

On the pretext of a conspiracy "discovered" against Ataturk in the summer of 1926, all members of the suppressed opposition party, both in and out of the assembly as well as the leading members of the UPC were arrested by the tribunal of independence. At the trial, political opponents were "assumed" to be conspirators by the mere fact of their being in opposition. "Kiazim Kera Bekir Pasha" (Nationalist), and Refet Pasha (Nationalist) and Ali Fuad Pasha (Nationalist) were acquitted by the pressure of the army...Several others who had been in the forefront of the "Nationalist Movement", were executed. Dr Nazim (Young Ottomans) was also executed. The Allies out-laws were eventually punished.

"O you who believe! When believing women come to you as emigrants, examine them; Allah knows best as to their faith...(Q, 60-10)

"Ayesha the wife of the Prophet said, "Allah's Apostle used to examine the believing women who migrated to him in accordance with this Verse..."(Sahih Al Bukhari, 6-414)

"And do not marry Al-Mushrikat (idolatresses) till they believe (worship Allah alone). And in deed a slave women who believes is better than a (free) Mushrikah (idolatress), even though she pleases you...(Q, 2-221)

How is it possible that Allah says something and it is not true! A little bit vibration from "Sirat Al Mustaqim" took us exactly opposite.

This is Freemasonry; they wait...wait...and wait, patiently and calmly. They have plenty of time, they endured for centuries, finally they captured "Muslim Khilapha" by a woman...yes..."Naqshe-Dil"..."Marie Martha Aimee Dubuc de Rivery" of Martinique. She did the job which millions of soldiers and numbers of "Crusades", could not.

Ataturk died on Nov 10 1938, after several month sickness, he was succeeded by his ex-Prime Minister, long term ally and right hand, General Inonu, another Masonic symbol. Ataturk's death did not finish Masonic rule in Turkey, in fact even the present elected President "Demirel" is also a high degree Freemason...Yes one of my Turkish friend Mr. X (identity not disclosed), formerly a Freemason himself, happened to visit Turkey a few years ago. Through his personal contacts he was invited to a dinner with Demirel. A Freemason: is not suppose to hide his identity (this can result in termination from Masonry), rather announce it through various phrases and movements. Demirel was "exposed" to Mr. X through verbal symbols.

Freemasonry still rule's Turkey!

Turkey's total debts to World Bank in 1998 were $79.8 billion.

Symbol of Skull & Bones Society

CH-14 SUEZ CANAL AND EGYPT'S FALL

NAPOLEON'S INVASION OF EGYPT

In 1795, Napoleon, applied for service in Egypt, it was turned down. This did not end his enthusiasm to excavate the historical land of Pharaohs. In 1796 Napoleon *(Illustrious Brother)* married Josephine, the widow of an aristocrat guillotined (beheaded) in the Revolution and mother of two children she was a cousin of Naqshe-Dil and an active member of Freemasonry's "Adoptive Rite". Two years after marrying her, in 1798, Napoleon invaded Egypt. Memlukes of Egypt charged at the French soldiers to recover their land in vain. To end Egyptian resentment, Napoleon changed his strategy and adopted turban, visited mosques and declared to support Islamic Law. "Liberty, Equality and Fraternity" were his slogans. Behind these slogans he actually re-formed the Egyptian government and Law. These re-forms of "Freedom" with the help of Josephine bought him a group of local Freedom-seekers. Along with this he was working on his statistics too.

"The French scholars he had brought with him began the scientific study of ancient Egyptian history...Napoleon's invasion was too short-lived to have any lasting impact, but it marked the beginning of a renewed European interest in Egypt".
(Encyclopaedia Encarta-96)

GRANDFATHER TO GRANDSON

Mohammad Ali (1770-1849), born in Kavala, Macedonia, an Ottoman officer and Mameluke arrived in Egypt with the Macedonian Brigade of the Ottoman Army that had been sent to resist Napoleon. He defeated Napoleon and assumed power. In the mean time, "Liberty, Equality and Fraternity" had worked its way through the weak Muslims and Napoleon's group was active amongst the elite class of Egypt. When Mohammad Ali's famous quote in history: "I have never had a master" is stated, it makes one wonder, was this when he was offered to work under a Grand Master of "Freemasonry"? Affirmation to this concept holds strong grounds when: In 1811 he invited all conspirators (Freemasons?) of his regime to a banquet in the "Cairo Citadel", closed all the doors and massacred them almost to the last man. His further cautious steps even make this opinion certain.

Because he understood exactly the Masonic policy of "New World Order", under covers of progress and modernisation, instead of bowing to them, he used them as a source of progress. His plans were different. His behaviour and ethics were intolerable to his Masonic opponents. One of Ali's advisors (FM) revealed to the political economist "Nassan Senior" about his social attitudes.

"The Fellah is an animal-kind docile, laborious; a higher sort of dog. The Bedouin too is kind of laborious, after his fashion". He continues; *"When we are talking of political life on a great scale, the Fellah and the Bedouin must be left out of the question".*

This was the time when Mehmut II, son of Naqshe-Dil was Sultan. We can understand, what; "political life on a great scale" is described here!

Nevertheless, Mohammad Ali was read stories of "Alexander the Great" and Machiavelli's "The Prince", (He did not read French, which was a set back for French Freemasonry) from which he declared that he had nothing to learn! True...Very much so. To criticise Shakespeare, one has to know better or at least good enough English. If a person, just basically familiar with English language, is read Shakespeare's literature, his lack of understanding compels him, to only appreciate Shakespeare. On the contrary, if Shakespeare is translated into his mother tong, he can, not only really appreciate, but also criticise. This is why Freemasonry "Introduced" French language to Ottomans. When you are in learning process your teacher is an ideal for you unless you become better. Once you know better, you start seeing your own ideal teacher's faults. This psychological warfare was deeply understood by Freemasons, so they tricked Turkish Muslims through Naqshe-Dil into French language. Naturally when, one is copying a whole culture he is sub-consciously feeling himself inferior. When this inferiority complex is triggered with knowledge of science and tainted hollow ethics and a show of etiquette, the learner has no choice but to completely surrender to his master. Since the time of 'Mahmut II', the royal servants were taught French and given orders in French. French became the ruling class language. Just like English is exercised world wide to keep third world or Non-Europeans in complex (though in some individual cases this complex does not work. This is a general example.)

"The Prophet said, 'You will follow the wrong ways, ways of your predecessors so completely and literally that if they should go into the hole of a mastigure, you too will go there'. We said, 'O Allah's Apostle! Do you mean the Jews and the Christians?' He replied, 'Whom else?" (Sahih Al Bukhari, Hadith 4.662)

We still can see the 19th century architect in Turkey, symbolic to the French. Look at the dress of majority of Muslims today, copy of Christians! Look at the heroes of the Muslim world today! Icons of Hollywood film industry. Yes this is an "Industry" to manufacture a generation of "Holy-Wood maniacs", which already exist.

When language complex spell was broken, by reading French stories to Ali, in his native language, he came out with his honest criticism. His steadfastness and strict Islamic law's enforcement made peace and brought prosperity. No power challenges or even peasant troubles erupted under his rule. He confiscated the "Religious Foundations" that had been the source of wealth for these troubles. No need to mention whom did these "Religious Foundations" belong to.

"And even to descend so low as to become a Jew among Jews, that you might be enable to gather together all information for the benefit of your order as a 'Faithful Soldier' of the Pope". (Ibid.)

All agricultural land was utilised, Mohammad Ali initiated agricultural techniques and crops, notably cotton. From 1812 onward, he set up a centralised economy in which sale and purchase prices were fixed. This control of exports and foreign trade provided between a quarter and a third of his budget receipts. First Arab printing press was opened in Cairo, in 1822, during Mohammad Ali's regime. Within 20 years it had published 243 books.

In 1826 he paid for a party of forty-four students to go to Paris, to learn the language and to attend trade schools and workshops (This is the Islamic way to seek knowledge, by not imposing their ideology on self). 1832, twelve medical students were sent, two of his own sons were among those, educated in Paris, one of them was Ibrahim Pasha. French historians of the time describe his both sons very critical towards French.

"In 1831 Muhammad Ali invaded Syria, thereby coming into conflict with his Turkish overlord. The Egyptians defeated the Ottoman armies, and by 1833 they were threatening the Turkish capital Constantinople. Once again, Russia, Britain and France intervened, this time: to protect the Sultan. Muhammad Ali's forces withdrew, but he was left in control of Syria and Crete". (Encyclopaedia Encarta)

This is the game! They were obviously working in corroboration with Turkish Dynasty. They were protecting their Sultan, Mehmut II son of Naqshe-Dil. By 1833 Mohammad Ali was employing 70 Italian officers, 70 French and about a dozen of British and Spanish. His Chief of Staff was "Octave Seve" a lieutenant under

Napoleon, later converting to Islam and named Suleiman Pasha. His statue is still in a square in Cairo.

Conscription into the army was considered a virtual sentence of death. By the end of his reign, he had 130,000 men under arms. His campaigns had been successful in Sudan, Arabia where Egyptians had reached holy cities, in Syria and Palestine, occupied for ten years under the rule of his son and heir, Ibrahim Pasha.

In 1839, he defeated the Ottoman Sultan, Mehmut II, son-of Naqshe-Dil in battle of Nezib. Britain and France had no choice after their puppet Sultan's defeat, other than signing a peace treaty with Mohammad Ali, which established that his power had reached its peak. British historians put this treaty in different words:

"The British and the French stopped him by certifying that he could keep what he had won for himself in Egypt".

This is the power of Islam; this is "Liberty, Equality and Fraternity". Only one 'just ruler' did the job that halted Freemasonry for decades. If you still have any doubts about Freemasonry's existence in Egypt; read this:

"Grand Lodge of Egypt was created in 1864, from Italian, Greek and French lodges, the earliest of which had been active since 1786". (2-52)

From their own book, from their own author and from their own Grand Master of Great Britain, this is the confession and evidence we were looking for. So now we know that in 1811, the conspirators massacred behind the closed doors of the banquet of Cairo Citadel, were for sure Freemasons! The religious organisations: that were confiscated, were being run by Jesuits. Freemasonry was active even prior to their admittance.

SUEZ CANAL

Mohammad Ali died in 1849, the barrier he put to Freemasonry, started sliding away slowly. His son Said Pasha became the next ruler. Suez Canal was the brainchild of a French Diplomat and engineer, "Vicomte Ferdinand Marie de Lesseps". Ferdinand convinced Said Pasha to build Suez Canal; as a result, Said Pasha left a huge debt when he died. To complete this project, Ismail Pasha was placed as Khedive (Viceroy) of Egypt in 1863. Ismail Pasha was second son of Ibrahim Pasha (the one who went to Paris for studies), and grandson of Mohammad Ali, born in Cairo and educated in "Paris" and he was:

"Grand Master of the Grand Lodge of Egypt. He presented an obelisk to US which was erected in New York". (2-235)

Apparently Suez Canal was built to halve the distance between Europe and Far East, and charge tax to passing ships. It was a brilliant idea as long as the motive was construction, but it was destruction, destruction of Egypt's economy, and with it to put burden on Turkey. Turkey was responsible for all the debts of its provinces, as head government. If Egypt is somehow under debts; then Turkey is under debts too. The debt, that swamped Turkey, floated through the waters of "Suez Canal". The Viceroy of Egypt, a Freemason and Grand Master himself, could betray his nation, his land, his religion, but could not break the oath to the Lodge.

"Ismail Pasha, increased the national debt by borrowing lavishly from European bankers to develop the country and pay for the Suez Canal...As a result of his financial policies, however, the government debt rose from £3 million in 1863 to £100 million in 1874". (E/Encarta)

Suez Canal's excavation began on April 25 1859 and it was opened to navigation on November 17 1869. Its total cost was $100 million. To start this project, a company was formed in 1858 named, "La Compagnie Universelle du Canal Maritime de Suez"

(Universal Company of the Maritime Suez Canal). This company had authority to cut the canal and to operate it for 99 years, after which ownership would return to Egyptian government. This was originally a private company and;

"Its stocks owned chiefly by French and Egyptian interests". (E/Encarta)

So how come Egypt was held responsible for the loans, taken personally by Ismail Pasha?

"Those who eat Rib'a (usury) will not stand (on the Day of Resurrection) except like the standing of a person beaten by Shaitan (Satan) leading them to insanity. That is because they say: "Trading is only like Rib'a", whereas Allah has permitted trading and forbidden Rib'a..." (Q, 2-275)

"And if you do not do it (i.e., stopping Rib'a), then take a notice of war from Allah and His Messenger but if you repent, you shall have your capital sums..." (Q, 2-279)

"And that which you give in usury (to Others), in order that it may increase (your wealth) from other people's property, has no increase with Allah; but that which you give in Zakat (charity) seeking Allah's Countenance, then those they shall have manifold increase". (Q, 30-39)

When Ismail Pasha borrowed heavily on behalf of the Egyptian government for the construction of Suez Canal, the British government and Lionel Rothschild (then head of London Rothschild bank) did not participate in this venture; they had a part to play afterwards.

After the Canal was complete and started profiting, the British government was held at ransom because of the (intentional) heavy duty put on them. This was the time when "Gladstone" was British Prime Minister. At this point, we open their game first, to understand how they worked their way through.

1- Somehow, Rothschilds had to buy the main stake of Suez Canal.
2- They needed some assurance on government level to ensure that their money does not sink. That meant to avoid a direct purchase of Suez shares.
3- The main stake (44% shares) was owned by Khedive (Viceroy) of Egypt, Ismail Pasha.
4- Then British Prime Minister "Gladstone" was not a Freemason but understood their bait, so he wouldn't agree.
5- The head of Rothschild House, Lionel Rothschild had a seat in the Commons and by virtue of "The Act of Privilege", MPs were prohibited to make a personal profit through government contracts.

The first obstacle! "Gladstone" who was popular for his re-formations, was removed from Premiership. Apparently people suddenly became too tired of his reformations. This was done through mass manipulation, "media control". Next "elected" Prime Minister "Disraeli" was the long time Rothschild family friend.

In 1875, when situation was set for a future Suez Canal share purchase, "Lionel Rothschild", resigned from The Commons. Government of Ismail Pasha was destabilised, in early November Ismail Pasha, in "desperate need of money" (for what?), decided to sell his personal 44% shares. Disraeli didn't take much time. He met Lionel Rothschild at 147 Piccadilly, London where he was a frequent visitor. On November 17 1875, the matter was discussed in the Cabinet. On November 24 1875 terms accepted by Cabinet and within hours, Disraeli reported to the Queen:

"The entire interest of Khedive is now yours; Madam!"

The Act of Privilege could not prevent Freemasons form playing their game, Lionel Rothschild, having resigned from the commons already, lent £4 million with 5%

interest, and two and a half percent commission. On the other hand Ismail Pasha was a Freemason and the Grand Master of Egypt, he was part of the game himself, how could he object? Rothschild's bank made £100,000 profit on the deal, which caused uproar in the Parliament: What was done was done!

Now Freemasonry had the main stake of Suez Canal and a right to intervene. On the other side, Ismail Pasha did not pay his previous debts despite the money he achieved by selling his 44% shares. On November 24 1875, Britain (Freemasons) bought the major share in the Suez Canal and by 1876 Egyptian government finance was in mess. This gave a right to International Committee to intervene. The Committee forced Egypt to submit the control of the economy to the creditors, which were Britain and France.

After creating this financial coup, Fraternity came to "help" Egyptian economy, yet with another loan, another "Package". This "Package" was eight and a half million pounds, more debts and more manipulation. It reminds me of economic experts of Pakistan, when after atomic explosion they were impatiently waiting for a new "Bail out Package" from IMF. Don't they know what is happening? Of course they do!

Anyhow, the Egyptian coup caused a rebellion amongst Muslims and wise men of agitators demanded expulsion of all foreigners, who included "Sir Charles Rivers Wilson" (English) and "Eugene de Blignieres" (French), who were "financial administrators". It is appropriate to quote here that by the end of Mohammad Ali's reign, 3,000 Europeans lived in Egypt; by the end of Ismail's the number was 70,000 half of them were Greeks, the remainder French or Italian. A proud Ismail states:

"My country is no longer in Africa, it is in Europe". (Ismail)

When this agitation started gaining power, the Khedive dismissed the overseas populace and resumed complete control. Ismail had completed his job, now he was to be separated from the game. River Wilson appealed to Natty Rothschild (in stead of British Government) to put on pressure by demanding his loans. As a result Britain and France put pressure on the Turkish Sultan. As a result Ismail was deposed in favour of his son, the young, 27 years old, Tewfik. Ismail later reverted, and abandoned Freemasonry! May Allah accept his repentance!

This change in the government quietened the agitators. This trick still works in the form of Democracy whenever a new President or Prime Minister is elected, even some times in the form of a military coup. If a head of army takes over, people expect new rulers to perform miracles, not realising that Presidents and Prime Ministers don't run countries! It is the Ministry!

Anglo French control was re-established, this time to cause a complete economic collapse. Tewfik's government far from solving the problem exacerbated it, arousing even greater anger among people. The country rapidly became non-governable and in 1881, Arabi Pasha raised a full-fledged threat to all foreigners and the security of Suez Canal. The agitation finally over threw the Egyptian government.

Now I hope the picture is clearer, that why Lionel Rothschild did not buy 44% shares in the Suez Canal himself! He needed security of the British government. After the British security, he didn't hesitate to lend a direct loan of an eight and a half million pounds himself and made an extra 2_ % commission. The result was inevitable, Britain had to defend her share and eventually recover his 8 _ millions too.

The following September, the British forces were in Egypt and Sir Garnet Wolseley defeated the few leftover forces of Muslims at Tel al Kabir. Wolseley restored the order and business became usual, for Egyptians as well as for Freemasons. The final nail was hammered in 1885 by French and British houses of Rothschilds, when they jointly arranged another loan of £9,424,000 to Egypt to re-set the Egyptian government on its feet. This loan was agreed by the major powers: "Britain and France".

In 1882 the British Protectorate was declared by William Gladstone, the then Liberal Prime Minister of Britain (once, Suez Canal problem was solved, people suddenly started liking Gladstone again), did so reluctantly. "Unable to explain satisfactorily to himself, let alone the others, why the government had taken this measure, with no permanent hope".

The biggest joke in Egypt's history was narrated, later by a financier:

"The Egyptian economy's potential for growth was not in doubt. Out of Panic! The Khedive- miscalculated".

Egypt's total debts to World Bank in 1998 were $31.4 billion.

Movie "The Pyramid"

CH-15 THE PROTECTORATES

As we have explained earlier, it is very hard to rule a conquered country permanently with conqueror's army and police. This overt control can be overturned and replaced by the natives at any time. Men-power is a vital element to maintain the rule. How could a minority rule the whole globe? For the west, this was a very important question. Over half of the world's population is in East and South Asia. Africa had 12%, North and South, America 14 % (including non-white). Europe and former USSR contained only 15 %. The share in population growth, of the developed countries is expected to fall to 17 % by 2025. According to a survey, nine out of ten being added to world population are living in the less developed countries.

These figures were well known to Masonic future planners. They decided to move to a "covert control". This is how "Protectorate" was introduced to the former European colonies. "Marshal Lyautey", the French resided "soldier" and protectorater of Morocco defined protectorate as:

"A country retaining its own institutions, governing itself with its own organs, but under the control of a European power which assumes control over its 'finances' and 'guides' it in its economic development".

Noteworthy point is that; besides being French, he does not mention France in particular, but particularly mentions; "any European power". This exhibit's the foolishness of the non-European world to believe in the slogan of "Nationalism", Especially "Muslims": who only have the concept of an "Ummah" and to Muslims, no nationality matters, the whole world is ours. Mohammad (PBUH) was a prophet for all the worlds: "Rahmatallil Aalamin"! This nationalism has become so deep-rooted that unconsciously or subconsciously when we mention our religion and nationality together to anyone, we call ourselves Arab Muslim, Pakistani Muslim or African Muslim. Thus: preferring our nationality to our religion by mentioning it first. Instead we should call ourselves: Muslim Arab, Muslim Pakistani or Muslim African. This is a very minute difference---but it matters---! On the other hand, Europeans were joining together as an "Ummah", to them, it did not matter which colonial country was under which European power---as long as it was---!

Protectorate seemed very non-practical. Why would an independent country take "guidance" and let any European power "control" her? The solution to this was to bring these countries to such a stage of inferiority that they are dependent on Western powers, by all means: **financially, scientifically and mentally.**

Fo**financial** dependency, wars, and banking system was chosen, run by **"International Bankers"** (see "Modern Banking System"), governed by "Brotherhood". To divide and monitor money World Bank and IMF were formed, to drain money from the remaining wealth of the world, Switzerland Banks were established with safest accounts in the world.

For**scientific and educational** dependency, **"Scholarships"** were introduced on world scale i. e. "Rhodes". This brain sucking system has got its needles injected in every big city of the world. Not contradicting the beneficial side of it, but future rulers are selected and observed closely in institutions like "Oxford", "Cambridge" and "Harvard", then brain-washed (in some cases blackmailed, see "Illuminati") into the class system of "ruling class" and "ruled class". From there either the geniuses are offered jobs in European or American organisations and permanently engaged, never returning to their countries; or sent as brain-washed rulers back to their countries. In their jobs as foreigners, they are not trusted entirely in the West and sometime have to escape for their country's need (i.e., Dr A Q Khan, In-charge and Founder of Pakistan Atomic Program).

For **"mental"** dependency, entertainment industry is used. People fall into this trap laughing and willingly. The "Dream Machine" takes them away from reality and discreetly passes the brain signals, only noticed by sub-conscious (see MK Ultra). News agencies mostly owned by the same group, globally assist and provide them background and make sure they believe and follow only, the Masonic propaganda and dogma.

Divide and rule policy still works in non-European countries, providing Brotherhood a chance to intervene and "help" through UN, World Bank, NGOs, Human Amnesty International and countless other disguised organisations.

Now, as we know their line of action, through fall of "Ottoman Empire" and "Egypt", we will travel through some countries and understand "Freemasonry's" presence and destruction of relevant countries. Brotherhood doesn't stick to one line of action, rather change strategy accordingly and moulds whenever and wherever required.

AFGHANISTAN

Afghanistan, with her limited resources enough for itself, never caught the British attention, which concentrated on wealth and permanent flow of profit. Yet Afghanistan's treaties with Russia were a threat to British rule in India, considering a consistent emergence of Indian rulers from and through Afghanistan in the past. Twice, Britain had to defend her Indian dominion by invading Afghanistan. Finally Amir Habibullah Khan fell prey to Freemasons he *joined Freemasonry (2)*. Thus a convention in 1907, between Britain and France pledged a mutual respect for Afghan territory. Habibullah was assassinated in February 1919.

Amanullah was the son of Habibullah. Amanullah was selected by Afghan nobles he declared war on the British in May 1919. The British were forced to sign an agreement at Rawalpindi, which recognised Afghanistan as an independent nation, not a protectorate.

ALGIERS

The French army of occupation arrived in Algiers in 1830. A French-artillery-man called "Leon Roches" expert in explosives also arrived with the army. This 22 years young man converted to Islam and also made a pilgrimage to Mecca. He even helped to upgrade an Algerian army to fight and resist French. This army for resistance to the French, was led by "Abdul Qadir":

"Abdul Qadir an Islamic holy man claiming descent from Muhammad, used hit and run tactics that were highly effective; he was not completely subdued until 1847, and remains a hero to modern Algerian nationalists". (E/Encarta)

Whereas protectorate was a union of Europe, Freemasonry was dividing the Muslim world with nationalism: Had the whole of Africa or Arabia got united to fight the European invaders for sure they would have defeated them. Brotherhood broke others union but made their own. Roches became Qadir's translator, advisor and even go-between with Marshal Bugeaud, his former commander in chief at the head of the French expedition. Roches was graded as:

"An unofficial minister of defence, he also opened a munitions factory in Abdul Qadir's capital at Togdempt. Eventually he returned to France, and in 1884 published a memoir, "Trente-Ans-a-Travers l Islam"" (Thirty years through Islam). (15-73)

I could not find his book or its translation, so I can't claim either he reverted or "converted" to Islam, if any reader gets the opportunity please go through it and inform others. On the other hand, Roches strengthened the relation between Muslims and French, as well as Qadir and Marshal Bugeaud.

"Marshal Bugeaud went so far as to make a present to Abdul Qadir of the hundreds of muskets with which armed resistance began". (15-74)

When Abdul Qadir took his place as a Chief of the tribe he exclaimed:

"Any Muslim who revolts against my authority. I, who accepted the title of Sultan, only in order to be able to chase the invaders from the land of the believers. By the sole fact of his rebellion gives help to our enemies and in consequence must be considered an enemy of Islam".

The question is that, were the French so polite and honest with their enemies that they provided them with arms to resist against their-own armies? Or was Abdul Qadir deceiving them and tricked to grasp ammunition?

The answer is that none of the above is true! Abdul Qadir was in fact a...Freemason! His Masonic services were highly regarded in France and he was awarded the "Legion d'Honneur". He was invited to join the lodge Henri IV, at Paris. He was finally initiated in 1864, when he became a "Master Mason" at Lodge les Pyramids, at Alexandria in Egypt. It takes a devoted career to Freemasonry and years of loyalty before you are initiated as a Master Mason.

After 1847, he spent 5 years as a "prisoner of war" in France (I bet he did), he settled in Middle East. In 1860 at great risk, he saved many Christians from massacre by Muslims at Damascus (even after being a prisoner of war). Finally he died in exile in Damascus.

In 1837: 25,000 colonisers were populated in Algeria. Two years later the first Bishop of Algiers was appointed. By 1847: 120,000 Europeans were already settled there. 1848: the French Republican Government decreed that under French-law Algiers was henceforth French-territory: divided into three departments of Algiers, Oran and Constantine. 1865: the status of Algerians had acquired this definition:

"The native Muslim is French. Nonetheless he will continue to be ruled by Muslim law. He "may be" admitted to serve in the land or Naval forces. He "may be" enrolled in tasks and civil position in Algiers. On request he "may be" granted the enjoyment of the rights of French citizens".

On the face it looks good but in reality the term was "*may be*" and not "will be". This "*may be*" was in fact to be used against them, on every occasion:

"The Muslim population, although benefiting from social services and economic development, remained a disadvantaged majority, subject to many restrictions. By French law they could not hold public meetings, carry firearms, or leave their homes or villages without permission. Legally, they were French subjects, but to become French Citizens, with full rights, they had to renounce their faith! Few did so". (E/Encarta)

As far as the *"French soul in touching goodness"* is concerned, could this **sole goodness** provide their enemies, weapons to fight them-selves?

I wonder when in Ottoman Empire, Muslim journalists and thinkers like Zia Pasha were shouting for personal and press freedom and praising their French lords, did they ever look back to this page of history? Or were they completely blinded by the Masonic enlightenment.

Algeria's total debts to the World Bank in 1998 were $33.3 billion.

TUNISIA

Ahmed Bey the ruler of Tunisia was the son of an Italian woman. From his mother he learnt Italian and through her he came to rely on the services of Giuseppe-Raffo, a Sardinian Christian. Ahmed Bey killed his cousins to inherit the rule (1842-1855). He invited a French military mission starting the "Bardo Military School".

In order to strengthen his infantry and artillery regiments, he was advised by his "French friends" to raise their number. A total of 26,000 were commissioned, out of them 16,000 were on active service. Equipment was imported from various European countries. All this was not enough; he was given a further advice to build some factories to be self-sufficient in munitions.

In 1853, on French engineers' suggestion, he ordered them to build and launch an "iron-clad frigate", but after completion she was never put to sea, the harbour mouth; happened to be too small---oops---!

Military modernisation finally bankrupted the treasury (this could not be the only reason). His treasurer absconded to Paris with funds and files or should we say! Transferred money to Swiss banks and took refuge in the West? In 1860, Ahmed Bey introduced a constitutional "autocracy". He built a palace, designed by an Italian architect with water gardens laid by a Frenchman. Finally 1881 was the year when the French declared a "protectorate" of Tunisia.

The President of Tunisia, "Bourguiba", studied in France, where he came in contact with professors, writers and politicians, who were quite "sympathetic" towards his country's "national aspirations". He not only came back with inspirations of a liberal idea of creating an atmosphere of the "University of Paris", but with a French woman too, as his wife! In his own words, *"Backwardness of Tunisians, that brings disgrace upon us in the eyes of the world".*

This is the same Bourguiba who made a speech in 1965, floating the idea of negotiations with Israel. Ahmed Shuqairi, then leader of PLO replied; *"Bourguiba is a traitor and therefore, I demand a punishment for the Tunisian President, commensurate with the gravity of his crime".*

MOROCCO

Sultan Abdul Aziz succeeded to the throne in 1894, at the age of twelve or thirteen. Charmed by modernisation, he started borrowing abroad. By 1903 he had a debt of £8000,000. Walter Harris, the correspondent for "The Times" of London in Morocco, a close witness of the events wrote:

"Grand pianos and kitchen ranges, automobiles and immense cases of corsets, wild animals in cages, and boxes of strange theatrical uniforms, barrel organs, and handsome cabs, a passenger lift capable of rising to dizzy altitudes, destined for a one storied palace. False hair, cameras of gold and of silver with jewelled buttons, carved marble lions and living macaw parrots, jewels, real and false, steam launches and fire works, ladies under clothing from Pairs, and saddlery from Mexico, trees for gardens that were never planted, or if planted, were never watered, printing presses and fire balloons, an infinity of all that was grotesque, useless and in bad taste".

This is what is called a teenage syndrome. These were the rulers of the Muslim Ummah! Martin Gilbert reports on the background of this purchase:

"The gullible Abdul Aziz had been persuaded to purchase this mass of material by European salesmen from whom he sought the symbols of 'civilisation'". (14, vol 1, 162)

European salesman exactly knew how to seduce a young king, so he did not offer him arms---but---toys. While the young king was busy playing with his expensive toys, in 1907 an incident at the port of Casablanca led to the murder of nine Europeans. The French Navy shelled Casablanca and then landed an expeditionary force. By 1912, Abdul Aziz had resigned in favour of his brother Hafiz and a treaty was signed to formalise a French "protectorate".

The first Masonic Lodge of Morocco was founded in 1867: by the Supreme Council of France. This was followed in 1882 by "Lodge Al Maghrib Al Aksa", founded at Tangiers by the "Grand Lodge of Manitoba", Canada.

MAKKAH

On 1st September 1908, the first railway link between Hijaz and Damascus was opened. This was a historical day for Ottoman Empire, then ruled by Abdul Hamit II. The railway was built by the contribution of tens of thousands of the Muslim's charity throughout the Ottoman Empire as well as the loans taken from Europe. These loans were given in form of European currency, the currency was then returned to European companies to pay the price for the railways. The empire had to pay these loans back in bullion with interest. In fact, Europeans paid them nothing and took their gold away. This is called a one-sided-match! Muslims were following the West madly and West was sucking their blood gladly!

Young Turks were active all over the Empire with media support. Beside all dangerous outcomes "The Hijaz Railways", was propagated, as an achievement by the Young Turks and the occasion was celebrated on their behalf with Masonic slogans.

"The Arab tribes along the rout, celebrating under the Young Turk's revolutionary banners of 'Liberty, Equality, Fraternity', took an oath to protect the railway". (14, vol 1, 161)

If we remember, this is the same slogan used by Napoleon Bonapart during his Egyptian invasion. And this is the slogan of "Fraternity"! How could the Brotherhood reach Mecca, where non-Muslims can't even enter?

The Dutch Orientalist "C Snouck Hurgronje" was one of the extremely rare Europeans ever to have lived in Mecca, able to pass as a Muslim under the name of Abdul Ghaffar and to "research" Islam there, during the1880s.

Lord Kitchener went ashore to Alexandria disguised as an Arab from the naval force as a "greasy levantine". Byrton disguised as Mirza Abdullah of Bushire, a pilgrim to Mecca. Charles de Foucauld, murdered during WW1 disguised himself as an Arab or a Jewish merchant. Mc Pherson occupied his leisure studying "Sufism".

They did their homework well before going to school, we Muslims didn't attend the school, we failed in the exams. We wanted to be "promoted" into the next class without any effort.

"Sherif Hussain, from Hashmite family was the leader of Arab Nationalist revolt. Near 1913,14, living in Istanbul [and there briefed by the British]. *The British paid him a monthly subsidy of £125,000 in gold". (15-109)*

In return, "Sharif Hussain" (Sharif-e-Mecca), was promised an independent country through T E. Lawrence. Sharif was not honest even to his comrades, and paid them a small amount, sometimes nothing at all. Eventually the tribes found out this fiddle and the Brotherhood started paying these amounts direct to the tribal leaders. This is how the promise made to Sharif-e-Makkah (Hussain-ibn-Ali) is stated:

"Great Britain and France secretly concluded a separate accord, known as the 'Sykes-Picot agreement', by which most of the Arab lands under Turkish rule were to be divided into British and French spheres of influence. The areas now comprising Syria and Lebanon were assigned to France, and those comprising Israel and Jordan were assigned to Great Britain". (E/Encarta)

The agreement took its name from its negotiators, Sir Mark Sykes of Britain and Georges Picot of France. The designated areas are still well known for their assigned influences. Sharif-e-Makkah got nothing as pre-decided in "Sykes-Picot agreement".

The policy of King Ibn Saud can be analysed through his sympathies with the Western powers when:

"He permitted construction of a US air base in Dhahran". (E/Encarta)

After his visit to the United States in January 1956, it was announced that:

"The United States would sell arms and supply other 'aid' to Saudi Arabia in exchange for permission to use the Dhahran air base. In April that year Saudi Arabia declared the Gulf of Aqaba to be territorial waters and announced that Israeli ships would be denied passage through the Gulf. ***Despite the declaration, no attempts were made to interfere with the passage of Israeli ships". (E/Encarta) Emphasis** added.*

Only slogans, is that what we Muslims were taught by our Prophet (SAW)?

The Gulf War of 1990s opened the way to the American army once more! This time, hundreds of thousands! To compensate for petrol losses from Iraq and Kuwait, Saudi Arabia enormously increased its oil output. United States insisted upon the Saudi government to pay the price of "Gulf War", costing the country $51 billion.

"War payments and declining oil prices forced the Saudi government to cut social and defence spending and to take out loans from international banks". (E/Encarta)

In actual fact loans from International Bankers!

AMMAN

Abdullah, native of Makkah, son of Sharif Hussain (Sharif-e-Makkah), marched out of Mecca with an excuse to help his brother King Faisal, to recapture Damascus for him with hundreds of tribal warriors. On the way to Damascus, he stopped on the station of Ma'an of Hijaz railways. There, these "warriors" got "arrested" (can you believe this?) by British officers. From there he gave up his brother's help and cancelled "jihad" to be:

"Moved in March 1921 to Amman. Styling himself as Emir. Reached an agreement with the, then British colonial Secretary, "Winston Churchill"[a Freemason], *that he could indeed establish his rule in Amman and even receive a subsidy of £5,000 a month for doing so". (The Closed Circle)*

Indeed the "Brotherhood" look-after their allies and their kinship. What else do you need? A little palace of your own and some money to spend! This is the entire purpose of life and this is what Allah (SWT) is going to ask us on the Day of Judgement, that how much did we make and if we were successful in our careers?

SYRIA

B'ATH PARTY: Before we visit Syria and Iraq, it is important to know who is ruling these countries and who was the founder of the ruling party. B'ath Party founded by Michel Aflaq and Salahuddin Bitar. Its proposals were, Liberation from the West, Arab unity and Socialism.

Salahuddin Bitar was a Sunni Muslim, European educated and Michel Aflaq was a European looking "Jew"!

Hafiz Al Asad (1928-2000) joined the party in 1946. Asad was born in Qardahah, educated in Syrian Military College and received "additional military training" in the "Soviet Union". He also completed a flying course in Soviet Union and often visited there openly or "secretly". He became general of the Syrian Air force in 1964, when B'ath party came into power after the coup of March 1963.

He seized power in 1970 and became president in March 1971. In December 1972, he formed a new cabinet, many of the new members of the government belonged to Alwite (Shi'a) sect; which are 11% of Syria's population. Between 1973 and 1983, Syria received Soviet arms worth $10 billion.

In 1970 a civil war in Jordan broke out, Salah Jedid sent troops across the frontiers on behalf of Palestinians, as commander of the airforce, Asad refused to provide an air cover to the field troops. As a result Jordanian army destroyed much of the Syrian armour. Asad blamed Jedid for the fiasco and imprisoned him for an indefinite time. Mohammad Umran was also murdered in March 1972.

"Mustafa as Sibai" was born in Homs in 1915, attended "Al-Azhar University" in Egypt. "Hasan Al Banna" was another student from "Al-Azhar". Together they both founded an organisation called "Muslim Brothers". "Shishakli", then president outlawed the Muslim Brothers in 1952. When Asad came into power, he passed "Law 49", which made it a crime punishable to death to be a member of "Muslim Brothers" (known today as Ikhwan-ul-Muslemin) or even to be associated with it. As many as 1,000 Muslim Brothers were butchered in one day in Palmyra prison.

In 1982, when "Muslim Brothers" mounted a rebellion in Hammah, 10% or more Sunni inhabitants were killed:

"Assad ruthlessly suppressed it at a cost of some 20,000 lives and near-destruction of the city". (16)

To make space for Alwi's and increase their immigrants number, hundreds more Sunnies were killed in Aleppo, Sarmada and Jisr-al-Shughur. In Hama, corpses of Ulema (Muslim scholars) were dug out of the ruins and defiled.

IRAQ

The same "B'ath Party" is working in Iraq whose member is Saddam Hussain. This side is a majority of Shi'a (about 60, 65%) and Christians, so the government is given to Sunnies. I am not trying to "cause frictions" rather pointing out the "caused frictions".

"King Faisal" Meccan native and the younger son of Sharif-e-Mecca, was first "exiled" to Damascus (where his elder brother Abdullah was coming to help him and got arrested by the British to become Emir of Amman) and then again "exiled" to Iraq. There he became a "king" too---Family business---!

It is said that Iraqi nationalists wanted monarchy so they "elected" Faisal as their king. Strange is this for nationalists to import a king from another nation. What kind of "Nationalism" is that? The same nationalists first urged Faisal to reject the French demands, over control of Syria. Conflict ensued between him and the French, resulting in his expulsion from Syria.

"Faisal went to London to complain about the French action". (16)

Poor little king---! Sir Arnold Wilson, the acting civil commissioner was famous for his dictations to King Faisal. Faisal became formally crowned king on Aug 23 1921. Wilson was succeeded by Sir Percy Cox, this Faisal-Percy combination, which was called a bizarre "Anglo-Sunni combination", started deporting Shi'as to Iran. At that time, Shi'as had formed a "secret society" to resent Faisal. It is also well known that the British had spent £40 million in Iraq---Why?

"The nationalists argued that there were two governments in Iraq, one foreign and the other national." (16)

The new Anglo-Iraq treaty was signed on June 30, 1930. It provided for the establishment of a "close alliance" between Britain and Iraq with "**full and frank** consultation between them in all matters of foreign policy which may effect their common interests". British communications were found essential to maintain and protect for Iraq's interest:

"Air-base sites for British troops were therefore granted near Basra and west of Euphrates". (16)

This treaty was for 25 years, to come in effect after Iraq joins "League of Nations", which Iraq did, on Oct. 3, 1932. That is how "League of Nations" was made a world monitor organisation. Countries---that did not join voluntarily, were conditioned in return of favours.

The ruling elite of Iraq could be said to have consisted of about 14 men who changed cabinet posts frequently. So was the change in the cabinet, in fact between 1920-1958, twenty-four cabi-nets were held.

One of the cabinet members was Nuri Said Pasha, who held cabinet posts 14 times. Nuri Pasha, born in 1888, son of an official, went to school in Baghdad. On graduation, he went to military college in Istanbul, took king Faisal as his sponsor (or we should say Brotherhood compelled king Faisal to look after him). Soon Nuri Pasha, Joined "Al-Ahad"---a "secret society". That was the time when in the Muslim world, the Brotherhood was working under the slogans of education and science:

"In 1865, the Alliance Israelits Universelle founded what is reputed to have been the best school in Baghdad; its graduates contributed to the great advances made by the Iraqi Jewish community during the next half century. Graduates of the government schools were expected to enter the provincial bureaucracy, and most did". (16)

We still have "Convent Schools" all over the world and also in various Muslim countries that are well reputed. Midhat Pasha (The secret source to Rothschilds) became the governor of Iraq from 1869-72:

"With a 'hand picked' corps of advisers and assistants". (16)

He formed the first 'savings bank' along with other upgrading works.

"Several new schools were opened, modern text books were printed on the press that Midhat founded, and Iraq's first newspaper, 'Az-Zawra', began publication". (16)

He was also the founder of the feudal system in Iraq, he claimed to distribute the land to peasants for cultivation, but:

"Most land was registered not in the names of individual peasants and tribesmen but rather in the names of tribal Shaikhs, urban based merchants, and former tax farmers". (16)

After the Young Turks revolution of 1908, in Iraq, however, there was scant nationalist opposition to Ottoman rule:

"Although some Iraqi Arab officers in the Ottoman army joined the secret 'Al-Ahd' society, which is reported to have advocated independence for the sultan's Arab provinces". (16)

This is the same "Al-Ahd", that Nuri Said Pasha, the 14 times cabinet minister was a member of. This was an equivalent society to Young Turks / CUP, working for Freemasonry.

Saddam Husain, born April 28,1937, in Tikrit, Iraq, joined Ba'th Socialist Party in 1957. He took part in an unsuccessful attempt to assassinate the then Iraqi Prime Minister Abdul Karim Qasim. Saddam got wounded but escaped to Syria and then to Egypt. After the Ba'thists took power in Iraq in 1963, he returned. The same year Ba'thsists were overthrown again, Saddam got arrested and spent several years in prison, eventually escaped from there. Again in 1968 when Ba'th Party came into power after the coup of 1968, in that coup, he played an active part. Then he effectively held power with President Ahmad Hassan al-Bakr.

After a long struggle of Communist and Socialist wings of Ba'th Party (although on the top level; working for the same cause), the Sunni majority formed their government. According to a historian of the Ba'th Party, any Syrian or Iraqi, who wished to be upwardly mobile, had:

"The avenue of the party bureaucracy, with its pyramidal structure, schools for cadres, and rewards for loyal service". (15-344,5)---Do these pyramids sound familiar---?

Inn 1979, Saddam Hussain's men placed Al-Bakr, then president of Iraq, under house arrest, took-over the "Broadcasting Station", "The Iraqi News Agency" and "The General Staff Headquarters". Compelled Al-Bakr to announce his resignation, under this camouflaged take-over operation. In July 1979, Al-Bakr's loyalists took the last stand by opening the "Ba'th Revolutionary Council's" agenda:

"For several years, this group has been preparing a malicious, conspirational design aimed at striking at the party and the revolution and the socialist and democratic gains of the masses and linking Iraq with the capitulationist design led by US imperialism in the interest of Zionism and the forces of darkness". Throughout the past phase, these plotters were in contact with a foreign side. The command believes it is not in the national interest to expose that side now. This group received funds from that side, received orders from it, and has co-ordinated its conspirational, criminal efforts with it (this group comprises) malicious pustules, the remedy for which is achieved by eradicating and eliminating them forever". (15-346)

We will come back to the after effects of this regime, working in corroboration with the forces of dark and their achievements to pave the way for "One Global Government" in chapter; "Committee of 300". Suffice is the quote:

"From 1921, real power has been in London. CIA overthrew the previous government and brought Ba'th party into power. Americans said: He (Saddam Hussain), is son of a bitch---but---our son of a bitch". (Paying the Price-ITV, March 6, 2000)

PALESTINE

Jerusalem was captured in December 1917, by British and Allies under the command of "Sir Edmond Allenby" (later 1st Viscount), the remaining area was occupied by October 1918, by the British.

In April 1920 anti-Zionist riots in Old Jerusalem resulted in the death of 5 Jews and 4 Arabs, which followed the replacement of military administration with a civilian in July 1920. Usually these incidents cause opposite results i.e. switching to military regime from civilian, but if we look at the resulted appointment of the high commissioner we understand why! The first high commissioner was:

"Sir Herbert (later Viscount) Samuel: a Zionist". (16)

In July 1922 the council of the "League of Nations" approved the mandate instrument for Palestine, stressing the Jewish historical connection with Palestine.

Article 2 made the mandatory power responsible for placing the country under such "political administrative and economic conditions as will secure the establishment of the Jewish National home...and the development of self-governing institutions."

Article 4 allowed the establishment of a Jewish Agency, full name:

" Jewish Agency of Israel, international body representing the 'World Zionist Organisation', created in 1929 by Chaim Weizmann ". (16)

This is the same Weizmann that Rothschild refers to, in his letter to "Dear Mr Balfour" in 1917. This agency also set up the "Youth Aliyah" program to resettle orphaned Jewish children from Nazi Germany.

"Upon the establishment of an Israeli state in 1948, the agency devoted itself primarily to problems of immigrations, settlement, the Youth Aliyah, propaganda and the cultural education of Jews outside Israel. These functions were retained even after 1951, when the Jewish agency became---legally---identified with the---'World Zionist Organisation'". (16)

On Sep 29 1923, the mandate officially came into force.

Amin Al-Husayni (1897-1974), born in Jerusalem took over the resistance to Zionist political ambitions in Jerusalem. He was appointed the Grand Mufti of "Supreme Muslim Council" by the British in December 1921, at the age of 24. This position enhanced his influence on Muslims to accelerate the rebellion against Zionism. After a long strive, against the British (the actual backing power for Zionism) and the other influential family of "Nashashabis" who were:

"More accommodating toward British"(16),

Amin succeeded to:

"Force Britain to make substantial concessions to Arab demands in 1939". (16)

Finally the British, Zionists or Brotherhood had to abandon the idea of establishing Palestine as a Jewish state. The other factor was that:

"Throughout the 1920s most of the British local authorities in Palestine, especially the military, sympathised with the Palestinian Arabs, while the British government in London tended to side with the Zionists". (16)

The first attempt for a Jewish state failed. Israel had to come into existence at whatever cost; let it be throats of 6 million Jews in Germany. No wonder, the Rothschilds and Chaim Weizmann were in London "close to the British government". No wonder, 6 million Jews were sacrificed to gain the sympathies of not only British military, but also the world population. Mass-manipulation!

Sympathies of British forces and general public towards Arabs meant; some more homework needs to be done before the large-scale immigration of Jews is possible. Suddenly the number of the Jewish immigrants dropped dramatically in late 1920s.

"In 1927 the number of Jewish emigrants exceeded that of immigrants, and in 1928 there was a net Jewish immigration of only 10 persons". (16)

This is not because all of a sudden anti-Semitism disappeared all over the world. This is merely due to fact that Jews were stopped to migrate by their elite, Zionists/Freemasonry. Nazism was rising! Poor Jews had to be slaughtered!

"In August 1929 negotiations were concluded for the formation of an enlarged 'Jewish Agency' to include non-Zionist Jewish sympathisers throughout the world". (16)

These negotiations were followed by the incident of the "Western Wall" of Jerusalem in the same month, in which 133 Jews were killed, 339 wounded. The Arab casualties were:

"Mostly at the hands of 'British security forces' [who were deployed there purposely], *being 116 killed and 339 wounded". (16)*

British favours to Zionists increased openly and the "Balfour Declaration", which was a promise to Zionism, started clashing with the obligations to the Arabs under Article 22 of the "Covenant of the League of Nations". "Passfield White Paper" which was issued on Oct. 20, 1930, finally not only called to halt the Jewish immigration but also recommended for Palestinian land to be sold only to landless Arabs. The possibilities of a Zionist State were fading away. In return to Passfield White Paper, Zionist pressure was so strong that "Ramsay MacDonald" the British Prime Minister addressed an "explanatory letter" to Chaim Weizmann, thus nullifying the Passfield White Paper.

PLOs

PLO was formed in 1964 to centralize various Palestinian groups. In the beginning it was sponsored by **Charles Helou (Alexander)** President of Lebanon (1964-70). Helou was a Christian, born in Beirut, educated at St. Joseph's University and received a law degree from the French faculty of law in Beirut. He founded two French language newspapers and served as an ambassador to the Vatican in 1947.

The other host country to PLO was Jordan, ruled by King **Hussain** who after 1967's "three noes" (No peace with Israel, no recognition of Israel and no "negotiations" with Israel) meeting in Khartum:

"Resumed his secert 'negotiation' with Israel over the disposition of the West Bank and East Jerusalem". (16)

He was responsible for killing thousands of PLO members in September 1970, remembered as "Black September". In Black September he not only called upon military assistance from the United States and the British, but also from Israeli military overflights to attack the Syrian forces fighting along PLO---This was a Muslim king-!

Hussain had been king of Jordan from 1953 till his death in 1999, educated partly in England, married to an English woman (another Naqshe-Dil?). He succeeded his father King Talal, who was deposed in 1952, because of---"mental illness"---very interesting---! For economic progress, Hussain was:

"Forced to depend on continual financial aid from the West...Hussain's socially conservative policies and his alignment with the Western powers were often criticized by other Arab leaders as well as by his domestic opposition". (16)

Till 1956 the Commander of the Jordanian Army was General John Bagot Glubb, a British officer. Hussain was forced to dismiss General John by the opposition. In the Arab-Israel war he lost the West Bank to Israel despite his army was being "helped" by Americans. In 1988, when Arafat started peace accords with Israeli government, Hussain surrendered Jordan's claim to the disputed West Bank as well as its role in representing the Palestinians living there.

"Israeli strategy was to induce the Lebanese to crush the PLO in their country as King Hussain had done in Jordan, but this policy did not succeed..." (16)

Israel did not need to induce King Hussain, but only to order! A country on continual financial aid from the West cannot disobey the rulers of the West, the Zionists! (Ibid.) This is a smoke screen to induce us---To induce you---!

Without going into details of the "Arab Israeli War" of 1967, which was a smaller set up as compared to WW1 and WW2, we go straight to the point. PLO came into prominence only after the Arab-Israeli war of June 1967. The movement is dedicated to the creation of a **"democratic and secular"** Palestinian state, **"not an Islamic state".**

Major organisations within or related to PLO include **"Fatah"**, the **"Popular Front for the Liberation of Palestine" (PFLP)** and the **"Democratic Front for the Liberation of Palestine" (DFLP). "Black September"** is also a group of Fatah and the PFLP-General Command.

Among other small groups "Fatah" is the largest, whose leader is "Yasar Arafat". **Yasar Arafat,** was born on Aug. 24? 1929 Cairo, Egypt (according to some others, born in Palestine). He received Nobel Prize for peace in 1994. Which he was given Jointly to him with his enemies, Yitzhak Rabin and Shimon Peres from Israel, for the peace agreement of 1993 (what a fighter)! Arafat Graduated as a civil engineer from the University of Cairo then got commissioned into the Egyptian army. From there he went to Kuwait where he worked as an engineer and established his own contracting firm.

He was named chairman of PLO in 1969. From 1974 Arafat advocated PLO's withdrawal from activities outside Israel. Same year the Arab heads of state recognized PLO as the sole legitimate representative of all Palestinians and given full membership of Arab League (a sub league of "Committee of 300" Ibid.) in 1976.

Arafat's leadership was challenged after his withdrawal from Beirut to Tunis and Lebanon, yet retaining some Arab leaders support. On Nov. 15, 1988 PLO proclaimed the "State of Palestine", thus founding a kind of government-in-exile. On April 2, 1989 PLO's governing body the Palestinian National Council elected Yasar Arafat as the President of the new quasi-state (a government in exile). The PLO during this period also recognized United Nations resolution 242 and 238 thereby acknowledging Israel's right to exist, finally giving-up its long time goal of eliminating Israel. In April 1993 Arafat made secret negotiations with Israel on possible peace settlements resulting Israel-PLO accords, signed on Sep. 13, 1993, including mutual recognition.

Al-Fatah; was founded in late 1950s by Yasar Arafat and Abu Jihad, with Syrian support (then ruled by Ba'th Party, a sub-organisation to Freemasonry, please see Syria and Iraq), became based in Damascus, where it developed a commando-type structure. On Dec. 31, 1964 it blew up the Israeli water pump installation (This was done to gain control over revengeful Muslims, once Arafat achieved this target, he condemned all so called, terrorist activities). By 1968 it had emerged as a large Palestinian organisation, thus becoming the major target of Israel. In March 1968 Fatah fought with Jordanians to drive off Israeli forces from their soils in Karameh. This was a big success after the Arab defeat in the Six-Day War of 1967 (another hero is being created just like Ataturk). By the end of 1960s Al-Fatah became the largest and richest of all Palestinian organizations and took over leading role in PLO. Thus taking a heroic lead on all other Palestinian organisations---You see---!

PFLP: Popular Front for the Liberation of Palestine, founded in 1967 by **Georges Habash**. PFLP is further divided within for the internal conflicts between its **Marxist and Leninist** ideologies. Georges Habash is a medical degree holder from "American University of Beirut", a member of the "Youth of Vengeance" group since 1950s and a **"Christian"!** Under his leadership PFLP hijacked many planes, including U.S. jet blown up in Sep 1970 which resulted in King Hussain's crackdown on Palestinian guerrillas in Jordan. **Abdul Abbas**, a Shi'a, was a member of PFLP, who headed the hijack of an Italian ship, "Achille Lauro" and murdered one of its passengers.

"Habash, a Marxist, visited China in 1970, finding Chinese leaders critical of the PFLP 'foreign operations', and Moscow in 1972. Following the Yom Kippur War of 1973, Habash became the leading voice of the 'Rejection Front' ". (16)

To cover the opposition to PLO Habash split from Arafat and founded his separate organization. The usual democratic strategy of Brotherhood: keep both sides under control, thus not ignoring any. Habash also founded the militant PFLP whose member was **"Wadi'ah Haddad"** another **"Christian"**. After disputes with Habash, Haddad split from him and became leader of all scattered Palestinian organizations. Haddad was the introducer of plane hijacking while working with Habash. His group included Laila Khalid, the first female plane hijacker. Haddad was also the man behind **"Karlos" (the jackal)** another **Christian**: who would threat any Arab Shaikh to get money from---and will get! At present Karlos is serving a prison sentence in Europe.

DFLP; is the "Democratic Front for the Liberation of Palestine". Making it one of many associated organizations with PFLP. Based on **Marxist-Leninist ideology**, founded in 1969 by a **"Jordanian Orthodox Christian"** named **"Na'if Hawatmeh"**. It took responsibility for the attacks in Ma'alot and Bet She'an in 1974.

"Hamas" came into existence in 1987 initially by the "Muslim Brotherhood's" members. Hamas is dedicated to the destruction of Israel and the creation of an **Islamic state** in Palestine. It also denounced the peace accords of 1993. Israel imprisoned its founder Shaikh Ahmed Yasin in 1991 and hundreds of its other members were arrested. Yasar Arafat tried to overwhelm Hamas, by including its members to leadership positions in Palestinian authority.

The question is; in case---who would succeed Yasar Arafat? The answer is Georges Habash!

This is how Brotherhood works; they spread confusion. A history of disputes and a number of organizations (all working for the elite group) ceased the interest of general public, till; people did not care any more who is doing what. Bulging choice makes a decision hard, you don't know who to trust and who to discredit. Only one loyal, Muslim congregation with Muslim leadership; dedicated to the cause, not only arises the interest in public but also block's the way leading astray. That is why:

"...He who swears allegiance to a Caliph should give him the pledge of his hand and the sincerity of his heart (i.e. submit to him both outwardly as well as inwardly). He should obey him to the best of his capacity. If another man comes forward (as a claimant to Caliphate), disputing his authority, they (the Muslims) should behead the latter..." (Sahih Muslim-4546. Narrated by Abdullah ibn Amr ibn al-'As)

First: Freemasonry supported violence by funding PLO through Syria, Jordan and Lebanon. Once they had their control on the top level of PLO; Brotherhood made them change their strategy and condemn violent attacks to look for a political solution. This had to have an opposition. They controlled opposition by appointing puppets like Georges Habash and Haddad. This gave them advantage to observe the incidents closely and in cases "orchestrate". Once two big organizations were formed and both in their hands, other small organizations like, "Abu Nidal" and "Hamas" were condemned widely or absorbed by these two. Thus leaving no chance for any real "PLO". **Once again Brotherhood is controlling "both sides"!**

Interestingly, all these famous organizations are not striving for Islam or Law of Islam, but democracy, communism or Leninism. The new generation in Palestine remembers "Karl Marx" and "Lenin" all by heart---but Hadith of Prophet Mohammad (SAW)---! Those who rise with slogan of Islam are out-casted as terrorists. To keep Muslims away from actual Jihad, mass manipulation was necessary. Countless incidents of hijacking and civilian casualties have drawn an image of "Muslim Terrorist". Red colours to this award winning painting are sprinkled by "Brotherhood media" and "Holy-Wood" film producers; by using the flowing blood of civilian casualties. As soon as one hears the term "Terrorist" he visualises a Muslim with half-covered face and a gun. Not mentioning the **Christians running these organizatoins and training these so called Muslims terrorists. Shall we call these leaders "FREEMASONS" Or shall we call them "JESUITS"?**

"And even to descend so low as to become a Jew among the Jews, that you might be enable to gather together all information for the benefit of your order as a faithful soldier of the Pope". (Jesuit's Oath)

FAHAD MIHYI

Out of countless victims to these mass-manipulations, one is Fahad Mihyi. He was born in Palestine in 1957. He spent his childhood playing in the open lands of Palestine's suburbs with suffocating feeling of Zionist regime. He witnessed Muslims being oppressed in their own land. He saw the in-just spread by Israeli army. He observed the poverty of his family and others like them. He looked at the hunger of the rightful owners of the harvest and luxurious lives of lazy businessmen.

All these unanswerable questions raised dissatisfaction in his restless soul. Walking on the uneven paths of his native soils he tried many times to untangle these knots, always ending up in extra bewilderment. With few education facilities he never had a chance to properly occupy his mind in progressive educational activities.

Past his childhood he stepped into his teenage, yet he saw no change in the atmosphere. Restlessness spread even farther when he realized the scale of oppression and the cost of day-to-day life. His father had already died his mother passed away in his youth. As a man he felt responsible towards his family, but there were no work opportunities. His background made him an easy prey for the recruiting members of PLO. This was the time when Habash had formed his separate group, "PFLP". Later on when Haddad formed his separate wing, he decided to keep "Fahad" with him.

After necessary brainwashing Fahad was given a "task" in England with another member of the organization. Their task was to blow the Israel airline's crew bus in which the crew travelled from Heathrow airport to their hotel in Central London. The suitable place their planners found, was the drop-off point of the hotel in Central London. Two youths stood there with guns and bombs in their hands. They were not skilled for the job; they were only playful energetic youths to be used for the elite purpose. As a result Fahad's companion died at the spot during the "task", when the bomb he was trying to throw---blew in his own hands---! Fahad left the job unfinished and ran. He was followed by a "cab driver", who "informed" the Police. Fahad was arrested while entering the sub-way station. Some how the source of information to the Police does not convince, with no mobile phones facilities in those days!

Fahad was charged for murder and given life sentence, recommended 22 years in prison. A youth, only 18, 19 years of age was to spend next 22 years of his life in Great Britain, a strange country, with a language he did not speak or even understand. Each minute spent in prison:

"I have to watch my back". (Fahad)

According to him:

"Time has slowed down, day goes like week, weeks like months...there is no one to look after me, no body has been to ask me how am I doing". (Fahad)

Time never stops, it never wait's for any one. It was 1976, when Fahad engaged himself in the incident. It was 1998, when he finished his recommended sentence. This is August 2000! He is still not released! He is still in Prison! He is not considered fit to live in a civilized society! His family has vanished! He has no news about his sisters and grand father who lived back home!

Fahad is abandoned: by all his friends---by all Muslims---by all of us!

CH-16 HINDUSTAN

VASCO DA GAMA

Vasco da Gama: (1460-1524) The Portuguese navigator opened up the sea rout from Western Europe to the East. Who could he be other than a Knight?

"Knight of the Order of Christ, [another sub-organisation of Templars] *identified as Vasco da Gama". (16)*

The sea rout started a race between European countries to monopolise the spice trade from East India to Europe. "Francisco de Almeida" and "Afonso de Albuquerque" were the successors of Vasco da Gama; they established a number of fortified posts to secure seaways. Albuquerque took Goa in 1510, Malacca in East Indies in 1511 and Hormuz (Ormuz) in Persian Gulf in 1515. These moves provided a strategic command of the Indian Ocean to Portuguese and financially damaged the Ottoman Empire by cutting her trade routs.

"Saint Francis Xavier" (1506-1552) was instrumental in establishing Christianity in India. He also belonged to the same cult: Here is the evidence of Saint Xavier's initiation and "Brotherhood's", activities in India:

"In Paris on Aug. 15, 1534, he pronounced vows as one of the first seven members of the 'Society of Jesus' or 'Jesuits', under the leadership of 'Ignatius of Loyola'... Xavier then performed the 'Spiritual Exercises', a series of meditations lasting about 30 days and devised by Ignatius in light of his own experience..." (16)

Ignatius Loyola was 15 years older than Xavier and a former soldier (This is the same Loyola described in Jesuit's oath), the founder of the Jesuits Order. Loyola shared a room with Francis. After completing his studies, Francis and other members of "Jesuits" reassembled in Venice, where he was ordained priest on June 24, 1537. From there amongst them, the "First Seven" went to the Holy Land to invite more people. After a year they came back to Rome with fresh recruits and joined the Pope. King John III of Portugal, a follower of the order proposed them to preach into his Asian dominions. On March 15, 1540, Francis left Rome for India. He started his missionary from Goa the centre of Portuguese activities in India. There he spent the next three years among the poor "Pravas", the pearl fishers, where 20,000 people were already baptised seven years before as a result of an early missionary. His "Oath of the Jesuits" helped him to convince or deceive another 10,000 men to seek salvation in the order of "Jesuits". He opened schools and turned "The College of Holy Faith" of Goa into Jesuits education base in 1548 with the help of other Jesuits who had arrived following him.

The "Dutch" made first voyage in 1595 with the help of "Jan Huyghen van Linschoten" who had worked in Goa for six years. Their objective was merely trade, not religion or expansion of their empire. They formed a trade circle to benefit from the spices. They went straight to business spots, for spices to the East Indies (Indonesia), for pepper and cardamoms to South India and for cinnamon to Ceylon (Sri Lanka).

DUTCH EAST INDIA COMPANY

The Dutch trade was operated through "Dutch East India Company" a much larger then the "English East India Company". The only problem they faced was the exchange in return to spices. West had nothing to offer to value the price of spices. In Indonesia, they needed textile (cotton or silk) to buy the spices. To buy the textile from India and China they needed silver.

"To work the spice monopoly, the Dutch developed an elaborate system of Eastern trade from Persian Gulf to Japan, the ultimate object of which was to 'secure the goods, with which to secure the spices, without recourse to scarce European resources'. It was this trade that brought the Dutch to India at Surat, the Coromandel Coast (Negapatam), Bengal, and up-country at Agra". (16)

In simple words, they wanted to spend---"nothing"---yet buy the spices. To solve this myth, "British East India Company" took control.

BRITISH EAST INDIA COMPANY

The initial capital that BEIC had, was only 50,000, which was even less than one-tenth of DEIC. The BEIC received its rights of trade in 1600. It included a group of London merchants, who sent separate voyages, which were replaced in 1612 by terminable joint stocks. In 1657 a permanent joint stock was established.

"The company's objective was the spices of the East Indies [Indonesia], *and it went to India only for the secondary purpose of securing cottons for sale to spice growers". (16)*

That is why it was called the "British East India Company" and not the "British India Company". This is how it was supposed to work:

Spices from East, paid by,
Cotton and silk from India and China, paid by,
Something from their own pocket!

The latter was impossible because the West had nothing, only a limited growth of cotton would not meet the requirement of spices and:

"The export of bullion was an offence to England's reigning mercantilist political economy". (16)

East Indians and Indians will not accept anything other than silver or gold in exchange for their goods. To solve the silver/gold problem the English had to develop a system. By virtues of this system they managed to achieve their target by------ **"DRUGS"**-----yes!

"Opium was shipped to Far East [China], *where it later became the basis of the Anglo-Chinese tea trade". (16)*

In fact tea was a cover up, actual trade was the drug trade. The questions are where this opium was coming from and how much income it secured for British? The answer is:

"Almost 13% of the income of India under British rule was derived from the sale of good quality 'Bengal opium' to the British- run opium distributors in China...The truth is that the supply of opium to China was a British monopoly, an OFFICIAL monopoly". (10-103)

Were Chinese already addicted to opium? No! Not at all!

"In China a market for opium was first created and then filled by opium from Bengal". (10-103,4)

To grow opium in Bengal, BEIC already had their "Factories" in Hindustan through, permission granted them in result of a naval victory over the Portuguese in 1612. Portuguese control of the sea routs was taken over by British, and the Mughal emperor allowed them to do "Business" in Hindustan in return.

"There followed through the 17th century a period of peaceful trading through factories operating under Mughal grants. This held good, for 'Surat' and later for 'Hugli' (1651) in Bengal. In the south, the factory at 'Masulipatam' (1611) was moved to the site of 'Madras'..." (16)

The myth was solved; this is how it was done:

Opium grown on Hindustani soils of Bengal, paid for;
Cotton and silk in China, paid for:
Spices from Indonesia!

To dismiss the danger of cotton production from Hindustan the British drug suppliers cut the thumbs of countless local Bengali Malmal (muslin) growers thus the Bengali economy depended on opium production. This also ended the danger of any direct cotton export from the sub-continent to the East Indies. The British opium trade was a well-kept secret like other conspiracies by Brotherhood up until recently. This is how information is controlled; they own all the newspapers. They own all the TV channels. They own famous authors. Brotherhood, are the "source of information". Any radical source of information is either neglected or ridiculed. **You only know what they want you to!**

"After 1700 the company found a new profitable line in the 'Chinese tea trade', whose imports increased (1706-50) from 54,000 to 2,300,000-odd pounds". (16)

I don't think, tea is so addictive---! The conquest of 1688-90 was the first try to take over the Mughal Empire but Mughal Emperor; Aurangzeb was too strong to be defeated. After this came the time of fortified factories surrounded by satellite towns. These factories were drug factories, the Madras factory and the 'Fort William' in Calcutta, built in 1696.

"The first opium shipments reached England from Bengal in 1683, carried in British East India Company 'Tea Clippers'". (10-110)

SINGAPORE AND DRUG TRADE

Sir Stamford Raffles, (1781-1826), was a Freemason, Knight and a fellow of the "Royal Society". He joined East India Company at the age of 14 as a clerk. At the age of 23, in 1804 he was appointed assistant secretary to the newly formed government of Penang. Raffles was initiated into Freemasonry in Java in 1811. On 11th Sep1811 Lord Minto (Freemason), the then governor general of India also appointed him lieutenant governor of Java.

On Jan. 29, 1819, Raffles acquired the island of Singapore for British East India Company:

"The Port of Singapore is a free Port, and the trade thereof is open to ships and vessels of every nation..." (16)

But how come he had all the authority to announce it as a free port? Why to announce Singapore a free Port on the first place? What was so special about it and why did it have to be a free port? ---Because, it was to be used for drug trade, a passage to China! If Singapore was not a free port, the goods passing through it will have to be checked by the Customs.

"To advance to more modern history, the Chinese-British partnership was solidified by the Hong Kong agreement which established an equal partnership in the opium trade." (10-114)

With Hong Kong its centre, still terms and conditions are the same. Still opium is traded in exchange with gold, because they don't except US Dollars. That is why very large volume of gold is traded in the Hong Kong Exchange (you may check it your self).

Mass supply of the drug to meet demands; is not carried out by little carriers, trying to make a few dollars. It is carried out under the supervision and banners of the "Committee of 300". For this purpose "European Economic Community" is doing an excellent job. EEC has got a special marker called "Triangle Internationale Routier", in brief, "TIR"! The trucks with "TIR" marker are exempted from any checking. These trucks are not supposed to be stopped at customs border posts.

"TIR trucks are allowed to carry only perishable items. They are supposed to be inspected in the country from whence they originated and documentation to this effect is supposed to be carried by each truck driver.

Under international treaty obligations this is what happens, thus Kintex trucks [a Bulgarian company], *were able to load their cargoes of heroin and certify it as 'fresh fruit and vegetables' and then make their way through Western Europe, even entering high-security NATO bases in Northern Italy." (10-119)*

This is the magic of the Masonic "Triangle"! "Brotherhood", geniusley display their signs everywhere, but to see them you have to know them! Next time when you see a truck with TIR mark, you know what could be going on! The drug trade was a well-kept secret by the elite. They formed subsidiaries, a net of different organizations to hide behind the veils.

"The trade was conducted by the illustrious British East India Company...The 300 members of the British East India Company's board were a cut above the common herd". (10-104)

This was, and is the "Committee of 300" which will be discussed in due course. The trade of opium brought Brotherhood enormous amount of wealth and money. With this money they were able to buy the native treacherous people, which enabled them to "divide and rule".

All the money from drug trade was going into the pockets of the elite. Remember this was not British Empire, this was not English drug trade: this was and is a Masonic Empire. The only brother to a Freemason is a Freemason! Don't be hostile towards the English, they were suffering like any other nation in the world. British Raj never benefited general public. At the peak of British Empire in 1908:

"The number of paupers at the beginning of the year in England and Wales was 928,671. If Scotland were to be included, the number was well over a million". (14, vol-1, p-178)

FIRST FREEMASON AND CORRUPTION

I am sure some people often think, that why there is so much corruption and bribery in the Sub-Continent? Is it because all people there are genetically overwhelmed by the instinct? Or is it because they were lead to believe that bribe is the magic stick? Where does this bribe come from? Who originated it?

It is all to do with a well-planned conspiracy! The BEIC's servants were privately engaged in their own businesses too.

"Their new authority and the company's power enabled them to exploit their trade with little hindrance. They had the means of using intimidations (through their agents) against Indian rivals like the indigo growers and Indian police, customs, revenue, and judicial officials. Presents and bribes were the price Indians had to pay for freedom from harassment". (16)

This is how "corruption" was introduced into India. On the basis of the same corruption, Third World countries' credibility is rated at present.

In 1762, Haidar Ali Khan from south of India, state of Mysure, became a threat to BEIC. In 1769 British had to make a peace treaty with Haider Ali Khan in Madras. The British were virtually helpless against Haidar Ali Khan, but they used their old Masonic techniques.

"The nawab of Karnataka had become by 'degrees dependent' on the company because he needed its support against the threat of Haidar and the nizam. Ingenious

and feckless, the nawab involved Madras in South Indian politics and the company in his affairs by borrowing from its servants". (16)

Madras was then under British/Brotherhood rule. The phrase "degrees dependent" used in Britannica CD 2000 is not a co-incidence; the author exactly knows what he means by this concealed announcement; which in fact, is an indication for "Brothers".

"The first Indian Mason, 'Omrat-ul-Omrah', Nabob of Carnatic [Nawab of Karnataca], *was initiated in 1775, but few others followed him (and those who did were Muslims) until the middle of the nineteenth century, when religious and social barriers began to break down". (2-206)*

He was the**First Freemason** in the sub-continent and this is the "degree" of dependency described in the quote above. The money he borrowed; pawned the whole population of Madras. In fact this degree of dependency was so high that:

"In Madras little could be done until the incubus of the Karnatic nawab's debts was removed..." (16)

Degrees of dependency of the Nawab, caused joblessness, this paved the way for frustration. Thus founding a class of people who became "middlemen" for the trade BEIC was carrying, lawful or unlawful, fair or unfair, cotton or drugs! These middlemen were only worried about their necessities.

"Up to 1750, the effects of the East India Company's operations were marginal. Production of cotton and silk goods, of indigo, saltpetre, and, later, opium was stimulated in particular areas like Bengal, Gujrat, and Mlawa, with some gain to middlemen but no sign of any general rise in living standards." (16)

To increase the frustration; extra revenue was enforced on zamindars (Landowners) which resulted in more pressure on the cultivators. In 1770 when the "Bengal Famine" occurred, which swept away the one-third population of Bengal, little attempt was made to help the effected, rather:

"The cruel severity with which the revenue was still collected at this time delayed recovery for many years. Economic recovery was further delayed by Warren Hastings' makeshift revenue arrangements'..." (16)

From 1774, "Warren Hastings" took control of all company's possessions in India. Warren Hastings---is listed in the gallery as a---Famous Freemason---! What shall we call it? British Raj, Company's Raj---or Masonic Raj?

In fact Freemasonry was present in India well before 1775 in the form of East India Company. But the actual Modern Freemasonry was there soon after the founding of the Grand Lodge of England, founded in 1723:

"First lodge in India was founded in 1730 at 'Calcutta'. Ten years later it was followed by 'Star in the East' Lodge (which is still working), and within 20 years lodges had also been founded at Madras and Bombay". (2-54)

Nawab of Karnataka borrowed money from Freemasons and sold the state. Same technique is used today through corrupt politicians of third world, or more appropriately, Masonic politicians!

NATIONALISM IN HINDUSTAN

In the early years of the craft in India, Hindus were not allowed to join the lodge, on the basis of worshipping several gods. In 1830's, when Masonic hold was firm with a possible total domination of the Sub-Continent, Freemasonry stepped ahead towards their "One World Government" target which they could not achieve, if Hindustan was united. A united Hindustan could be a threat in future, with mass population, vast land and countless resources: It was necessary to divide it and divide it further into small pieces, until a big power threat is permanently dissolved. For this purpose,

Nationalism was cultivated in Hindustan. Nationalism was needed, to divide Hindustan into two, with the help of religious division, Muslims and Hindus!

Muslims and Hindus had been living together in Hindustan for centuries, in peace and harmony. Other than some individual conflicts, there had never been a confrontation on a national level. It reminds me of a story, which I read in childhood, about unity.

Long time ago, there was a woodcutter he had five sons. When the woodcutter was on deathbed, he feared about his five sons' future. There upon he called his sons, gave them a bunch of wood sticks and asked them each in turn to break the bunch. Each one of them failed. Then he separated each stick and asked them to break the individual sticks. This time they succeeded easily. So the woodcutter advised them; "if you stay united and together like a bunch, no body will be able to defeat you, but if you split you will be defeated easily".

Freemasons must have had read this story, so they decided to break the Hindu Muslim Unity. This is their strategy step by step.

1. To inspire Hindus by Masonic theories and for this, Lodges must open their doors to them.
2. To introduce "Nationalism" and promote Hindus into politics, so they could be able to run their own government and become parallel to the Muslims (Latter already experienced with governing affairs).
3. In the mean time, instigate Hindus against Muslims and vice versa, to cause a conflict on "Nations-level".
4. Thus to enforce the "Two Nations Idea".
5. With Two Nations Idea, first, split them half instantly, and in the long run divide further, until small provincial governments come into existence.
6. Once all five sons of the woodcutter are split and weak, they will be easy prey for "One World Government".

First of all, Duke of Sussex, then Grand Master of the "Mother Lodge" in Britain, over ruled the condition on Hindus, to join them into the Craft. He described that, "gods of Hindus were really personification of aspects of the same Supreme Being, and Hindus could quite properly be made Masons". Soon after this in 1844, Dr George Burnes, the Provincial Grand Master for Western India, under the Grand Lodge of Scotland, founded a lodge at Bombay for the general admission of Hindus.

Along with manipulating Hindus, it was necessary to capture the "Mughal dynasty". For this purpose the *"descendants of Aurangzeb"*, were given a chance to join Freemasonry through membership of *"Committee of 300" (10-242)*, a sub-organisation of Freemasonry. History tells us what the British did with Mughals in the end: when they chopped the heads of all throne claimants and presented those heads to "Bahadur Shah Zafar", the last emperor---in a tray!

To emphasise the Masonic propaganda, in the literature was "Rudyard Kippling" (1865-1936), the English writer and poet. He was awarded the "Nobel Prize for Literature" in 1907 ("Nobel Prize" is named after "Alfred Nobel" who was the inventor of the "Dynamite Explosive" and owned 93 Dynamite Factories by the year of his death in 1896). Most of Kippling's writings, both prose and verses concern India and praise Masonic ideology. Masonry has been subconsciously inspiring children and adults, through the mask of art and literature. Among Kipling's most popular works are his stories for children, "The Jungle Books", "Just so stories" and "Stalky and Co". Other works contain, "Kim", "The Man who would be King" and the famous poem, "Mother Lodge". Kipling was initiated in "Hope and Esperance Lodge" No 782, Lahore, then in India, in 1887.

CH-17 RELIGIOUS AND POLITICAL MANIPULATION IN HINDUSTAN

Along with other techniques, Freemasonry used religions to divide mass people, sects and cults to divide them even further. Some of these sects already existed and some, created by Freemasonry Raj. They used their wealth and natives' minor differences to confuse and lead astray.

To manipulate the peoples, some heroes and leaders were required, the already existing leaders were too staunch to be controlled or diverted. New production was necessary. Many people have new ideas; the problem is to introduce their ideas to the rest of the world. For this, massive media coverage is required which was, and is not possible, without a strong backup. Freemasonry does this job—free of cost, you only have to abandon your faith---and adopt theirs!

Swami Nerendramah Vivekananda (1863-1902) was a production hero of Freemasonry. Nerendramah was the Indian ascetic who became the leading exponent of both Hinduism and "Yoga" in the West (I am sure there were many others who were more expert in yoga, specially looking at his short life span, he died at a tender age of only 39). Nerendramah was initiated in "Hope and Anchor" Lodge No 1 Calcutta, in 1884. In 1893, he attended the "Parliament of Religions" at the "World's Fair" in Chicago.

THEOSOPHICAL SOCIETY AND CONGRESS

Congress has been the longest ruling party in India. When a party makes a government it has to abide by the party rules, different Prime Ministers from the same party have to work within the party lines. That is why it is said that such and such party has to form its government in so and so country. The party rules are set from the foundation and are rarely changed. In simple words, the first presidents and general secretaries of the party (who form party rules), inspire it eternally. The Indian National Congress held its first meeting in December 1885 in Bombay. Looking at the date and the arranger of the first meeting (PS see the quote after), we can also conclude:

"Thus, just as the British Indian Empire attained its outmost limits of expansion, the institutional seeds of the larger of the two national successors was sown"..."Provincial roots of Indian nationalism, however, may be traced to the beginning of the era of the crown rule in Bombay, Bengal and Madras". (16)

Yes! The grounds for nationalism were already set to bring the future ruling class, the elite of Hindustan! Which will enforce the Masonic law in the country and through this elite, the Freemasons' elite will rule until "One World Government" target is achieved. To check the roots of Indian Congress we have to study the "Theosophical Society". This will help us to understand the people, who founded the Congress, and through them the charter of Congress, that have to be followed by every new Prime Minister. Let it be male or female---patriot or treacherous---with an IQ of---150 or---10.

"One of the key men who helped arrange the first meeting of the Congress was a retired British official, 'Allan Octavian Hume' ... Allan retired from ICS in 1882, in 1881 Allan had joined the "Theosophical Society" as had many young Indians." (16)

Allan Octavian Hume: Famous for his "Mysticism" and "Theosophy". According to the Oxford Dictionary, theosophy is:

"Any of various philosophies, professing to achieve a knowledge of God by spiritual ecstasy, direct intuition, or special individual relations, especially a modern movement following Hindu and Buddhist teachings and seeking ***universal brotherhood".***

The word "Universal Brotherhood" sounds familiar! Let us check further. "Theosophical society" was:

"Founded in New York City in 1875 by Helena Blavatsky of Russia (and Henry Steel Oscott, an American). It had as its original inspiration ***Kabbala*** *(Jewish esoteric mysticism), Gnosticism (esoteric salvatory knowledge), and other forms of Western occultism...The society survived serious accusations of charlatanry levelled against its founder and certain other leaders". (16)* ***Emphasis*** *added*

Is it the same "Kabbala" that Freemasons were and are accused of or, was it a total independent society, nothing to do with "Brotherhood"? Describing the leadership of Annie Besant (the successor of Helena, the first leader), Britannica states:

"Under her guidance, many Theosophical **Lodges** *were founded in Europe and the United States". (16)*

O! No! The word "Lodges" gave the game away. The hidden message is clear for those who know! The teachings of the "Theosophical Society" are described as they:

"Emphasized human service, a spiritual evolutionism drawn from both Eastern and Western esoteric philosophy, and the role of 'superhuman masters of wisdom'..." (16)

"One of the society's most controversial claims concerns the existence of a ***'Brotherhood' of 'Great Masters'****, or Adepts, who, it is asserted, have perfected themselves and are directing the spiritual evolution of humanity". (16)*

If you still have any doubts in recognising the **Freemasons International Brotherhood** with **Grand Masters** controlling their **Lodges** and practicing **Kabbala**"; then may you have all the peace of world and enjoy your life!

Theosophical Society is also called:

"Theosophist Society", which is an organization direct responsible to "Committee of 300". (10-226)

"Swami Dayananda Sarswati" (1824-83) was a Hindu reformist who started "back to the Vedas" Hindu society called "Arya Samaj" in Bombay in 1875. His objective was to revert to the actual scriptures "the Vedas" and reject the corruption adopted by Hindus including idolatry, the cast system and infant marriage. Swami's "Arya Samaj" society was kidnapped by "Helena Blavatsky" the above-mentioned Russian-born co-founder of the "Theosophical Society".

Helena Petrovna Balvatsky (1831-91): Born in Yekaterinoslav, Ukraine: Russian Empire and died in London. At the age of 17 she got married to a Russian military officer and provincial vice governor, "Nikifor V. Blavatsky" but separated after a few months---why not---she had a greater cause. After separation she travelled throughout Asia, Europe and the United States; she also claimed to have spent several years in India and Tibet studying spirituality under Hindu Mahatmas.

" She went to New York City in 1873, where she met and became a close companion of H.S. Olcott, and in 1875 they and several other prominent persons founded the 'Theosophical Society' ". (16)

Helena published a book called "Isis Unveiled" in 1877. The "unveiled Isis", however, did not catch the public **eye** and the society dwindled.

After that, the society went to India in 1879. There, Helena became a follower of "Swami Dayananda Sarswati" and sat in his feet. Once she was known in the spiritual-circle she soon rose from her Swami's feet, and stood on her own, by establishing her own "Samaj", the "Theosophical Society", whose headquarters were outside Madras city, at Adyar, which still serves as the international headquarters for the society.

Helena claimed that she possessed extraordinary psychic powers, which she was suspected for. When she travelled to Germany and Paris, Indian press accused her of being a fraud, although she had a warm welcome back in Hindustan on her return. The "Hodgson Report" was the finding of an investigation in 1885 by the "London Society for Psychical Research", which declared her a fraud.

This does not mean that those who came after her, held real power, rather this means that the certificate of the "London Society for Psychical Research" made the difference; it worked! Once Indian press suspected Helena, she would rather be abandoned than defended. Once "LSPR" gets the vote of confidence from public, next psychic healer will be certified by the "LSPR", thus not suspected, and recognised by public: as genuine! This is how Freemasonry works! This is what keeps them successful! They keep the power of decision!

I wondered why "Theosophical Society" had many *"young Indian followers"* and why is it particularly mentioned? My suspicion was answered when I imagined a Russian lady sitting "frankly" in the middle of youngsters. Situation got clearer, when I found out that Helena's successor was "Annie Besant", another lady---this time an English!

Annie Besant (1847-1933): The most famous leader of "Theosophical Society" and the first and only British woman to serve as president of the **"INDIAN NATIONAL CONGRESS" (1917)**---Naqshe-Dil---is everywhere---! To top up the situation the general secretary appointed for the Congress, for the first 22 years was---"Allan Hume" the organiser of the first Indian National Congress meeting and a "Theosophist"!

Annie Besant was the wife of an Anglican clergyman, separated (another one) in 1873. After separation she became an associate of the atheist and "social reformer", Charles Bradlaugh. She was an early advocate of birth control, and in the late 1880s she became a prominent "Fabian socialist" under the influence of George Bernard Shaw. She was also an Indian independence leader. She was international president of the "Theosophical Society" from 1907 until her death in 1933. She also established the "Indian Home Rule League" in 1916.

What shall we call this? Indian National Congress! Or! **Masonic Ritual Congress!**

To make Congress representative of Indian population, reverse psychic was used. If your opponent refuses something, you are bound to think that this is where it hurts. This way you are led to believe, the path you have chosen is the right one and is damaging your enemy. First meeting of Congress on Dec. 28, 1885: was attended by only 73 representatives as well as 10 more unofficial delegates. Hume, the organizer was the only British delegate.

"Most Britons in India, however either ignored the Congress and its resolutions as the actions and demands of a 'microscopic minority' of India's diverse millions or considered them the rantings of disloyal extremists". (16)

British Government's opposition had to bring favour from the Indians and it did, within two years it had 600 delegates. In 1888, their number increased to 1,248. Still British officials continued to dismiss its significance. The new Viceroy, Curzon's strong opposition helped Congress to become heart favourite.

"Curzon, however, inadvertently helped to infuse the Congress with unprecedented popularity and militant vitality by his own arrogance and by failing to appreciate the importance of human sympathy in his relentless drive toward greater efficiency". (16)

To invoke and test the nationalism in heart of every Indian, Lord Curzon moved ruthlessly! He divided Bengal into two parts on Oct. 16, 1905. Forming Western Bengal, Hindu majority, with its capital in Calcutta and Eastern Bengal, Muslim majority, with its in Dhaka. This division was also a forecaster of the results for the future major division of Hindustan itself. However, the division raised a severe love for the motherland and "Bande Mataram" (Hail to Thee, Mother!), became the Congress' national anthem.

Karamchand Gandhi was well aware with the outcomes of so-called modernizaton of Hindustan, and the slogans of nationalism. Throughout his political career, he pleaded for Hindu-Muslim unity. In an article, first published in 1909 in "Indian Opinion", he quote's:

"The British Government in India constitutes a struggle between the Modern Civilization, which is the Kingdom of Satan, and the Ancient Civilization, which is the Kingdom of God". (14, vol-1, p-198)

The intellect of that time knew what they were being led to, but could not pin point the enemy. That is why Freemasonry is so much secretive. That is why Satan does not appear to us in person, but works within us, through our greed! The biggest trick Satan use's, is to assure us that ---he does not exist---!

MIRZA GHULAM AHMED

For British, it was necessary to deface the Muslims compulsion of Jihad, so they could avoid the biggest threat to their rule. This was thought vital after the Freedom Fight of 1857 (the so-called 'great mutiny' or "Ghadar"). For this purpose they appointed many puppets to justify British rule, and nullify the necessity of sword.

Mirza was born in 1839, in Qadian, India and died on May 26, 1908. Mirza Ghulam Ahmad not only claimed that he was Mahdi, and a reappearance of the Prophet Mohammad SW, but also that he was Jesus Christ and the Hindu god Krishna returned to earth. In his book "Kashti-e-Nooh" (Boat of Noah), he exceeds the limits and even claims to be Maryam AS (Mary) as well, and then from him/her-self through pregnancy he is born again to be Isa (Jesus). On page 90 he writes:

"In the third part of Brahin-e-Ahmadia, He [Allah SWT] *named me Maryam. Then as the name Brahin-e-Ahmadia suggests I nurtured in the characteristics of Maryam for two years and grew in a cover. Then as two years passed over that, just like Maryam, the spirit of Isa (Jesus) was blown into me as it is written (Brahin-e-Ahmadia vol 4, p-496), and made me pregnant metaphorically. After several months, which are not more than 10, through inspiration as written in Brahin-e-Ahmadia vol 4 p-556: I was transformed into Isa (Jesus) from Maryam. (Translation from Urdu)* [Brahin-e-Ahmadia, was also written by him]

What a unisex prophethood he had---! He claimed his falsehood in Lahore. Near that time he was working in one of the administration offices of the British government. For his claim, he was fully supported by the government and helped to publish hundreds of books that praised the glory of the Queen and her Raj. His teachings emphasised a total surrender to the British and abrogation of Jihad. According to him British Raj was a mercy of Allah SWT.

He also claimed that in the second verse of Surah Muhammad of Qur'an, and others Allah (SWT) addressed him and not Muhammad (SW). He was also a poet and had published a book of poetry containing his poems. His book "Kashti-e-Nooh", includes his two poems, one is about plaque and other about the "Glory of Islam".

"We have not instructed The (Prophet) in Poetry, nor is it meet for him..." (Q-36-69)

The explanation of this Ayah according to Ahmadia English translation of Al-Qur'an, by his followers, clearly states that; *"a messenger or a prophet can not be a poet. If a poet claims to be a prophet he is a liar"*; thus nullifies his claim by his own followers.

The revelations of Mirza, which he thought he received from an angel called "Teechee Teechee", are compiled in a book called "Majmooa-e-Ilhamat" (Compilation of Inspirations). Although Mirzais (his followers) say that they believe in "Al-Qur'an" but this is the book, which, they actually believe as their Qur'an. Its first edition was published in 1935, now a second edition is compiled by "Abdul Latif Sahib Bahawalpuri" and published by their authorities under the banner of "Al-Shirkatul Islmiah Ltd".

In this book, Mirza mentions:

"When I focused about death, after a little drowsiness, it was inspired to me that:

Freemasons will not be appointed to kill him.

About Freemasons I was inspired: ***Those with secret intentions.*** *" (P-424/425)*

Mirza feared to be accused of Freemasonry, so he used a reverse psyche. He accused Muslim scholars who opposed his falsehood publicly, as Freemasons with secret intentions. Noteworthy point is that for a fact, we all know that he did not receive any inspirations from any angel, even his followers' translation of Qur'an proves that he was not a prophet but a liar. As he was not a prophet he could not receive any revelations or inspirations. Then how did he know about Freemasonry and their secret intentions? This establishes a fact that he was in a close association with Freemasonry. So close that he not only knew their secrets but even whom they will kill and whom they will not! This is so important for him that he describes them in his "holy book".

A book called "Sirat al Mahdi" compiled by "Qamar al Anbiya", one of Mirza's sons explains in "Report 966":

"Sethi Ghulam Nabi informed me that he went to the promised Messiah, Mirza Ghulam Ahmad, revealing to him his inner depression and worries, and the promised Messiah said to him: "I have prepared an "Araq", (an alcoholic drink), so drink it daily. Yes alcohol is forbidden, but this I prepared myself and therefore it is permitted".

Ghulam Nabi also added that the promised Messiah continued to send him a glass of Araq in the morning and another in the evening for one month. When Ghulam Nabi asked Mirza to give the recipe to make it, Mirza said:

"*You will not be able to do it. Come and take it from me whenever you need it".*
("Ahmadiyya Beliefs and Experiences"—by Hassan Bin Mahmood Odeh p-167)

Report No 929 reveals:

"Dr. Mir Muhammad Ismail, (one of Mirza's close companions) told me that the promised Messiah had confirmed to him that Opium had many strange and odd benefits, and he (Mirza) had personally prepared, from opium, a medicine called 'Divine Cure', which he also used to give to his friends". ("Ahmadiyya Beliefs and Experiences"—by Hassan Bin Mahmood Odeh p-167)

What would you call a man, who consumes alcohol, supplies drugs to his followers and is in a close association with Freemasons?

His son and successor, Mirza Bashir-uddin was deputed in Kashmir to induce Muslims into his father's religion. It is worth quoting that the invitation of Ahmadiyyat is restricted only to Muslims and never made to Christians, Hindus and Sikhs, which should not be the case, if their mere purpose was not to lead only Muslims astray.

In Kashmir, Sheikh Abdullah helped Mirza, and Muslims were only heard if they came via this combination. Any other leadership was totally neglected by the British. This Mirza-Abdullah combination resulted in Kashmir occupation by India, when Abdullah, the Masonic icon, voted in favour of India on behalf of millions of Muslims pining to join-in with Pakistan.

These treacherous characters are responsible for deaths of millions of Muslims in Kashmir and still are supported by the British. In 1975, when "Mirzies" (the cult of Mirza), were announced as a minority in Pakistan and thrown out of Muslim Ummah, they found no other place in the world other than Britain, their overlords and founding sponsors. The Ahmadi headquarter is based in Wimbledon, London they have named it "Islamabad". They also have a facility of a private TV channel called "MTA", (Muslim Television Ahmediya), supported by the British, which still poisons the less informed Muslim minds. Their new field of mischief has spread into Far East. Indonesia is now their main target, all sponsored by the government.

AGHA KHAN III (SULTAN SIR MUHAMMAD SHAH)

Born on Nov. 2, 1877, in Karachi, then in India, died on July 11, 1957, in Versoix, Switz. He rapidly acquired a leading position among India's Muslims as a whole. How did he do it? Of course, with the help of Brethren!

In 1906 he headed the Muslim deputation to the viceroy, Lord Minto (who initiated Sir Stamford Raffles into Freemasonry in 1811, in Java), to promote the interests of the Muslim minority in India. This deputation included some 36 Muslim leaders and was set by "Sayyid Mahdi Ali" Popularly known by his title "Mohsin-ul-Mulk" the successor of Sir Sayyid. This deputation was merely a fake one that got nothing but a promise:

"To protect and advance the political rights and interests of Mussalmans of India". (16)

But in return it affirmed the Muslim loyalty to the British government, Support for the Bengal partition and condemnation of the boycott movement (which started as the condemnation of the Bengal partition). Basically betraying the rest of the Indian population, who were fighting against British rule!

Agha Khan III also served as president of the All-India Muslim League during its early years and initiated the fund for raising the Muslim College at Aligarh to University status, which was effected in 1920. In the First World War he supported the Allies against Turkey.

"He played an important part in the 'Round Table Conferences' on Indian constitutional reform in London (1930-1932)... He was appointed president of the 'League of Nations' in 1937". (16)

How a Muslim, loyal to Islam could do all this? Why did he betray the Muslims of India? The answer once more comes from the book of Freemasons. This is how he is introduced in the Freemasons book with his photo as a Freemason:

"The Third Agha Khan, Sultan Sir Mohammad Shah (1877-1957), the father of the United Nations High Commissioner for Refugees and Spiritual Leader of Ismaili cult". (2)

He did all this only because he was a Freemason---!

MAULANA FAZLE-RASOOL (BADAYOONI)

Maulana Fazle-Rasool was the first Muslim who opposed "Shah Wali-ullah", "Maulana Ismail Shaheed" and "Maulana Shah Muhammad Ishaq Muhaddis Dehelvi". He introduced the word Wahabi in Hindustan to label these re-nouned scholars as the followers of Shaikh Muhammad bin Abdul Wahab of Najd, who was against all the innovations (Bid'ah) in Islam. The mere purpose of erecting these puppet scholars was to lead Muslims astray from Sirat-al-Mustaqim by introducing new things in Deen, the "Bid'ah".

Muhammad Yaqoob Alqadri, one of the followers of Maulana Fazle-Rasool wrote his biography, in which he states:

"Maulana (Fazle-Rasool) was worried about his earnings when British held his hand...For this purpose he planned a journey to the state of Gwaliar...Nawab Mohi-uddola helped to fix 17 Rupees per day, since that time this money is fixed as 11 Rupees per day from the State." (Akmal Tarikh, vol-2, Quote from 17, vol-1, p-188)

Fazle-Rasool's sons Abdul-Qadir and Abdul-Muqtadir carried on enjoying this 260 Rupees per month grant, but the actual successor of Fazle-Rasool was Ahmad Raza Khan Brailwi.

AHMAD RAZA KHAN (BRAILWI)

Ahmad Raza Khan was born in Braili, India (1856-1921). Raza was a follower of the same Aastana (school of teaching) as was Maulana Fazle-Rasool Badayooni. He stepped forward from his predecessor by not only labelling the true scholars as Wahabies, but by decreeing them as "Kafir" (non-believer) and whosoever doubts their Kufr, is a Kafir too. These fatawas did not even spare the true leaders like, Dr Iqbal and Muhammad Ali Jinah. His follower and biographer Ahmad Qari Pili Bheti wrote:

"Maulana Ahmad Raza Khan strove for continuos 50 years, till two permanent school of thoughts established, Brailwi and Devbandi". (Swaneh Aala Hazrat, Quote from 17, vol-1, p-193)

This was a division within Muslims on a large scale, before this there was only one group of Muslims in Hindustan and that was "Devbandi". Devbandi itself was never a school of thought! Devband was only a school to teach. Devband taught the teachings of either of 4 Imams: Imam Abu Hanifa, Shaf'ee, Malik or Hanbal. Those who follow either of these 4 Imams, are called "Ahle-Sunnat Wal-Jama't", the main body of Islam. Raza's strive for fifty years was not for the unity of Muslims but for division!

Raza Khan continuously abrogated Jihad in his publication from Braili he quotes:

"For the Muslims of Hindustan, the order of Jihad and Qital (to kill in the path of Allah) is not applicable". (Dawam-ul-Aish, p-14, Quote from 17, p-199)

The eleventh of the month is still recognized as a sacred date to Raza's followers. Although on every Thursday night they arrange a "Khatm", but the special one is on the 11th of every month. This is called "Geyarwin Sharif" (the noble 11th). Dr Allamah Khalid Mahmood, one of the leading Muslim scholars at present and a researcher on "Brailwi-ism" quotes:

"Maulana Ahmad Raza's 11th [as was of Maulana Fasle-Rasool's] *is also related to 11 Rupees, not 11th the date". (17, p-189)*

In those days, a paper named "Mashriq" started from "Gorakh Pur". With reference to that "P. Hardy" admits the services of Maulana Ahmed Raza Khan and writes:

*"It is not clear where the Bariely had its strongholds but the Mashriq of Gorekhpur and Al-Bashir took note of the **pro-government fatwas** of Ahmad Raza Khan and it seems that the school's permissive thinking on Islamic practice appealed especially to the certain low groups in Muslim Society." (The Muslims of British India, p-268 Emphasis added)*

Francis Robinson also describes Raza as a pro-British:

"Nevertheless his normal stand was of support for government and he supported it throughout world war one, he opposed the khilafat movement and in 1921 organised a conference of anti-non-cooperation Ulama at Bareily. He had considerable influence with the masses but was not favoured by educated Muslim. (Separatism among Indian Muslims p-422)

Ahmad Raza not only introduced hundreds of Bid'ahs into Deen but also accused any one who does not follow him as a "Kafir". To know the Brailwi school of thought and damage they did to Muslims in Hindustan, please refer to "Mutalia-e-Brailwiyyat" (A study of Brailwi-ism) by Dr Allamah Khalid Mahmood MA, PhD. Director Islamic Academy Manchester UK.

CH-18 EDUCATIONAL AND POLITICAL MANIPULATION IN HINDUSTAN

Allah SWT has described Islam as a "Deen", not a faith, and not a religion. Deen is a complete way of life, starting from child's birth till death. Deen involves not only religious teachings but also explains how to conduct worldly affairs, how to do business, how to educate yourself and others. All aspects of a practical human life have been explained in "Qur'an" and "Sunnah".

Wherever Muslims adopted a way, other than of Allah and His Prophet, it brought nothing but disasters. We have proved in the previous chapters of this book that the results of leaving the "Sirat-al-Mustaqim" (The Only Straight Path) and innovating our own, led us straight into the grip of "Kuffars".

The first revelation that came to Prophet Mohammad (SA) was:

"Read! In the Name of your Lord who has created (all that exists)". (Q-96-1)

Unfortunately we have adopted the only first word, which is **"Read"**! And left the rest, which is **"in the Name of your Lord".** When a child is born his or her parents strive to get him/her the best, preferably a Western education school, European or American. Very rare are the parents who wish him to get the religious education first, thus fulfil the whole commandment of Allah SWT, so he can classify between Halal and Haram, so he can understand Deen first to protect him/her from wrong inspirations of the society. The education system enforced on us is Masonic, it does not care about Halal and Haram, it slowly brain washes us and solely enslaves our souls. Thus we forget our Deen and adopt theirs!

*"The universities of Bombay, Bengal and Madras had been founded in 1857 as the **'capstone'** of the East India Company's modest policy of selectively fostering the introduction of English education in India". (16)*

The **"Capstone"** here is the capstone of the Masonic pyramid. On "Masonic dollar", this capstone is not set on the top yet. It will come down on dollar when dollar will totally dominate the world currency, and no other currency will exist, which is not too far if we don't wake-up. The Euro dollar is a step up on the pyramid, the final target is---No Currency at all---! However, the pyramid of "Masonic ruling system", described above is complete with its founded education system. Why a nation would be interested in educating another? Just being good? O yes, I am sure! Especially when the former wants to rule the latter then why to educate them and alert the awareness; so they can stand up and throw the ruling class away? This is not possible and intellect can never accept this. So what else can be the cause to be so kind towards their subjects? --- Let me tell you the objective was not to educate them but to lead them astray and to create a new class, the "Middle Class". This middle class was necessary to work in the offices, to carry on record keeping and run Masonic suggested governments not understanding anything beyond their work lines; just live their lives working for their livelihood and die!

The bigger cause this education system serves is that it enables Brotherhood to monitor "future ruling class" from childhood! Yes---the future leaders are selected and closely monitored right from childhood till they "successfully" achieve an NOC (no objection certificate) in form of a "degree", from Harvard, Cambridge or Oxford. The students of these first Masonic founded universities in India were:

"Convinced that, with the education they had received and the 'proper apprenticeship' of 'hard work', they would eventually inherit the machinery of British Indian Government". (16)

Among the first handful products of these universities was "Surendernath Banerjea", who joined the ICS and later was dismissed. He went on to become the founder of "Indian Association" in Calcutta and Editor of "The Bengali" newspaper, thus monitoring the Masonic interests on political and informational sides. In 1833 he convened the first "Indian National Conference" in Bengal. The first partition of Bengal in 1905 promoted Banerjea, as a national leader of "Swadeshi Movement".

Mahadev G. Ranade also graduated from Bombay Universities in 1862. He taught at "Elphinstone College", edited the "Indu Prakash" newspaper and helped to start the "Prarthana Samaj", the Hindu reformist society.

"Ranade was one of the early leaders of India's emultive school of nationalism, as was his brilliant disciple 'Gopal Krishna Gokhale", later revered by Gandhi as a political guru". (16)

Gokhale was also an editor and teacher at "Fergusson College" at Puna. In 1905, he was elected president of the "Congress".

Gokhale's colleague at the Fergusson College was "Bal Gangadhar Tilak". He took the lead of revolutionary side in reaction to the British rule on behalf of Indian Nationalism. Gangadhar was also Poona's most influential journalist. His newspaper:

"'Kesari', became the leading literary thorn in the side of British...The orthodox Hindu character of his revolutionary revival alienated many within India's Muslim minority and exacerbated communal tensions and conflicts". (16)

In 1909, British found necessary to bring their Indian, British styled educated breed, into governing body. Lord Minto, who opposed "Congress", was also responsible for the reforms, which will bring Indians into many levels of government. This is the way these reforms were done:

"The first Indian to be appointed a member of the Viceroy's Executive Council, Satyendra Sinha, took his place on the council in March. In choosing Sinha as against Minto's own first choice, Dr A. Mukerji, the Vice-Chancellor of Calcutta University – a Bengali. Minto, wrote to the Secretary of the State for India in London: 'Please do not think me terribly narrow, but Sinha is comparatively white, whilst Mukerji is as black as my hat!'" (14, vol-1, p-195)

I am sure you must be thinking, what a discrimination! You are right! But the actual message is far more dangerous! It is the confidence on the educational capstone of the "Masonic pyramid system"! Any one passed through the long brainwashing process of Masonic education; does not make a difference! They all are equal! Master Brothers can pick their choice as suits them, like a butcher selects a sheep from a herd!

The other co-founder of Theosophical Society, Henry Steel Olcott (1832-1907) was born in Orange, N.J., U.S. and died in Madras, India. He was agricultural editor of the "New York Tribune" (1858-60). From 1863-66, he was special commissioner in the U.S. war and Navy departments. After settling down in India in 1879, he worked with Helena and then assisted Annie Besant in establishing the "**Central Hindu College**" at Banaras. Thus dividing Hindus from Muslims on educational basis.

"In Ceylon, he saw three colleges and 250 schools established as a result of his efforts". (16)

SIR SAYYID AHMED KHAN AND ALIGARH

Sir Sayyid Ahmed Khan b. Oct. 17, 1817, Delhi, d. March 27, 1898, Aligarh, India was a Muslim educator, author and jurist. Founder of the "Anglo-Mohammedan Oriental College" at Aligarh, UP, India, later named as Aligarh Muslim College, which eventually became Aligarh Muslim University in 1920.

British used the word Mohammaden for Muslims, to psychologically balance them with Christians, subtracting the name of God and leaving the prophet's. So the followers will eventually become, worshippers of their prophet. Muslims are not Mohammadens, we are Muslims: Islam is the Deen given by Allah, and Allah has chosen Islam as Deen for Muslims. Muslim scholars noticed this point soon and raised it to West, but still it is in practice by some fundamentalist Western writers.

Sir Sayyid helped the in-happened phenomena, by selecting the name "Mohammaden" and even tried to mix it with Anglo philosophy by naming it "Anglo Mohammaden".

Sir Sayyid's father received an allowance from the Mughal administration, his maternal grandfather was twice Prime Minister of the then Mughal emperor and:

"Had also held positions of 'trust' under the East India Company". (16)

To hold a position of trust with untrustworthy East India Company means and tells a lot---. These positions of trust became hierarchy and enabled Sir Sayyid's brother to establish one of the first printing presses at Delhi and start one of the earliest Urdu newspapers to propagate the western ideology. However, the death of Sayyid's father was followed by financial difficulties. Then Sir Sayyid:

"Started as a clerk with the East India Company in 1838". (16)

Later on he qualified as a subjudge and served at different places in the judicial departments. After the freedom fight of 1857, he wrote a pamphlet, "The Causes of the Indian Revolt". In this pamphlet he pointed out the reasons for the revolt and weaknesses of the British government.

"During the Indian Mutiny of 1857 he had taken the side of the British". (16)

This was the point when Muslims should have understood his tendencies and stayed alarmed. Like many others this chance was not availed and later Sir Sayyid was able to cause a lot of damage, politically and educationally.

"He began a sympathetic interpretation of the Bible". (16)

Sayyid wrote Islamic books and translations of Qur'an as well. His*sympathetic interpretations* of Bible meant his faith on the death of Jesus (Isah AS), thus notwithstanding the teaching of Islam and infiltrating the Christian believes in Islam. Further on the account of Jihad he interpreted:

"That Jesus died a natural death and was not assumed into heaven as Islamic orthodoxy believed, and that 'Jihad' by the sword had been abrogated and replaced with 'Jihad of the Pen'". (16)

This ideology of "Jihad of pen" was later adopted by many other Masonic encarved idols, who had faces like, of Muslim scholars. The British-paid scholars pleaded Hindustan as "Dar-ul-Amn" (dominion of peace), whereas the true scholars agreed upon Hindustan as "Dar-ul-Harb" (dominion of war).

When Sayyid, solemnly declared himself an ally to the British East India Company, they bestowed on him all the financial support. He started establishing schools at Muradabad (1858) and Ghazipur (1863) he also founded the "Scientific Society" which issued a bilingual journal in Urdu and English.

"In 1867 he was transferred to Banares". (16)

How come an independent owner of two schools and well-established owner and founder of a newspaper is *"transferred to Banaras"*, and who transferred him? The consequences tell us! Describing his transfer, Britannica quote's further:

"At about the same time a movement started at Banares to replace Urdu, the language cultivated by the Muslims, with Hindi. This movement and the attempts to substitute Hindi for Urdu in the publications of the Scientific Society 'convinced' Sayyid that the paths of the Hindus and the Muslims must diverge". (16)

In other words, he flared up the situation in his own publications of the bilingual journal of the “Scientific Society”. If some issue is not attended, it dies after a while Freemasons knew this mass-manipulation technique, that is why Sayyid was deputed in Banaras, to introduce Muslims with the new born problem and even to exaggerate the situation.

What does he do next? He visits England (1869-1870) and comes back with an idea of "a Muslim Cambridge". He set up a committee for the purpose and founded another influential journal, "Tahzib al Akhlaq" (Social Reform) through which he could advertise the Masonic ideology. He visited Oxford again in 1874. Finally a "Muslim School" was established at Aligarh in May 1875 on Oxford model. Following year he retired but still "devoted" to enlarge the school into a college. The Viceroy of India laid the foundation stone of the school!

"In 1886 Sayyid organized the 'All-India Muhammaden Educational Conference', which met annually at different places to promote education and to provide the Muslims with a common platform. Until the founding of the 'Muslim League' in 1906, it was the principal national centre of Indian Islam...Sayyid advised the Muslims against joining active politics and to concentrate instead on education". (16)

Why not so! He was confident on brainwashing of the Masonic education system. His advise; was generally followed by Muslims for several years and those who joined "Indian National Congress" in these years, were strongly opposed by Sayyid. This was a planned set back for Muslims, they fell prey for a while but soon leaders like Quaid-e-Azam and Dr Allamah Iqbal woke their conscience.

All these services, proved "Sir Sayyid Ahmad Khan" to be worthy of a bounty from Masonic paradise, so:

"In 1888 he was made a Knight Commander of the Star of India". (16)

In simple words: He was made a Grand Master of the “Star of India” Lodge in 1888. This is the same “Star of India Lodge” that is still operating (Ibid.). The hidden message like “degrees dependent” reveals it all. I am sure you are shocked! So was I.

“I heard the Prophet say: ‘Before the Hour comes, there will be years of deceit, in which a truthful person will be disbelieved and a liar will be believed; and the insignificant will have a say.” (Ahmad narrated by Abu Hurayra Quote from 20-93)

These are the founders of modern education system. This is the message from schools; you are absorbing right from your childhood and now, are your children! That is why this system wants your child at earliest age, in Kinder Garden and Nursery: To indoctrinate their brains at “Nurse-rey”. Can you do anything? Can you afford to send your child to learn Qur’an, and Fiqh first: and then the secular education? That is the way our ancestors did---they ruled the world---! We are doing opposite to the command of Allah--- the world rules us---!

“Read! In the name of your Lord who has created (all that exists)”. (Q-96-1)

QAID-E-A’ZAM AND MUSLIM LEAGUE

Where Hindus were gathering around “Indian National Congress”, chances were there that Muslims also would find it necessary to have a congregation of their own. This could lead to a group, free of Masonic influence. To cover both sides, left and right wings, Grand Masters decided to move first! Thus was formed the “All India Muslim League”! Agha Khan the 3rd, a Freemason, was found a suitable person as its president. It was founded in the same year when Agha Khan headed the deputation of 36 Muslim leaders to surrender to the demands of “Lord Minto---another Freemason”!

"The Muslim League was founded in 1906, in 1913 it adopted the self-governing rule of India with a call for Hindu-Muslim unity. It was not until 1940, that the League called for the formation of a Muslim State". (16)

Muslim League held its first meeting in Dhaka. Aligarh presented the creed ready to take the responsibilities of political reformation. This lot of Aligarh was not totally Masonic there were of course those who will not bow. British did not need the total domination of the League, but a few on the top to inspire, likewise in the Congress. League and Congress were working for separate states of each, which was Masonic agenda anyway.

"Aligarh became the intellectual cradle of the Muslim League and Pakistan". (16)

Once the basic concept of "Two Nations" was implanted, it was easy to orchestrate the future consequences. Whole India was working against unity. Hatred, enmity and dislike for each other became stronger then ever. Media: the main Masonic tool was helping to ignite the situation. Fake leaders like Agha Khan, Sir Sayyid, and Mohsin-ul-Mulk were the mass-inspirations, call for Hindu-Muslim unity did not have any significance.

"Hindu Muslim riots in Malabar claimed hundreds of lives in1924...Wherever rumours of Muslim 'cow slaughter', the polluting appearance of dead pig's carcass in a mosque, or other clashing doctrinal fears ignited the tender of distrust ever lurking in the poorer sections of India's towns and villages". (16)

By that time "Masonic Lodges" were established in all major cities, Freemasonry was at its full, British Raj was at its peak! Still some genuine leaders like Jinnah and Gandhi were picking thorns from India's body, but for how long? Can you imagine the situation when every one is opposing you and you are a stranger in your own land! This is exactly what happened:

"Jinnah, alienated by Gandhi and his illiterate mass of devoutly Hindu disciples, instead devoted himself to his lucrative Bombay law practice". (16)

In late 1920s, when the agitation in India rose to a stage that the British had no points to argue in their defence to prolong their rule in India, Freemasonry used a different technique. This time, their defence came through an unusual cannon, never used before, but proved very effective, only because its shells were noticed. It was to be noticed, because it was written merely with this purpose. I have used term "written", because it was a book!

Kathleen Mayo was an American journalist who travelled through the subcontinent and apparently came across many cruel practices never known to "civilized" Europeans. The book was called **"Mother India"**, published in 1927. This book was justified by "Bolly-Wood" the Indian film industry, by making a film in which the theme of the book was reversed by representing a devoted family woman as "Mother India". However the book "Mother India" set out the details of the abuse of child brides and live women's burning with their husbands, on their husbands' death. To use this book as an excuse to prolong the British rule:

"There were others, who found such aspects of Hinduism as child marriage – often as early as the age of ten – and the burning of the young widows on their husband's funeral pyre, which Kathleen Mayo had documented – to be a reason of British rule. And the elimination of these evident (From a Christian or humanitarian viewpoint) malpractices". (14, vol-1, p-722/3)

The other attempt to disrespect Muslims and Prophet Mohammad (SW) was made in the same year in 1927 by a Hindu. The author of the article, that ignited the Hindu-Muslim riots in Lahore; was murdered by "Ghazi Ilm Deen Shaheed"! Loyalty of Qaid-e-A'zam could not tolerate this injustice and:

"In an attempt to lessen the immediate tension, and to find a long term solution to Hindu-Muslim violence, the head of All India Muslim League, Mohammad Ali Jinah, convened a Hindu-Muslim conference, known as the 'Unity Conference', at Simla. But despite the earnestness of its deliberations, it was unable to find a way forward to halt the communal riots, which continued, week by week, to take their toll in human lives". (14, vol-1, p-723)

This is not a co-incidence, two publications in the same year, both attacking two major religions in the subcontinent, not only caused unrest and enmity in the public but also served as an excuse to prolong British rule. This rule was to be maintained, however, by hook or crook, till World War Two, which was already decided on papers!

Two years later, in 1929, under the chairmanship of a "distinguished Indian lawyer", "Sir Moropant Joshi", a "Child Marriage Bill" was voted in making fourteen the minimum age of marriage and sixteen for the first sexual intercourse after marriage. This two years gap between husband and wife represents the psychological supremacy of Masonic law! A couple, although legally married, cannot be together because law does not allow. For two years they will constantly feel personally restricted by law, thus subsequently turn into law slaves. That is why "Joshi" is named a "distinguished Indian lawyer". The religious freedom; Hindus had in their land and which was maintained throughout the Muslim rule, for centuries, was gone with in 50 years of Masonic rule!

The indistinguishable flames of hatred, overwhelmed each individual striving for anti-Masonic cause, the adversity afflicted Muslims as well as Hindus:

"By 1930s a number of Indian Muslims had begun to think in terms of a separate statehood for their minority community". (16)

Knowingly and not-knowingly, mass brainwashing with the help of media infiltrated all genuine solution seekers and they were compelled to use the only exit left open, purposely, by the captors.

Allamah "Mohammad Iqbal, while presiding over the Muslim League's annual meeting in Allahabad in 1930, proposed the separate state for the Muslims". (16)

Jinnah, the Agha Khan and other important Muslim leaders were at that time in London attending the "Round Table Conference" (another sub-organization of Freemasonry), still looking for a single federation solution to India. Templars were sitting on the corner of this round table as Grand Masters; Jinnah alone could not do much when his own companion, Agha Khan was a "Fellow" to the "Round Tablers". Next step also came from England:

"In 1933 a group of Cambridge Muslim students, led by Choudhry Rahmat Ali, proposed...'Pakistan'". (16)

I am not trying to dishearten the readers from Pakistan or necessity of its foundation, but only portraying the actual facts, which caused Pakistan. The way every one was led to believe that Pakistan and India is his own dream, was in fact a creation of Masonic dream machine, the "Media"! Now this dream machine is very sophisticated and we pay --"them"-- to buy --"our"-- dreams, we are addicted to it; it is called "TV"! We are wasting our lives in "TV--Trance"!

I have explained the reasons, why Pakistan was necessary for Freemasonry in "Nationalism in Hindustan", and am explaining now, how Pakistan was allowed to come into existence. We can feel the pre-decided "Division Conspiracy" through the movements of Qaid-e-A'zam, who; till last moment was looking for a solution for Hindu-Muslim conflicts, and not joining the demand for Pakistan, but:

"Jinnah's hopes for a reconciliation with the Congress virtually disappeared, when Nehru refused to permit Muslim League to form coalition ministries with the Congress majority provinces and elsewhere after the 1937 elections. Nahru insisted: 'There were but 'two parties' in India, the Congress and the British Raj'". (16)

The unstoppable work of Muslim League proved Nehru wrong within two years of Congress Raj. A massive campaign started by Muslim League, reporting the Congress errors in papers published in 1939, which proved the dangers of Hindu Raj.

"For many Muslims soon viewed the new 'Hindu Raj' as biased and tyrannical and the Hindu led Congress ministers and their helpers as insensitive to Muslim demands or appeals for jobs, as well as to their redress of grievances... The Congress partiality toward its own members, prejudice toward its majority community, and jobbery, its leadership's friends and relations all conspired to convince many Muslims that they had become second-class citizens in the land". (16)

This is only tip of an ice-burg. The actual trials Muslims suffered during Congress Raj; were far more devastating. Their religious rituals like Azan (call for prayer); were banned, especially in Hindu-majority lands; it was hard even to reach mosque for five time congregational prayers. All these afflictions made, a strong personality like Jinnah also feel bitter, but still:

"Jinnah did not join in the Pakistan demand until after the League's famous Lahore meeting in March 1940". (16)

Once he did join, the chorus, he did not vary his tune. Up until now the call for Pakistan did not hold any rigid grounds or threat for Congress, but conversion of Jinnah, as "The Leader" of Indian Muslims rang alarm-bells in Congress formations. British were waiting for this moment for a long time, which came click-on to, with their WW2 program. Round Tablers did not wait more to announce their "Division Conspiracy". In World War Two, which was a set-up (Ibid.):

*"Churchill's war cabinet, fearing the imminent possibility of a Japanese invasion of India, sent the socialist Sir Stafford Cripps, a **'close personal friend'** of Nehru, to New Delhi with a post-war proposal in March 1942". (16)*

Keeping in mind that "Pearl Harbour bombing" on December 7, 1941 had already brought America into the war, now with a zero chance of "Japanese invasion of India", and as we know that the results of WW2 were pre-decided. On the other hand if Japan invades India, what is Britain loosing, if she has already decided to evacuate India! The "Japan Invasion" was never to happen, it was never a threat on the first place. The only threat present at that time was atom bomb, which was being prepared in America's, area 51 (see area 51 in UFOs). In fact the time had come to release India under "Protectorate" after dictating masses with political and educational systems.

The "post-war proposal" suggested that any province could vote to "opt out" from the Congress dominion if it preferred to do so (i.e. to be with Pakistan, or stay independent). Nehru refused this proposal and felt "angry" on Cripps for his readiness to give so much to Muslims. Gandhi called this offer: "A post-dated check on a bank that was failing".

Elections in 1945-46 proved the leadership of Jinnah by winning all 30 seats reserved for Muslims in the Central Legislative Assembly and most of the reserved provincial seats as well. The results of these elections proved Congress wrong of being "the only party of India".

Finally on August 14, 1947 Pakistan appeared on the world map, which followed the bloodiest migration in the history of Hindustan.

"And (remember) when the dis-believers plotted against you (O Muhammad) to imprison you, or to kill you, or to get you out (from your home, i.e. Makkah); they were plotting and Allah too was plotting; and Allah is the best of those who plot". (Q-8-30)

Nothing in this world happens without Allah's consent! As the Ayah above explains, the disbelievers plot and plan their way through our weaknesses. This is the Mercy of Allah SWT that He saves us from their worst conspiracies by plotting on our behalf. The tribulations we suffer are because of our own ignorance from our Deen and varying and splitting our ways from "Sirat-al-Mustaqim".

"Whatever of good reaches you, is from Allah, but whatever of evil befalls you, is from yourself..."(Q-4-78)

By adopting Masonic deen (I call it deen because they have plotted against Islam, for this they needed something with a complete way of life from birth to death, from serving to governing and from learning to educating. How perfect their system is, we can see through the wide spread evils in the world.), we invited wrath of Allah, so the evil fell on us. The good came from Allah in shape of Pakistan, because "they plotted and Allah plotted and Allah is the best of those who plot".

"...And never will Allah grant to the disbelievers a way (to triumph) over the believers". (Q-4-141)

Beside there were many treacherous people among Muslims, there were those who were pious and travellers of "Sirat-al-Mustaqim". Allah fulfilled His promise by granting their supplications in form of Pakistan; thus disbelievers did not triumph over the believers and Pakistan came into existence.

After the Independence when most of Britons left the country, Craft's activities went underground; Craft does not cease to exist:

"But in 1961, the Grand Lodge of India was inaugurated. Today Freemasonry flourishes through India..." (2-207)

Remember! Freemasonry only discloses its secret existence when it is in full control. This means India's population, her government, her elite, and the next generation totally dominated by Freemasonry!

The total debts of India are $89.8 billion.

CH-19 PAKISTAN

"But in 1961, the Grand Lodge of India was inaugurated. Today Freemasonry flourishes through India, but not so in case of Pakistan". (2-207)

As for as Pakistan is concerned, do we believe their statement? Freemasonry never ceased to exist anywhere! Simply they changed their masks. In Pakistan they changed the name of their "lodge" to "Jadoo Ghar" (Magic House). This "Jadoo Ghar" was situated next to the "Zoo" of Lahore; probably it was the same old Lahore Lodge building with a different name. "Jadoo Ghar" was painted black and had sign of "Skull & Bones", the same old sign of Templars, Freemasons or Skull & Bone Society. This sign of Skull & Bones was made common by introducing it on high voltage electrical poles and wires in the Sub-Continent. This is another example of mass deceiving, "thing that you want to hide, display, in a visible spot".

Another thing famous about "Jadoo Ghar" was that; those who were taken in, never came out. Further investigation revealed that these 'taken in people' were mainly politicians and specially those, who were working against the Western interests. Jadoo Ghar was discreetly clearing the loyal political Pakistani leaders. Do you believe the Government of Pakistan never knew this? I am sure you do believe it---So do I!

GENERAL ZIA-UL-HAQ

Freemasonry was there in the time of Quaed-Azam Mohammad Ali Jinah, this sign was there when Ayyub Khan ruled, it was there when Zulfiqar Ali Bhutto ministered. It was only removed in General Zia-ul-Haq's time. Zia-ul-haq ordered to raid their office and other offices related to Freemasonry, confiscated their records and banned Freemasonry, Zia-ul-Haq was martyred:

"The Club of Rome, acting on Committee of 300 orders to eliminate General ul Haq, had no compunction in sacrificing the lives of a number of U.S. Army Defence Intelligence Agency group headed by Brigadier general Herber Wassom. General ul Haq had been warned by the Turkish Secret Service not to travel by plane, as he was targeted for a mid-air bombing. With this in mind, ul Haq took the United States team with him as 'an insurance policy' as he commented to his inner circle advisors". (10-9)

When Zia-ul-Haq's plane took off, shortly before that a warning from control tower was issued to security base, concerning a suspicious looking truck seen close to the hanger. Unfortunately, by the time of reaction, job was done, Zia-ul-Haq's C-130 was already airborne, and truck had left. A few minutes later the plane started looping, till it hit the ground and turned into a fireball:

"There is no explanation for such behaviour by the C-130 an aircraft with a marvellously reliable record, and a joint Pakistani-United States board of enquiry found no pilot error or mechanical or structural failure. Looping-the-loop is a recognized trade mark of an aircraft hit by E.L.F. fire...The truck seen near the C-130 hanger undoubtedly carried a mobile E.L.F. device of the type the Soviet Armed forces are known to possess". (10-10)

Zia-ul-Haq was not listening to Brotherhood, he was getting out-of-hands, he knew too much about them, he raided their offices, closed their recruiting agencies...He got martyred! The Zia case was never investigated thoroughly by the CIA, despite the deaths of top America's high-class citizens. It is the same America that chases her enemy round the world. Zia-ul-Haq was the third person in the history that charged Freemasonry, first was King Philippe of France and second was Hitler!

Do you think the elite of Pakistan does not know this----They are all part of it---! This is democracy. They are speechless in front of their democratic lords! They are following "Masonic System"!

GENERAL PERVEZ MUSHARRAF

The new ruler of Pakistan is General Pervez Musharraf. He claims that his ideal is "Mustafa Kamal Ataturk", whom we know now as the "Grand Master" of "Turkish Lodge". What do you expect from Musharraf?

Musharraf's first appearance on TV showed him, hugging a Chinese dog, a newspaper in the USA labelled him a China lover. As I am writing this chapter, Musharraf is dividing the power of central government into provincial; thus initiating the final target of Freemasonry to *" divide it further into small provincial governments"*.

On 14th of August 2000, "The Pakistan Day"; General Pervez Musharaf the Chief Executive of Pakistan went first on to the grave of "Sir Sayed Ahmed Khan" and made a visit to the tomb of "Mohammad Ali Jinah" after wards. In his speech he emphasised to follow the footsteps of "Sir Sayed". The photos of Sir Sayed are hung in the government offices for the first time in the history of Pakistan. He also became the first ruler of Pakistan to visit Sayed's grave on the "Freedom Day" of Pakistan.

General Pervez Musharraf stated that all the reports concerning Nawaz Sharif's exile from Pakistan could not be disclosed, because of their confidentiality.

"Musharaf has also directed the sell-off of state enterprises and ensured the transparency process. The government is scheduled to privatise PTCL, UBL and nine oil wells by the end of 2001. PSO, OGDC, Pakistan Petroleum and NIT would be disposed off by next year. The government hopes to get $ 4 billion from their sale, which is much lower than its initial estimate of $ 10 billion.

PTCL alone was valued at $ 8 billion in 1994; it is now expected to fetch not more than $ 2 billion. Moreover, PTCL, after the improvement in its management, has been turned into a profit-earning unit. The same goes for NIT, which registered market improvement by 16 percent and 4 percent in 1999-2000, 2001-2002, respectively. Then there is the factor of national security, particularly in PTCL." (Editorial The Pakistan Post Thursday August 16 2001)

What goes-on on the upper level, public hardly has any idea! People think and blame individuals for the damages caused to the country during that individual's regime. Actual matters and factors are not even whispered in front of public. Every lip of the elite is sealed in this respect; ink of every critical pen is frozen.

Regarding the latest scapegoat of Pakistan, "Nawaz Sharif"---"General Pervez Musharaf" says:

"Some things are so confidential that can not be disclosed for country's betterment".

He refused to even-*"Disclose the source of secret pressure on him to release Nawaz Sharif in exile". (Nawa-i-Waqt UK Thursday 28 Dec. 2000)*

Lt General Moin-uddin Haider is the Interior Minister of Pakistan, he stated:

"I feel this is good for Pakistan. I am not following any one else's agenda. Pakistan ought to become a progressive, modern and tolerant 'Secular State' ". (Khilafah magazine Issue-1, vol-II, Sep, 2000)

According to "The Oxford Popular English Dictionary", "Secular" is!

1-Concerned with the affairs of this world, not spiritual or sacred.

2-Not ecclesiastical or monastic!

These are the claims of Pakistan's elite; they want Pakistan to be a secular state, which has got nothing to do with religion. In simple words only the majority of the inhabitants will be Muslims, not Pakistan. Let us see what does The Elite of the elite, Allah SWT claims about these people:

"...And whosoever does not judge by what Allah has revealed, such are the Kafirun". (Q-5-44)

"...And whosoever does not judge by that which Allah has revealed, such are Zalimun". (Q-5-45)

"...And whosoever does not judge by what Allah has revealed (then) such (people) are Fasiqun". (Q-5-47)

"And whoever seeks a Deen other then Islam, it will never be accepted of him, and in the Hereafter he will be one of the losers". (Q-3-85)

When Moin-uddin Haider says; *"I am not following any one else's agenda"*, we can tell in the light of The Holy Qur'an, whose agenda is he following. Is he not following the Kafirun, Zalimun and Fasiqun?

NGOs

Since Freemasonry is banned in Pakistan, after "Jadoo Ghar", they have been working through and in semblance of different organizations. Non Government Organizations are the latest veils Freemasons are hiding behind although not all of the NGOs are Freemasonry. NGOs employ boys and girls from poor and backward areas of Pakistan, particularly spinsters among the girls. They take these employees for fieldwork in form of mix groups and stay overnight wherever the night comes! These organizations are not only converting the illiterate Muslims into Christianity but also creating a feeling of insecurity about the government; that has failed to solve their problems. Even Hindus living in Pakistan are complaining the conversion of their fellow Hindus into Christianity.

A young man called "Shahid Hamid" who felt obliged to do something for Pakistan, to strive he gave-up his long time job as an accountant and joined an NGO. His work consisted of collecting the information of every individual living in the suburbs who could influence minimum 10 people. This information consisted on to that man's status, education, religion, children and interests. Thinking, this information is vital to solve the problems of poor, he worked day and night with enthusiasm. He did not know that he was being used to collect "DATA" to feed into the "Super Computer" of the "Total Surveillance Program" by the "One World Government"! He realized that all the information he is dispatching is met with a complete silence from the NGOs directors...nothing is being done. This situation lasted, even after he repeatedly enquired about the use of this information. After many attempts to solve the myth he got disheartened and eventually returned to his old job. Luckily his boss was understanding and took him back with a smile.

They are not collecting this information only through these NGOs, but also by stealing the Personal Data Disks:

"An Inquiry about the Theft of Nurses Records"
Islamabad (Jung Reporter)
"According to reliable sources a hard disk and computer ram, containing the data of thousands of nurses has been stolen from the 'Pakistan Nursing Council Headquarters'. It is reported that a meeting of 'Pakistan Nursing Council's Executive Committee' has taken place headed by Mrs Faiz Alam, who stopped Islamabad police department from investigating the theft" [I wonder why?]. *(Jung London, Tuesday 29 August 2000)*

This is not any maniac interested in women details; this is a conspiracy in full swing. In 1998/99, an American company was taking measurements of Pakistan's streets inch by inch. This company completed its job, packed its stuff and zoom…it was gone! No official or unofficial in Pakistan dared to ask them the purpose for these, minute measurements.

Canada Lottery is another bait Freemasonry is using to collect the data and possibly fingerprints from the third world. Every year three countries are included in this lottery. Only 70,000 (I have never come across any one) are the lucky ones who will win the residence-ship in the "Promised Land", the land of opportunities, the land of Freemasons! The Canada of the America!

The total debts of Pakistan are $ 40 billion.

CH-20 MODERN BANKING SYSTEM

Every nation in the world is under debts; every country is borrowing, let it be rich or poor, west or east, first, second or third world. Russia was helping poor countries, when she was herself on the brink of bankruptcy. America is helping nowadays, while she is heavily under debts. England has her own debts. Yet we have classified some countries rich and some poor.

So when we call a country rich, what do we exactly mean by that? Is it that the country has extra natural resources, or is it that the people of that country don't pay tax?

Arabian and Asian countries are considered to be highly resourceful countries the former because of oil and latter by virtue of agriculture. South Africa is supposed to be the richest in the world, with mines of gold and diamonds. Surprisingly all these countries are under debts.

As far as the tax-exempted nation is concerned, it simply does not exist. Rather developed countries like England and US enforce excessive tax on their subjects with an assurance of collection by their tax collecting system i.e., VAT, Sales Tax and National Insurance Tax (in some cases refundable).

So, what is a rich country? And where is it?

There is nothing such as a rich country, and it is nowhere!

Total National Debts of UK in 1996 were £374,636,000,000. And Total National debts of US in 1998 were $5,516,800,000,000. So where is all this money going? Who is benefiting? Who is lending all this money? Who is the debt collector? Who is so rich?

The only rich is a small group of **"International Bankers",** that lends money to the governments---and---makes the governments. Before they were called "king makers" now they are "government makers". This is the modern form of "Early Banking System", more sophisticated and sheltered constitutions working in corroboration world wide, with their subsidiaries named as State Banks, Central Banks and Federal Banks.

When Goldsmiths introduced the first deposit system (please see 'early banking system'), they realised that only a few clients came to demand their deposits back at any one time. That meant, a lot of gold was lying in their possession unused and inactive. There came a time when goldsmiths had had a credibility among people and started printing money instead of issuing written chits and notes. This currency was circulated in public on behalf of "inactive assets" lying in 'goldsmiths' possession. Careful statistics showed that they could afford to lend out more money to the public, than the actual assets they had in their deposits, and "charge interest" on it. This was the birth of:

"FRACTIONAL RESERVE BANKING"

In modern banking system this fractional reserve banking allows banks to print out **"TEN TIMES"** more money than they have in their deposit and **"CHARGE INTEREST"** on it. For example: if you deposit £1, 000 or equivalent value of bullion in the bank, the bank can print £10, 000 in paper money and draw interest on it.

"Fractional Reserve Banking is allowed to every United States Bank that; to loan out 10 times more than its deposits". (18)

They are simply loaning out the **"money they don't have"** and charging interest on it. If you or I would do this, we will be charged for falsifying!

MODERN MONETARY SYSTEM

To decide the quantity of currency of a country "monetary system" is established, which carefully monitors the flow of cash and issuance of bank notes.

"Monetary Systems are today very much alike in the major countries of the world. They consist of three levels:

1- The holders of money (public)--individuals, businesses, government units.

2- Commercially banks (privately or governmentally owned), which borrow from the public and make loans to individuals, firms, or governments.

3- Central banks, which have a monopoly on the issue of certain types of money, serve as the bankers for the central government and the commercial banks, and have the power to determine the quantity of money". (16)

Noteworthy point is that this monetary system is followed in most of the countries, that means central banks or state banks have total *power to determine the quantity of money,* as well as they *serve as bankers for the central government and the commercial banks.* So all matters due to money are totally subject to these Central Banks.

CREATION OF MONEY, THE CURRENCY VIA BONDS

First of all, government issues "Bonds", which are only a promise by the government to pay at the end of "bond's term", with interest.

People buy these bonds to get a secure rate of interest.

At the end of term, these bonds are paid with interest and destroyed.

How these bonds are converted into money or currency and then distributed into public, is a four step process:

Step 1: The "Central/ Federal Open Market Committee" (it varies names in different countries), approves the purchase of government bonds.

Step 2: Committee purchases these bonds from the open market, whoever is offering them.

Step 3: Central/ Federal Committee pays for the bonds with electronic credits/checks to the seller's bank. These credits/checks are based on nothing! The Fed just creates them.

Step 4: The banks use these deposits as reserves. Now they can loan out over ten times the amount of their reserves to new borrowers. **All at interest!**

This way a purchase of $1 million turns over to $10 millions. The Central / Federal **Committee creates the 10% of non-existing money and the banks create the rest 90%! ---------------------------------100% illusion--!**

To reduce the amount of money in the market, same process is reversed!

Step 1: Committee sells bonds to the public in the open market.

Step 2: The money flows out of the purchaser's local banks.

Step 3: Loans must be reduced by 10 times of the sales.

Step 4: Committee's sale of bonds one million worth; results in 10 million less money in the economy.

"In most of the countries the bulk of the currency consists of notes issued by the central bank. In the United Kingdom these are Bank of England notes; in the United States, Federal Reserve notes and so on. It is hard to say precisely what 'issued by the central bank' means. In the United States, for example, the currency bears the words 'Federal Reserve Note', but these notes are not obligations of the Federal Reserve Banks in any meaningful sense. The holder who presents them to a Federal Reserve Bank has no right to anything except other pieces of paper adding up to the same face value. The situation is much the same in most other countries." (16)

In simple English this means; although "Bank of England" and "Federal Reserve Bank", have total authority to issue currency notes, they are not bound to value them. They can refuse them any time they want!

Because "Bank of England" and "Federal Reserve Bank of the United States" are the models for other "central/State banks" on the globe, we will explore their history and system to find out the roots of "world wide banking system".

BANK OF ENGLAND (ENGLAND'S BANKING SYSTEM)

After the Templars had pawned every monarch in the Europe and their dominion was expanding through their subsidiaries, i. e. British East India Company and Virginia Company; they realised that loaning money to a king is dangerous. This could be wiped out as a personal loan of the predecessor by any successor of the throne. For this the whole people of the country had to be responsible somehow. In other words, they held thrones and now had to hold people. If the general public "elect" a government, they are responsible for the government's deeds. So any loan taken by "elected government" is actually taken by the whole country and her subjects.

On the other hand, if a consistent institution is formed, which is responsible for printing and manipulating the currency, free from any "elected government's" pressure then the loans of former government can be downloaded to the successor. Brotherhood had achieved their first target as Parliament was already working, so now they only had to form the constitution with a permanent monopoly on the currency.

William of Orange, also called William Henry, stadholder of the United Provinces of Netherlands, was ruling Great Britain, jointly with the actual Queen of England, "Mary II". She died in 1694 at an early age of 32.

"Mary administered the government in her own name, but she relied entirely on his [William's] *advice. In the periods when William was in England she willingly retired from politics". (16)*

William was brought to the throne of England purposefully, to retire the Queen from politics and finally from life. Apparently she died of smallpox. Co-incidentally 1694 (the year the Queen died), was the same year when Bank of England was incorporated.

"The Bank of England was incorporated by act of Parliament in 1694 with the immediate purpose of raising funds to allow the English government to wage war against France..." (16)

The war was not on but expected to be on.

"He [William III], *directed the European opposition to Louis XIV of France and, in Great Britain, secured the triumph of Protestantism and of the Parliament". (16)*

Here again we find other purposes of William: to lead English into French enmity, create the feeling of insecurity thus forming the background of war, as well as complete the hold of Parliament, and found the first bank, "The Bank of England".

The "Bank of England", was in fact never owned by England. The name England was used merely for deception!

"It was privately owned, like any other private corporation it sold its shares to get started". (18)

The private owners of the bank were suppose to put one and a quarter million British pounds as to get it started and rest 10% was the responsibility of the government. Government carried out with her responsibility, but as far as private investors are concerned:

"Only £7,000 were ever received, despite that the bank was duly chartered and started loaning out to the politicians several times the money it had—on—interest. The loans were secured by the direct taxation of the British people ". (18)

Poor British---! By 1698, the British debts grew from one and a quarter million pounds (which these private investors were 'supposed' to put in and never did), to a staggering 16 million pounds. In mid 1700s they were 140 million pounds!

In the years to come these "money changers", joined by the "Rothschilds", orchestrated wars after wars till they sucked all the bullion from Europe and then from all over the world. Nathan Rothschild was never wrong when he bragged that in 17 years in England he has increased his original £25,000 to 2,500 times.

Rothschilds financed "Cecil Rhodes", to dominate the diamond and gold in South Africa, which they still do. In America, they financed the "Heriman's" and "Vanderbilt's" in railroads, and "Carnigee" in steel industry. During "World War One", "J. P Morgan" was thought to be the richest man in the United States. J P. Morgan owned the wealthiest shipping company that had biggest ships of the time, "Olympic" and "Titanic"--- "Gigantic" was on the way to completion when "Titanic, the ship that *"even god can not sink"(as they claimed)*---the "Unsinkable"---sank!

Allah O Akbar!

J.P Morgan's will was made public after his death, which disclosed that he only owned 19% of the "J. P Morgan Company". He was only a lieutenant by "Rothschilds", who owned the rest of the company.

By 1850, James Rothschild the heir of the French branch of the family was said to be worth 600 million French Franks; 150 million more than all other bankers put together in France!

"There is no evidence that their predominance standing in Europe or world finance has changed". (18)

The Bank of England was first located in Mercer's Hall and then in Grocer's Hall, but it was moved to its present location on Threadneedle Street in 1730s where now it is guarded by military! The City of London has its own police too! In early years even Queen had to ask permission to enter the "City of London"!

Every country in the world has a privately owned "central bank" on the model of Bank of England. These central banks quickly take over the economy control and put in the hands of the "Rich".

"The Bank of England was the first modern central bank, serving as the model for many others. It was established as a private bank in 1694 but quickly came to be largely an agency of the government". (16)

This is how they conceal the truth: *"but quickly came to be largely an agency of the government"*. I wonder what does the writer mean by an agency of the government? In fact he gives the game away just after a few lines:

"...The bank was privately owned until 1946." (16)

What do you call this? A source of genuine information or a source of censored information! This is how "Fraternity" has been fooling you for centuries! The Bank of England is still not a government bank; it is a private bank!

"Immediately after the congress held at Vienna [after the battle of Waterloo}, *the international bankers forced Britain to set up a new bank of England, which they controlled absolutely, and which they still control to very this day". (The History of Illuminati, by Myron Fagan)*

And:

"Generally speaking, there is no formal limit to the amount of notes and deposits that a central bank may have as liabilities." (16)

This means "Bank of England" is a loose dragon in civilized economy!

HISTORY OF AMERICAN CURRENCY

After the birth of Virginia "the First State of USA" in 1604, small banks began operating in each new founded state. These banks were independent of any constitution and working merely as moneychangers on the basis of good will they had in public. There was no central bank as to enforce the rate of interest and different states would exchange their currency on reasonable exchange rates, agreed-on from both sides. This was the introduction of currency to the "New Founded Land". It was going very smooth for banks and public, Brotherhood didn't like it. They had to pull the strings but after the currency introduction was matured. Brotherhood waited for nearly 60 years. Everything had to come in formation.

In 1764, British Parliament hurriedly passed the "Currency Act", which they could not for the past few years, because of "Earl of Bute", who had an influence on "George III" and was Prime Minister of Britain 1762-63.

"George IV, William IV, Edward VII, Edward VIII and George VI, were all Freemasons. Over 300 aristocrats, princes and royal dukes and marquesses, earls, viscounts and barons were Freemasons". (23 p-136)

Freemasonry has been the ruling class, yet Freemasonry calls itself "revolutionary".

"Its highest offices are always held by royal dukes or by earls while a peerage or knighthood is almost 'de rigeur', even for the rank of 'Junior Grand Warden'." (23 p-137)

British Parliament passed the "Unlawful Societies Act in 1799" that outlawed all organizations, "the members of which are required to take an oath not authorized by law". Amazingly, they spared Freemasonry by giving the same excuse that "how can there be a society 'revolutionary', with its members from royal family"?

Earl of Bute was also responsible for signing the "Treaty of Paris" that ended the seven-year war with France (1756-63). Earl of Bute had to resign within a year as a Prime Minister; he was doing too well for Britain. Next came George Grenville (1763-65):

"He entered Parliament in 1741, one of the "cousinhood" of men interrelated by blood or marriage...Started the train of events leading to the American Revolution". (16)

Now the time was right, British Prime Minister was one of "Brotherhood". Benjamin Franklin: "*an enthusiastic Freemason*" had nearly completed his homework for American Revolution. British Parliament passed the "Revenue Act" in 1764 and the "Stamp Act" in 1765, which: Prohibited American Colonies to print their own money and obliged them to pay the future tax in silver and gold coins. The result was a disaster and "American War of Independence" was on. In his own biography, Benjamin Franklin states:

"The inability of the colonies; to get power to issue their own money, permanently out of the hands of George III and the 'International Bankers', was the prime reason for the Revolutionary War". (Benjamin Franklin's Autobiography. A quote from 18)

1ST BUS TO DISASTER

In 1791, the first Congress passed a bill under the presidency of George Washington. Same George Washington; who was responsible for igniting the "Seven Year War" with France which resulted in heavy taxes on American Colonies, and a Famous Freemason. This bill gave a charter to "1st Bank of United States" (1st BUS).

Unlike "Bank of England", in this the share of the Congress was 20% and 80% was given to private investors. The 20% share of Congress was not given to sit on the driving seat of the 1st BUS rather scene is more like the same as it was in the Bank of England case:

"The private stockholders never paid their full share. The government put up their initial 2 million dollars in cash and those were the actual assets the 'First Bank of United States' had!" (18)

In modern business and economics, there is a formula, called "Twenty-Eighty Formula". This formula applies in every practical field, i. c. Business, studies and research. It is defined as; "Eighty % of the outcome is from 20% work". For example: 20% of your business brings your 80% income. This is very true and "BUS" is the base, where this formula comes from!

Like the "Bank of England" the names of the private investors were never revealed. 1st BUS was given a monopoly to print the "US Mint"! The name "Bank of United States" was deliberately chosen to hide the fact that the bank was privately owned:

"It was a common saying that the Rothschilds were the actual power behind the Bank of United States. " (18)

The first five years, US government borrowed $8.5 million from the bank and in the same five years, prices rose by 72%.

"End of the nineteenth century an economist claimed that Rothschilds, owned half of the world's wealth". (18)

People were not ready to give-up yet, the 1st BUS had to be taken "off the road" and scrapped.

"Antagonism over the bank issue, grew so heated that its charter could not be renewed in 1811". (16)

2ND BUS TO DISASTER

After 25 years of 1st BUS launch, in 1816, 2nd BUS was put on the road. Opposition to the BUS was still too strong and any thing could happen. Both sides needed to be covered, "support" and "opposition". To support, Congress was enough; opposition was handed over to Andrew Jackson (1829-1837), who was to become the seventh President, merely on the basis of opposing the "International Bankers". This is the same Andrew Jackson, who:

"Initiated in Lodge No 1 at Nashville, Tennessee, and became a Grand Master of the Grand Lodge of Tennessee, October 1822-October 1824". (Ibid.)

This is the same Andrew Jackson who supported Freemasonry when "William Writ", the lawyer and a Freemason himself, took the charge of "Anti-Masonic Campaign" in America! (Ibid.)

Once again "Twenty-Eighty Formula" was applied and the private stockholders stayed anonymous. But it was a well-known fact that 1/3rd of the stake was sold to foreigners.

"A substantial interest in the bank was also purchased by the Europeans". (16)

The Grand Master Andrew Jackson stood-up and took his campaign against the "International Bankers" and not against the Freemasons, to the streets of US. He was welcomed by the people, became hero and a messiah. This messiah: concealed the truth about the actual enemy, "The Freemasonry" and diverted people's attention towards "International Bankers", thus: maintaining the actual oath of secrecy! So the researchers blame individuals, and not Freemasonry:

"The Rothschilds had taken control of Bank of England, as well as of 2nd Bank of the United States". (18)

After becoming president of US, instead of voiding all the national debts, which did not exist any way, Andrew Jackson the Grand Master paid them all! All this money---the actual existing assets went in the vaults of---"Freemasonry", via---"International Bankers".

GREEN BACKS

Abraham Lincoln came into power in 1861. He only attended school for one year through out his life, so he was not brainwashed. He understood the dangers America had because of these moneychangers. He was determined to solve this problem once and for all. The only solution was to print own money, "Free of Interest", so he did. This money was called "Green Backs", because the back of the dollar was printed in green. In 1862,63 he printed 450 million dollars with no interest to the federal government. These dollars helped to stabilise the economy of America, as well as means to purchase the arms. How prosperous was the idea, we can judge by the critics from an editorial of London Times, which was at that time and still is owned by Fraternity!

"If this mischievous financial policy, which has its origins in North America shall become endurated down to a fixture, then that government will furnish its own money without cost. It will pay off debts and be without debt. It will have all the money necessary to carry on its commerce. It will become prosperous without precedent in the history of the world. The brains and the wealth of all the countries will go to North America. That country must be destroyed or it will destroy every monarchy on the globe". (18)

Do you believe this? This is the power; interest free money can bring to a country-------Is there any country in the Muslim world---in the whole world---that want to adopt this system----? The system, given to us by Allah! The system, which dismantled the Roman and Persian Empires! The system, that is interest free, the system that takes money off the rich, and gives to the poor! Not the system, that takes money off poor and gives to, rich. The system of "Zakah" and not of "Tax"!

We all adopted the system of interest and because of its web spread all over the world our brains get sucked into it. Every thing goes back to its origins, our intellect takes the West as a modal; this idea is hammered into their brains right from Kinder Garden. The Masonic system is a complete manipulation from A-Z, built for total control. It is complete on the surface but its foundations are weak. You can demolish this entire plaza: it takes only "LA ILAHA ILLALLAH"!

The modal for the West; Abraham Lincoln stated about this system:

"The money power preys upon the nation in tunes of adversity, it is more despotic than monarchy, more insolent than autocracy, more selfish then bureaucracy". (18)

Abraham was getting too dangerous for Fraternity they had to do something about him---they did---! On April 14th, 1865, Abraham Lincoln was murdered. On his death, "Otto von Bismark", the man later responsible for re-union of Germany, said:

"...I fear that foreign bankers with their craftiness and tortuous tricks will entirely control the exuberant riches of America, and use it systematically to corrupt modern civilization. They will not hesitate to plunge the whole Christendom into wars and chaos in order that the earth should become their inheritance". (18)

Very much so, the years that followed proved each and every word of the statement true.

The green backs were enormously popular among public. They were in the market till 1994. Gerald G McGeer was an attorney in Canada in 1934 he revealed that:

"Lincoln's murderer was a mercenary hired by the international bankers". (18)

Next President, Andrew Johnson (1865-69) was a Freemason, so was James A Garfield (1881) the 20th president of the United States. Working as a Masonic President, came a point that Garfield could not take it any more, he had to come out with the truth. The cruelty of Brotherhood forced him to slam the moneychangers publicly, or probably it was yet another attempt to divert public's attention from their actual enemy---- the "Freemasonry". In 1881 he said:

"Whosoever controls the volume of money in any country is absolute master of all industry and commerce...And when you realize, that the entire system is very easily controlled, one way or another, by a few powerful men at the top. You will not have to be told how periods of inflation and depressions originate". (18)

Within a few weeks, after this statement, on July 2nd 1881, Garfield was assassinated!

FEDERAL RESERVE (UNITED STATES BANKING SYSTEM)

Federal Reserve's headquarters are in Washington. The name "Federal" is selected again for nothing else but deception! It has got nothing to do with the government. It is a privately owned institution. In Britannica "Federal Reserve System" is stated as:

*"Central banking authority of the United States. It acts as a fiscal **agent** for the U.S. government, is custodian of the reserve accounts of commercial banks, makes loans to commercial banks, and is authorised to issue Federal Reserve notes that constitute the entire supply of paper currency of the country. Created by the Federal Reserve Act of 1913..." (16)*

The same term ***"agent"*** is used again to conceal the private ownership of the whole system. We will prove the privacy of the Federal Reserve System along the way. First we will concentrate on how this draconian blood-sucking bill of 1913, went unnoticed through Congress. The bill was called "Federal Reserve Act" and was passed in 1913 as mentioned in Britannica, what is not mentioned is the date that bill was passed! The date was 23rd December! Bill was presented to the Congress on 22nd and quickly passed on the following day when:

"Most of the members were gone on Christmas holidays, after being assured by the leaders; that nothing will be done until long after the Christmas holidays". (18)

Those who came to know about it before it was signed by the President, warned:

"This Act establishes the most gigantic trust on earth. When the President signs this bill, the invisible government by the 'Monetary Power' will be legalized. The people may not know it immediately, but the day of reckoning is only a few years removed...The worst legislative crime of the ages is perpetrated by this banking bill". (Congress Rep: Charles Lindbergh. Quote from 18)

"A super-state controlled by 'international bankers' and 'international industrialists. Acting together to enslave the world for their own pleasure". (Congress Rep: Louis McFadden. Quote from 18)

Beside these and many other warnings, "Mr President" did sign the bill! ---- Why? ---Because--- "Mr President"--- was Mr Woodrow Wilson! --- A famous Freemason! Listed in the Famous Freemason's Gallery.

During his first term in the office, three years after passage of the bill "Mr President" said:

"We have come to be one of the worst ruled, one of the most completely controlled governments in the civilized world—no longer a government of free opinion. No longer a government by ---a vote of majority, but a government by the opinion and duress of a small group of dominant men.

Some of the biggest men in the United States, in the field of commerce and manufacture, are afraid of something.
They know that there is a power somewhere, so organized, so subtle, so watchful, so interlocked, so complete, so pervasive, that they had better not speak above their breath when they speak in condemnation of it". (18)

What do you conclude from this? A defeated President? Reverted President? Or A hidden threat: from President?

Mr President was elected again for a second term! ----Long live Democracy! Did you ever think that why the law prevents a President or Prime Minister to stand for a fourth term? One person can be head of the state for maximum three terms! The reason is that in fifteen years he can understand how the country is run: He becomes Dangerous!

The "Commercial Banks" are liable to the "Federal Reserve Bank" which has 12 branches and controlled by the "Federal Reserve Board", that consists nine directors, six; from "Federal Reserve Banks" and three; appointed by the government. This whole system is called "Federal Reserve System".

A say about the "Federal Reserve Board" by "Louis T McFadden", a Congress rep:

"We have in our country one of the most corrupt institutions the world has ever known. I refer to the 'Federal Reserve Board'. This evil institution has improvised the people of the United States, and has practically bankrupted our government. It has done this through---the corrupt practices of the moneyed vultures who control it". (18)

Talking about the Board and whole system, "Charles A Lindburg" another Congress Representative stated:

"The financial system---has been turned over to---the 'Federal Reserve Board'. That board administers the finance system by authority of---a purely profiteering group. The system is private, conducted for the sole purpose of obtaining the greatest possible profits from the use of other people's money". (18)

FEDERAL RESERVE BANK OF USA (MODEL FOR CENTRAL, NATIONAL AND STATE BANKS)

Britannica introduces "Federal Reserve Bank" as:

"A Federal Reserve bank is a privately owned corporation...It is governed by a board of nine directors, six of whom are elected by the member banks and three of whom are appointed by the Board of Governors of the Federal Reserve System." (16)

We have explained the "Federal Board System" and its corruption earlier. Albeit, the appointment of three impartial members from the "Board" (if they are impartial) will not have much say among six corrupts, majority is the authority. Whereas in this case the whole system stinks!

"The way in which a central bank increases or decreases the total amount of money is, typically, by making loans or by buying or selling the government securities [open-market operations]. *If, for example, the Federal Reserve purchases $1,000,000 of government securities* [i. e. government bonds], *it will pay for these securities by a check on itself* [means not paying in assets but a peace of paper], *adding $1,000,000 to its assets and $1,000,000 to its liabilities. The seller* [the one who sold those government bonds in the open-market] *can take the check to a Federal Reserve Bank* [privately owned], *which will exchange for it $1,000,000 in Federal Reserve Notes* [Thus actually paying him nothing but pieces of paper]. *Or the seller may deposit the check at a commercial bank, and the bank will in turn present it to a Federal Reserve*

Bank, which will 'pay' the check by making a book entry increasing that bank's deposits with it by $1,000,000 [Again paying no actual assets]. *" (16)* [Added]

There are no real assets in the whole process. There are no real assets in the whole dollar system. This money is created out of thin air. This dollar does not exist. This dollar has got no real value or credibility. This dollar is an illusion-----Yet this dollar rules the world----This dollar was created, owned, and controlled by "Brotherhood". They spare themselves from its ugliness, staying behind the label of "International Bankers". Let it be "Skull and Bone", "International Bankers", "East India Company", The "International Drug Traffickers", it is all Freemasonry. These are the same people waiting to raise their "Master", "The one who will establish His kingdom for ever". They can afford to hide all this from us because:

"By World War One, the moneychangers [Freemasonry] *had ceased the control of the 'National Press', with their dominant wealth". (18)*

"These 'International Bankers' and 'Rockfeller Standard Oil' interests control the majority of newspapers and magazines in this [US] *country". (John Hylan, Mayor of New York, 'New York Times', March 26, 1922. Quote from 18)*

This is true not only in case of the United States, but everywhere in the Europe and in the rest of the world too!

The Federal Reserve banks are in Boston, New York, Philadelphia, Chicago, San Francisco, Cleveland, Ohio, Richmond, Va: Atlanta, Ga: St. Louis, Mo: Minneapolis, Minn: Kansas City, Mo: and Dallas, Texas.

"Federal Reserve is the most powerful central bank in the world". (18)

MONEY DEPRESSION

Because the power holder behind this illusionary money system in one, it can control the consequences. First it could only control Europe and America, now it can the whole world. The market crash in Japan is an example, which people would not have forgotten yet. Recession of early nineties in Europe and States has its effects still haunting the small investors. This is how recession is created and controlled.

First step is **"EASY MONEY";** when the bankers give easy loans, people borrow heavily and expand their businesses. Money circulation expands.

Second step is **"TIGHT MONEY";** the moneychangers tighten the money supply, make hard to borrow. Certain debtors fail to pay back their previous loans because the number of currency notes in the market has decreased, and cannot take out new loans (as a result of tight money) to pay their previous.

This process of easy and tight money results in some people's **"BANKRUPTCY"** and banks take-over their real properties and existing assets, for nothing**----They are taking your real properties for and by the money that does not exist-----!**

This is what "James Madison"; the main author of the American constitution has to say about the Brotherhood:

"History records that the moneychangers have used every form of abuse, intrigue, deceit and violent means possible to maintain their control over government by controlling money and its issuance". (18)

This not only is happening in the United States and Europe; it is happening everywhere in the world, this is happening in your country ----RIGHT NOW----!

'ABA", is the "American Bankers Association" that "look afters" the interest of general public and makes sure that unjustly interest does not corrupt the market by bankers or by the federal. The following memorandum issued by "ABA" will reveal that this association in fact is a deceit! ABA asked bankers to create a depression on a certain date, **three years in the future.**

"On September the 1st, 1894, we will not renew our loans under any consideration. On September the 1st we will demand our money. We will foreclose and become mortgagees in possession. We can take two-thirds of the farms west of the Mississippi, and thousands of them east of the Mississippi as well, at our own price...Then the farmers will become tenants as in England". (1891 American Bankers Association as printed in the Congressional Records of April 29, 1913. Quote from 18)

If you still don't believe that the "Federal Reserve" is a private "***agency***", then pick-up the telephone directory of the States, you will find "Federal Reserve" listed in **"WHITE BUSINESS PAGES",** which is for only private businesses, and not in the "Blue Pages" which refer to the government organizatons.

The biggest families in the Banking System are six: three from Europe and three from United States. These families are interconnected to each other by intermarriages. Among the Europeans, are **"the Rothschilds, the Warburgs and the Schiffs"!** Among the Americans, are **"the Morgans, the Rockefellers, and the Aldriches"!**

THE BIGGEST THEFT OF HISTORY

Franklin D Roosevelt became the President of the US in 1933. He was a Freemason and his three sons were master Masons too (Ibid.). He campaigned in the traditional manor, opposing international bankers. Surprisingly just after two days in the office, he announced a bank holiday. His job was even dangerous than the international bankers themselves. He was supposed to loot all the gold from American public, so there is no real bullion left in the country. How could he do it? ---By just passing a bill---the same year:

"Roosevelt outlawed private ownership of all gold bullion and all gold coins with the exception of rare coins". (18)

Most of the gold, Americans stored: was in the shape of gold-coins. This new decree was in fact a confiscation of all gold. Those citizens, who didn't comply, risked as much as 10 years in the prison and a $10,000 fine, which is equivalent to a 150,000 today. Those who turned in their gold were paid the official price of $20.66 per ounce.

This confiscation order was so unpopular that no one in the government would take the "honour" to introduce it. At the signing ceremony, even President Roosevelt made it clear to all present:

"That he was not the author of it and publicly stated that he had not even read it". (18)

Even the secretary of the treasury said:

"He never read it either". Saying, it was; *"What the experts wanted". (18)*

Who were these experts—do you know them---? Does any body know them---? Finally it was Roosevelt who as a President had to take the liability to seduce people into give up their gold because:

"Pulling the nation's resources was necessary to get America out of depression". (18)

Who caused this depression---do you know them? It was Roosevelt who ordered to build a new "Bullion Depository" to store all the gold, government was confiscating "ill-legally". By 1936, the "U. S. Depository" at "Fort Knox" was completed, It is a major U.S. military reservation 110,000 acres in Meade, Hardine and Bullitt counties, northern Kentucky, 30 miles Southwest of Louisville. Fort Knox is a solid square bombproof structure with mechanical protective devices. In 1937, the gold began to flow in. The rip-off of all the ages started proceeding.

In 1935, when all the gold was turned in, the official price of gold was raised to $35.00 per ounce. But the catch was that "only foreigners" could sell their gold at the new price. The gold in fact was already purchased by foreigners and shipped out:

"Over the years it was sold to the European moneychangers at the price of $35.00 per ounce. This was done during the time when it was ill-legal for Americans to buy any of their own gold". (18)

The same gold was then brought back and sold to Fort Knox at the new price. More debts on government---more debts on public---more tax on public! All this for what! Only for a rich group of people!

All the gold people had, was gone into the hands of "Fort Knox". The assets at the Fort Knox were suppose to be audited annually, it never happened, but only once in 1951, by the order of President Eisenhower.

By 1971, all the pure gold had been secretly removed from Fort Knox and [according to some researchers] drained back to London.

"Once the gold was gone from Fort Knox, President Nixon closed the gold window by repealing the Roosevelt's Gold Act of 1934, making it legal once again for Americans to buy gold". (18)

Within nine years the price of gold rose to $880.00 per ounce, 25 times the price, the gold was sold for. Nathan Rothschild's wealth increased once more 25 times, he must have benefited from it again! This time upstairs though!

Most Americans believe that the gold is still here at Fort Knox. At the end of "W. W. 2", Fort Knox contained 700 million ounces of gold, 70% of all the gold in the world.

President Ronald Regan took office in 1981, his party members advised him to return to gold standard, as a solution to the economic problems. Convinced with the idea, Regan appointed a group of men to study the gold situation and report back to the Congress. This commission was called the "Gold Commission". What Regan's "Gold Commission" reported back to Congress in 1982, was the following shocking news concerning gold!

"The U.S. Treasury owned-----no------gold-----at all. All the gold that was left at Fort Knox was now owned by the Federal Reserve, a group of private bankers as collateral against the national debt". (18)

The land of opportunities became the poorest land of disasters!

The actual division of USA

Scottish Rite - Northern & Southern Jurisdictions

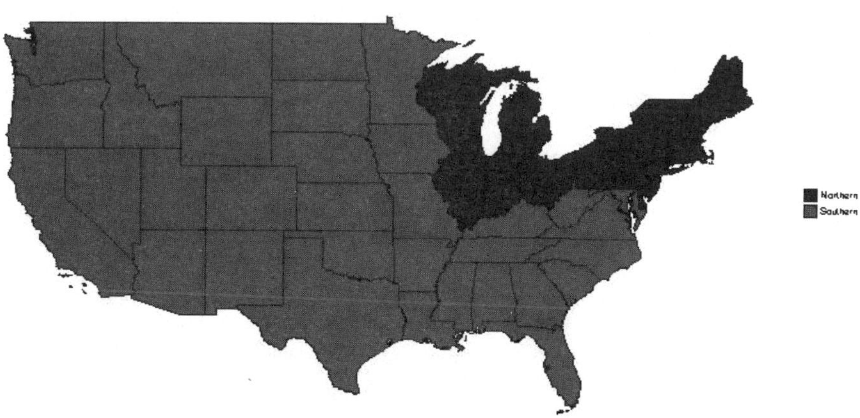

CH-21 ONE WORLD GOVERNMENT

The final target, the Brotherhood want to achieve is total domination. Let it be economical, educational, mental, religious, natural resources or personal. For this target they have worked for centuries. How close are they from their goal? Unfortunately not too far! Every day, every hour, every minute and every moment, we are wasting, achieving our personal petty benefits and flaring mutual differences, they are getting closer to their final countdown!

This is not a single maniac from James Bond version, trying to dominate the whole world by one advance scientific invention. This is a network of sophisticated, educated, literate and highly advanced people, holding maximum available resources in their hands to manipulate our weaknesses. We fall into their trap, whenever we stray from "Siratal Mustaqim".

They have created differences among nations and sustained them to create wars, so nations keep on consuming their ammunition, loans and aid. Thus paralysing themselves into Brotherhood's hands. Look at what happened in East Timor!

If any terrorist activity happens in Pakistan, people blame India and vice-versa. The situation is same in Africa, Middle East and other parts of the world. Some aware people can trace these conspiracies back up to America, no one goes beyond that, because beyond that is all misty, and that is where the spider of the world-wide-web sits! For example our helper and hero is America, a rich country that can afford to help poor nations by giving them loans, like she did in 2nd World War, by providing loans to Britain and Europe. In fact America is as poor as any other country in the world, rather poorer than some real poor countries. Look at the amount of "Federal Tax" people are paying there. "Federal Tax" is another illusion, enforced on American public; there is no law of government that allows these private agencies to collect tax from the public. The name "Federal" is another deceit! Anyhow: while America was giving loans to other European countries, she was getting under debts herself:

"After the World War 2, U.S. federal debts went from 43 billion in 1940 up to 257 billion in 1950, an increase of 598%! (18)

So who was loaning to Europe, Japan and America? This question is never asked and never answered! Now you know--- why---!

2nd World War not only helped Brotherhood to put half of the earth under their debts, but it also divided it into two economic systems. Communist and capitalist! The economic domination, which is a vital step towards "One World Government", was to come in three phases:

1- *Central Bank domination of national economies, world--wide!*
2- *Centralize regional economies through organizations such as the "European Monetary Unions" and "Regional Trade Unions", such as NAFTA.*
3- *Centralize the world economy through a 'World Central Bank', a world money and abolition of all national independent tariffs through treaties like 'GATT'. (18)*

The first two targets are achieved utterly. Look at the currency notes of your country: who issues them? Government or "Central/State or National Bank? Third phase is complete as far as "World Bank" is concerned. "One World Money" or "One World Currency" is half way achieved through the strong position of the dollar and world economy's dollar-standard, free of gold. Rest of this is done in Europe via "Euro Dollar", and on world level via, "American Travellers Checks", which are massively used to exchange black money. To review the relations with Iraq, leaders of six Gulf countries are holding a seminar in Bahrain. In this seminar:

"They will also consider the chances of issuing 'One Currency'". (The Daily Jung London Sunday 31 Dec. 2000)

The abolition of "national independent tariffs" is being done through "UN Forces". When a country is under debts and in non-payment position, UN Forces have full right under liabilities to IMF and World Bank, to walk in and assure the solution to the economic and corruption problems. "IMF" is already the biggest economic power in the world!

"Amongst central banks, the largest holder of the gold is 'IMF'". (18)

This is because international bankers are "IMF". A large part of stolen American gold; is now owned by IMF!

Another thorough research shows the detailed strategy of the Brotherhood:

1- To enforce a world authority called the "United Nations" (with associated bodies like the "World Health Organization"), which could evolve it into a world government with powers to control the lives of everyone on the planet.

2- To continue to cause conflicts across the world and to use the fear like Soviet Union, to massively increase spending on nuclear weapons and "Conventional Weapons". Thus adding to the terror of nuclear war and demands for global security. To set-up an American-European defence alliance (which was called the "North Atlantic Treaty Organization or in brief, NATO), and a "United Nations Peace keeping Force", which through the engineering of conflicts, would eventually be fused together to form the "World Army".

3- To create three "Free Trade Regions" in Europe, America and Asia, which would be sold to people initially as merely economic groupings. Gradually, however, these would be evolved into centralised political unions, with one central bank and one currency. These would be stepping-stones to the introduction of the same institutions on a global scale. The "European Economic Community (EEC)", and the "European Union" was the first of these, but the others are under-way.

4- To advance the control of public opinion and to research and expand the understanding of how to manipulate the human psyche, individually and collectively. Today this agenda includes the "Micro-chipping" of people and their permanent connection to a global computer.

5- To create a welfare state while destroying alternatives to the economic system and, when the desired dependency had been achieved, to dismantle the state welfare support, so creating a vast "Under-Class" without help or hope.

6- To make fantastic amount of money in the course of realising all of these ambitions via the Elite-controlled companies and banks.

7- To continually add to the debt burdens of people, business and state; thus increasing the control exerted over them.

(4-141)

The clearest of all scenarios we get from Dr. John Coleman's "Conspirators' Hierarchy". He defines the One-World-Government in real depth and actual form and you will find it familiar in so many ways. As we are well introduced to their actual targets through different organizations and their slogans, although they do not announce it openly. So far many of these things have taken place and we are well aware of them though, thinking them prosperous and beneficial for all humanity. We have seen this happening in so many futuristic Holy-Wood films that we take this as fiction. But believe it or not, this is **serious stuff!** (The name Hollywood comes from the pagans' Holy Wood, which they used to worship)

"A One World Government and one-unit monetary system under permanent non-elected hereditary oligarchists who self-select from among their numbers in the form of a feudal system as it was in the Middle Ages. In this One World entity, population will be limited by restrictions on the number of children per family, diseases, wars, famines, until 1 billion people who are useful to the ruling class, in areas which will be strictly and clearly defined, remain as the total world population.

There will be no middle class, only rulers and servants. All laws will be uniform under a legal system of world courts practising the same unified code of laws. Backed by a One World Government police force and a One World unified military to enforce laws in all former countries where no national boundaries shall exist. The system will be on the basis of a welfare state; those who are obedient and subservient to the One World Government will be rewarded with the means to live; those who are rebellious will simply be starved to death or to be declared outlaws. Thus a target for any one-who wishes to kill them. Privately owned firearms or weapons of any kind will be prohibited.

Only one religion will be allowed and that will be in the form of a One-World Government Church, which has been in existence since 1920... Satanism, Luciferianism and Witchcraft shall be recognized as legitimate One World Government curricula with no private or church schools. All Christian churches have already been subverted and Christianity will be a thing of the past in the One World Government. To induce a state where there is no individual freedom or any concept of liberty surviving, there shall be no such thing as republicanism, sovereignty or rights residing with the people. National pride and racial identity shall be stamped out and in the transition phase it shall be subject to the severest penalties to even mention one's racial origin.

Each person shall be fully indoctrinated; that he or she is a creature of the One World Government with an identification number clearly marked on their person. So as to be readily accessible, which identifying number shall be in the master file of the NATO computer in Brussels, Belgium, subject to instant retrieval by any agency of One World Government at any time! The master files of the CIA, FBI, state and local police agencies, IRS, FEMA, Social Security shall be vastly expanded and form the basis of personal records of all individuals in the United States.

Marriage shall be outlawed and there shall be no family life, as we know it. Children will be removed from their parents at an early age and brought up by wards as state property. Such an experiment was carried out in East Germany under Erich Honnecker, when children were taken away from parents, considered by the state to be disloyal citizens. ***Women will be degraded through the continued process of "women's liberation" movements. Free sex shall be mandatory.***

Failure to comply at least once by the age of twenty shall be punishable by severe reprisals against her person. Self-abortion shall be taught and practiced after two children are born to a woman; such records shall be contained in the personal file of each woman in the One World Government's regional computers. If a woman falls pregnant after she has previously given birth to two children, she shall be forcibly removed to an abortion clinic for such an abortion, and sterilization to be carried out.

Pornography shall be promoted, and be compulsory, showing in every theatre of cinema, including homosexual and lesbian pornography. The use of "recreational" drugs shall be compulsory, with each person allotted drug quotas, which can be purchased at One World Government stores throughout the world. Mind control drugs will be expanded and usage will become compulsory. Such mind control drugs will be given in food and/or water supplies without the knowledge and/or consent of the people. Drug bars shall be set up, run by One World Government employees, where the slave class shall be able to spend their free time. ***In this manner the non-elite masses will be reduced to the level and behaviour of controlled animals with no will of their own and easily regimented and controlled.***

The economic system shall be based upon the ruling oligarchical class allowing just enough foods and services to be produced to keep the mass slave labour camps going. *All wealth shall be aggregated in the hands of the elite members of the Committee of 300* (Freemasonry). *Each individual shall be indoctrinated to understand that he or she is totally dependent upon the state for survival. The world shall be ruled, by Committee of 300 Executive Decrees-which become instant law... Courts of punishments: and not courts of justice shall exist.*

Industry is to be totally destroyed along with nuclear powered energy systems. Only Committee's members and their elitists shall have the right to earth's resources. Large populations in the cities shall be forcibly removed into remote areas and those who refuse to go shall be exterminated in the manner of the One World Government experiment carried out by "Pol Pot" in Cambodia. Euthanasia for the terminally ill and the aged shall be compulsory...At least 4 billion "useless eaters" shall be eliminated by the year 2050 by means of limited wars, organized epidemics of fatal rapid-acting diseases and starvation. Until the world's population reaches a manageable level of 1 billion.

All essential and non-essential pharmaceutical products, doctors, dentists and health care workers will be registered in the central computer data bank and no medicine or medical care will be prescribed without express permission of regional controllers responsible for each city, town and village.

No central bank save the bank of International Settlement and the World Bank shall be allowed to operate. Private banks will be outlawed. "Bank of International Settlements" dominates the scene, private banks are fast disappearing in preparation for the "Big Ten Banks" that will control banking the world over under the guidance of "BIS" and the "IMF". There shall be no wage disputes allowed, nor any diversion...Those who break the law will be executed.

There shall be no cash or coinage in the hands of non-elite. All transactions shall be carried out by means of a debit card (Finally by "micro chip plantation"). *The cards of outlaws will be suspended. Such persons will find when they go to make purchases, that their card is blacklisted and they will not be able to obtain any services. Attempt to trade "old" coins shall be treated as a capital crime and subject to death penalty. Out laws who fail to surrender to the police or military after a declared- period of time, shall have a former family member selected at random, to serve prison terms in their stead.*

Rival factions and groups such as Arabs and Jews and African tribes shall have differences magnified and allowed to wage wars of extermination against each other under the eyes of NATO and UN observers. *The same tactics will be used in Central and South Asia, Sikhs, Muslim Pakistanis, and the Hindu Indians. These wars of attrition shall take place BEFORE the take-over of the One World Government". (10-161-9)*

Another research discloses:

"The third World War is to be fomented by using the so-called controversy; agents of the Illuminati would stir up between political Zionists and the leaders of the Muslim world. *That war is to be directed in such a manner that all of Arab, and political Zionism, Israel, will destroy each other. While, at the same time the* *remaining nations, once more divided on this issue, will be forced to fight them-selves into a state of complete exhaustion-physically, mentally, spiritually and economically. The stage will be set to put the One-World-Government into operation. (The History of Illuminati-Myron Fagan)*

The policy of the Third-World-War has long been established. In fact it was established along with the blueprint of 1st World war. That if necessary second and third world wars will be orchestrated to achieve the target of One-World-Government! The Second World War target has been achieved, and the Third has to come yet and seems inevitable! If you are following news of these days (November 2000) you can clearly notice that the media is gradually portraying "Israel" as a villain, showing the killings of innocent Palestinians. Israeli soldiers have been killing innocent civilians in Palestine for last 50 years, but it was always concealed or ignored by the media, now it attended and vastly displayed---why---? This is a slow process as always is the case with the "Brotherhood". These news will be used as an evidence to reason the Third World War between Muslims and Jews. However, such a war, has clearly been predicted by our Prophet Muhammad (PBUH) in the signs of Qayamah:

Allah's Apostle said, "The Hour will not be established until you fight with the Jews, and the stone behind which a Jew will be hiding will say: 'O Muslim there is a Jew hiding behind me, so kill him". (Sahih Al-Bukhari, Hadith 4.177)

Allah's Apostle (peace be upon him) said: The Last Hour would not come unless the Muslims will fight against the Jews and the Muslims would kill them until the Jews would hide themselves behind a stone or a tree and a stone or a tree would say: Muslim. or the servant of Allah, there is a Jew behind me; come and kill him; but the tree "Gharqad" would not say, for this is the tree of the Jews. (Sahih Muslim, Hadith 6985)

"Genetic Bomb" is already achieved. Jews (Bani-Israel), being the only racial religion in the world can be predicted as an only target of this destructive weapon; that attacks a certain gene. This seems the reason for a total wipe out of the Jews (Wallaho-Aalam).

A leaflet by the name of "The New Millennium" distributed door to door, shows the statistics of the future deaths. According to its figures taken from different surveys, pollution, sickness and poverty is going to cause unimaginable number of deaths. Figures about future war are more devastating:

"Violence within (various lands) could reach unprecedented levels. Generated by ethnic, tribal and religious (divisions)...such violence will form ...the most common type of conflict in the next quarter century...killing hundreds of thousands of people each year". ("New World Coming: American Security in the 21st Century". U.S. Commission on national security/21st Century)

Interestingly this leaflet is from a "Biblical Organization". The layout of the leaflet is sympathizing but in fact this is a pre-brainwashing for their future plans, to introduce people with the "creation" of the problem. This is going on through every source. The worst thing is that general public is---numb---! They don't care any more. What they have in their plate is enough. People are on that stage that they don't want to even think about any body else's problem.

We have discussed Parvez Musharraf (chief Executive of Pakistan). In his recent speeches on the border of India and Pakistan he has declared an effective response to India's aggression. "Putine" the Russian President made a speech on a visit to India following the purchase of Russian aircrafts, India has made. In his speech he threatened any disorder to the Indian line-of-control with a severe response.

Atal Bihari Vajpie, the Indian Prime Minister also delivered a similar statement on this occasion, which is usual. The shocking bit was the phrase they both used in their speeches alike, and that was:

"We are working for a New-World-Order!" (BBC News 5/10/00)

A program on BBC 1, called "The Future Wars", showed the exercises of U.S. Army. These exercises were carried out in South Carolina. In these exercises the army soldiers were practicing how to get control of a city, divided into two groups fighting with each other.

That means: U.S. or UN will come into war after, when it has been decided or near to a decision and take over the control of the cities, indulged in civil war.

Among many other signs of Qayamah, which we will discuss thoroughly in the next chapter Insha-Allah, yet we have come across another one, which we find appropriate to discuss here:

"The economic system shall be based upon the ruling oligarchical class allowing just enough foods and services to be produced to keep the mass slave labour camps going".

"In this manner the non-elite masses will be reduced to the level and behaviour of controlled animals with no will of their own and easily regimented and controlled".

The Hadith clearly defines the time, when these people will inhibit the earth:

*"...I heard Allah's Apostle (peace be upon him) as saying**: Only the wicked people will survive and they will be as careless as birds with the characteristics of beasts.** They will never appreciate good nor condemn evil. Then Satan will come to them in human form, and would say; don't you respond? They will say; what do you order us to do? He will command them to worship the idols but**, in spite of this, they will have an abundance of sustenance and lead comfortable lives**. Then the trumpet will be blown and he who hears it will bend his neck to one side and raise it from the other side..." (Sahih Muslim Hadith 7023, narrated by Abdullah Ibn Amr)*

The book "Conspirators' Hierarchy" was published in1992, it must have been an effort of years research. Until now many foretold satanic scenarios have come true and forced "lawfully" by democratic governments. Others are on the way in guise of moral, humanitarian and health care grounds:

Women will be degraded through the continued process of "women's liberation" movements. Free sex shall be mandatory.

Failure to comply at least once by the age of twenty shall be punishable by severe reprisals against her person. Self-abortion shall be taught and practiced after two children are born to a woman; such records shall be contained in the personal file of each woman in the One World Government's regional computers. If a woman falls pregnant after she has previously given birth to two children, she shall be forcibly removed to an abortion clinic for such an abortion, and sterilization to be carried out.

This seems a far future plan, but it is not! In fact it is well on the way in UK by sympathetic health authorities that, are concerned about--- **"OUR CHILDREN":**

Mass genetic testing of pregnant women on the way

A NATIONAL genetic testing programme for pregnant women is being set up in a move that could lead to mass screening of the population.

*New guidance has been sent to health authorities telling them to offer a range of genetic tests to pregnant women who could be carrying a disorder. They have also been advised that **counselling about an abortion should be given** as a matter of course if the foetus is found to be abnormal.*

The recommendations, drawn up by the government's "Advisory Committee on Genetic Testing", call for a dramatic expansion in the number of women tested on the National Health Service.
Every body with a family history of illness and ethnic groups more susceptible to particular disorders should be tested automatically. *(The Daily Telegraph. 11/3/2000)*

This is just the beginning of "Eugenics", which will be fully enforced in the near future. At the time when the book (Conspirators' Hierarchy) was published in 1992, this all seemed very fictitious and ridiculous. Now this is happening!

To describe and disclose each and every conspiracy of Freemasonry and the organisations that carried on these conspiracies or their future planning will take millions of pages to write and read. Each organisation deserves a whole book, however; some of the secret organisations and societies are vital to discuss, as they have a direct effect on general public and future of humanity's own existence. For a full view of their network please see the chart. Remember this is only a brief introduction to their vast activities.

COMMITTEE OF 300

This Committee is the direct subordinate of Freemasonry along with "Global Elite", "Black Nobility" and "Illuminati". Committee of 300 gets its works done through "Club of Rome", "Skull & Bones" and other secret societies, which are at the 4th level from the top, so can other 3rd level organizations. As I said this is a complicated network yet very individual and secretive. Members of different societies work on the same project through **"Compartmentalization"**, which means: "you should only know what is sufficient for your job". A big project is broken down into different phases and given to various departments. Departments don't know the part of machine they are preparing fits into which machine or even what will the whole machine look like or used for. This system is used in U.S. army, NASA and all scientific projects as well as in all secret societies and intelligence agencies. Just like "Jesuit's Oath"!

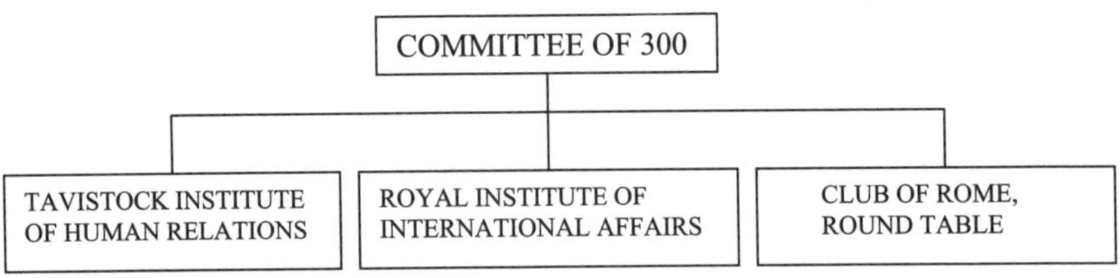

With the arm branches like these, "Committee of 300" directly influence's or owns 166 different institutions and sub-organizations including "Arab Bureau", "Arab Higher Committee" and "Asian Research Institute". This Committee is known to have been existing for 150 years and is a direct descendent of the "Council of 300" which was the policy body for "British East India Company" and activated the "Opium trade" in China.

"The BEIC is gone but the descendants of the Council of 300 linger on in the membership of the Committee of 300". (10-116)

There are at least 40 known branch offices of this committee. "P2" was the Italian Masonic Lodge, which apparently on papers was separated from the main body of (Aluminised) Freemasonry (4th level) 4 years prior to the murder of "Aldo Moro". The leader of Italian Democratic Party, Aldo Moro was five times Premier of Italy, who was responsible for the economic and industrial progress of Italy. After his murder, "Guerzoni", a close associate of Moro, testified in open court that Henry Kissinger, was the man responsible for Aldo Moro's assassination. Dr. Coleman writes:

"Thanks to the sworn testimony of Guerzoni, Italy and Europe, but not the U.S. learned that Kissinger was behind the death of Aldo Moro". (10-8)

Henry Alfred Kissinger the former "Mr President of the United States", is a member of the "Club of Rome", the "Council on Foreign Relations-CFR" and an important agent of "Royal Institute for International Affairs-RIIA". This Mr. President is the same man responsible for threatening "Zulfiqar Ali Bhutto" the Prime Minister of Pakistan to reverse the nuclear program otherwise---!

George Bush the American President during "Gulf War", a personal friend of "Saddam Hussein" is also a *member of "Committee of 300", (10-244).* George Bush is the one who ordered the brutal slaying of 150,000 Iraqi troops, in a convoy of military vehicles, carrying white flags, on their way back to Iraq under "Geneva Convention" rules of agreed disengagement and withdrawal. He is also responsible for ordering to bury 12,000 Iraqi soldiers-------alive-------!

Bush did not deliver these orders as "Mr President of the United States", rather carried these orders as a "Humble Servant" to the "Committee of 300"!

Bush is also responsible on behalf of the "Committee of 300" to drop the bombs with "atomic radiation warheads" on Iraq during the "Gulf War". These bombs are still emitting atomic radiations! Because the UN has put a restriction on Iraq to clear the battlefields, this radiation: is carried through contaminated sand, and 34-40 people are dying of cancer in **only one hospital** every month! Children are born disfigured! Altogether 4,000 Iraqi children under the age of five are dying every month! According to an official report: "Half of the population can be effected by the uranium, present in weapons"! The contaminated sand is carried through permanently blowing wind in all directions! To make sure of their death; UN has prohibited "Vaccine" in Iraq, as it "could" be used in chemical weapons! The aid from different countries of a billion and a half is on hold and not being let delivered!

According to the UN's own reports: "24,000 combat missions have been carried out which dropped 36,000 bombs between May 1998 and 1999, at a cost of £60 million (of your money), half of the casualties were civilians".

Surprisingly these attacks were not even authorised by UN, or as they say. The number of people died during these sanctions and combats; has exceeded the number killed by two atom bombs on Japan! The world still mourns about 6 million Jews, killed in Germany. All these figures were tallied with the ITV program "Paying the Price" showed on March the 6th 2000.

George Bush is responsible for all these inhuman monstrous acts, so is the Committee of 300, so is Freemasonry--- so are you and I--- for letting this happen!

ILLUMINATI

Founded by "Adam Weishaupt", in 1760s, who was a Catholic priest but defected from the Catholic Church. Sponsored by the "international bankers" he organized "Illuminati". This secret society openly opposed church and nullified all communities of Christianity, Talking about the church reforms, Britannica states:

"The political and social prerogatives of the church were also threatened by the 'Enlightenment', especially when it was allied with the expanding claims of an 'autocratic enlightened despotism'. The brotherhood taught by such groups as the Freemasons, members of secret fraternal societies, and the ***Illuminati,*** *a rationalistic secret society, provided a rival to the Catholic sense of community". (16)*

Illuminati is also known as **"Moriah Conquering Wind"** and **"Mumma Group"** by her sister society, the "Committee of 300"!

"Interest in the French Revolution was enhanced by the waning of the reformist impulse of the 1780s in the Italian states. During the 1780s, Masonic lodges had begun to replace the scholarly academies and agrarian societies emerged, modelled after the Illuminati (Enlightened Ones) founded in Bavaria by Adam Weishaupt, a professor of canon law, which promoted free thought and democratic political theories". (16)

These were the same schools and academies, of Europe, praised by the Muslim world, that "Ottoman Turks" sent their future ruling class to seek "knowledge" and "Modern Education" from. These academies are no different today! They are still brainwashing our future ruling class!

Weishaupt was defected from the Church in 1760, and soon he started a project with satanic plan to dominate the world. He officially completed this plan on May-1-1776; this day was called "May Day". This "May Day" is celebrated in many countries with different legacies, somewhere it is called bank holiday somewhere labourer's day, peasant's day and so on, but this is the reality behind the "bank holiday of the 1st May".

In the mottoes this society is no different to "Jesuits". The main mark of the plan was the destruction of all existing-governments and religions. This target was to be achieved by dividing masses of people into opposing camps via economic, racial, religious, language and political issues, provide them with arms and ammunition; thus increase the enmity and decrease the unity. The main points of Weishaupt's plan are:

1- *Monetary and sex bribery was to be used to obtain control of men already in high places in the various levels of all governments and other fields of endeavour* [Are these teachings of a religious sect?]. *Once influential persons had fallen for the lies, deceits and temptations of the Illuminati, they were to be held in bondage by application of political and other forms of blackmail. Threats of financial ruin, public exposure, and physical harm: even death to them-selves and loved members of their families.*

2- *The Illuminati who were on the faculty of colleges and universities were to cultivate students possessing exceptional mental ability and who belonged to well-bred families with international leanings, and recommended them for special training in Internationalism. Such training was to be provided by granting scholarships, like the "Rhodes Scholarship", to those selected by the Illuminati. All such scholars were to be first persuaded and then convinced that men of special talent and brains had the right to rule those less gifted on the grounds that the masses do not know what is best for them physically, mentally and spiritually.* [This is how a future ruling class is prepared for every country]

3- *All influential people who were trapped to come under the control of the Illuminati, plus the students who had been specially educated and trained, were to be used as agents and placed behind the scenes of all governments as experts and specialists. They would advise the top executives to adopt the policies, which would, in the long run, serve the secret plans of the Illuminati's one world conspiracy. And bring about the destruction of the governments and religions they were elected or appointed to serve.*

4- *They were to obtain absolute control of the press so that all news and information could be slanted to convince the masses that a 'One-World-Government' is the only solution to our many and varied problems. They were also to own and control all the national radio and TV channels! (The History of Illuminati, Myron Fagan)*

Main groups of newspapers in different countries are owned or "strictly observed" by "Brotherhood". Behind newspapers, national TV channels or satellite, are the same faces. For example "The Times" believed to be the most trusted newspaper with a high standard of authentic news sources all over the world, *is owned by "News International" which also owns 40% shares in "BSky B" (The Times London 7-10-99). "News International"* itself is a big group that owns many other newspapers and magazines.

News agencies on national level control news in every country. These agencies are responsible to, and monitored by, the "International News Agency" which is an offshoot of brotherhood. That is why there is so much confusion in the world.

Hundreds of organizations are working under this Dajjalic system completing different tasks. One of the examples is "MK Ultra" (please see MK Ultra). Once again I must say that to disclose all their conspiracies will take millions of pages to write and read. However, this little program (MK Ultra) carried on, on behalf of the state for public benefit, will give you merely a glimpse of scenario, that how we are being lead into a total darkness---unaware---!

SHRINERS

I have already exposed the intentions of "Freemasonry" taking care of our children, spreading forms of evil, i. e. pornography, Sodomy, anything and everything for Satan, against the command of Allah.

They want to originate a generation that has no categorization between good and evil. If there is no sensitivity of sin: sin does not exist any more. We only know sin because we are educated about the good and evil.

To brainwash the world is a long-term plan, for that one has to start from children, toddlers and infants. To interest children you have to amuse them, to amuse them you have to entertain them to their standards, physically, mentally and morally.

What else could be appropriate other than hospitals for children, circuses, funfairs and singing clowns? That is how, "Shriners" are designed!

Freemasonry may not be "so" corrupt at the lower degrees. The actual Freemasonry starts when one is raised and the "Word" is whispered into his ears. This is the "initiation" or "raising" of a "32nd degree Mason" in the "Scottish Rite" or a "3rd degree Knights Templar" in "York Rite".

"Shriners" is an organisation only for Freemasons who are either 32nd degree or Knights Templars. "Shrine" is reward for the followers of Dajjal, for people who devoted their entire lives for cause of the "Craft" and now they are free to act for Dajjal, with Freemasonry backing them up.

I quote their history from their own version:

"The Shrine, or more properly the Ancient Arabic Order of the Nobles of the Mystic Shrine (A.A.O.N.M.S.), was founded in New York City in 1872 by Billy Florence, an actor, and Walter Fleming, a physician. The idea was to create a society that would provide a fun outlet. As they were both 32nd degree masons, they envisioned it as an extension to this body, which elaborates on the basic tenets of Freemasonry. As it stands today, a man must first be a Mason in order to become a Shriner.

In setting up the new society, Fleming and Florence realized it needed a colorful exciting backdrop. As the legend goes, Fleming attended a party in Marseilles, France, hosted by an Arabian diplomat. At the end of the party, the guests became members of a secret society. Florence realized this might be the ideal vehicle for the new fraternity, and he made copious notes and drawings of the ceremony. When Florence returned to the States, Fleming agreed and together they created the elaborate rituals, designed the emblem and costumes, and formalized the salutation. Though the Shrine is not itself a secret society, it still retains much of the mysticism and secrecy of its origins.

As part of the requirements for membership, Florence and Fleming decided that all members must be either a 32nd degree Scottish Rite Mason or a Knights Templar York Rite Mason. These groups are concordant bodies of Freemasonry, which is the oldest and most widely known fraternity in the world. It dates back hundreds of years to when stonemasons and other craftsmen on building projects gathered in shelter houses or lodges.

The basic unit of Masonry is the Blue Lodge, where members earn the first three Masonic degrees. ***There is no higher degree than that of Master Mason but for those who wish to further explore the allegory and symbolism learned in the Blue Lodge, the Scottish Rite and York Rite elaborate on the basic tenets of Freemasonry.***

Charity was a part of the Shrine almost from the beginning, but over the years Shriners kept looking for something more as an even greater purpose. In 1920 the organization voted to adopt its own official philanthropy, dedicated to providing free orthopaedic medical care to children in need, and the first Shriners Hospital was built in Shreveport, La., in 1922. There is never a charge to the patient, parent or any third party for any service or treatment received at any of the hospitals. The Shrine's philanthropy now consists of 22 "Centers of Excellence" including three Shriners Burn Institutes.

This is just a brief synopsis of the History of the Shrine. For more detail on both the Shrine and its philanthropy, you can go to the Shrine page at the Shriner's HQ Web Page". ***(Emphases added)***

www.al-azhar.ab.ca/shrine.htm

Question rises that why do they mention an *"Arabian diplomat"* the host of the party and do not mention his name in any quotation, yet the name of the other two founders is mentioned. The answer is in "Psychology".

In case there comes, another "Friday the 13th", this time Muslims should be blamed for child molestation.

For this purpose the name Shrine and Shriners are chosen carefully because they are used in Muslim terminology.

For this purpose al-azhar is used as the name of the website.

For this purpose they wear Fez (Turkish Hat) in their rituals and gatherings.

For this purpose they have got an open help line for missing, abandoned and sick children.

For this purpose Freemasonry has used excessive number of Muslim names and terms for their Shrines and on some occasions word "Mosque" for their Temples.

"With the first Divan they are shown in the large framed picture in the entrance to the Mosque".

"In 1966 the Jackson Street Mosque was destroyed by fire and we moved to the Hotel Jayhawk". (Arab Shrine History)

For those who have an access to the inter-net I have quoted their web-site above, I quote it here again (www.al-azhar.ab.ca), go and explore it yourself and you will find out a lots of other things.

Those who don't have an access to the inter-net I am listing their hospitals.

SEARCH
Tell a friend!

Home | Shrine | Shriners Hospitals | Hospital Directory | What's New
Patient Success Stories | Patient Education | Prevention | Research
For Shriners Only | Message Board | Imperial Potentate's Message | Archives

Shriners Hospitals Directory

If you know of a child Shriners Hospitals might be able to help, please call our toll-free patient referral line: In the U.S.: **1-800-237-5055**. In Canada: **1-800-361-7256**.

Shriners Hospital-Boston (burn) Job listing (Last updated April 03, 2001)	51 Blossom St. Boston, MA 02114 617-722-3000
Shriners Hospital-Canada (orthopaedic)	1529 Cedar Ave. Montreal, Quebec, Canada H3G 1A6 514-842-4464
Shriners Hospital-Chicago (orthopaedic and spinal cord injury) Job listing (Last updated March 23, 2001)	2211 N. Oak Park Ave. Chicago, IL 60707 773-622-5400
Shriners Hospital-Cincinnati (burn)	3229 Burnet Ave. Cincinnati, OH 45229-3095 513-872-6000
Shriners Hospital-Erie (orthopaedic)	1645 W. 8th St. Erie, PA 16505 814-875-8700
Shriners Hospital-Galveston (burn) Job listing (Last updated April 02, 2001)	815 Market St. Galveston, TX 77550-2725 409-770-6600
Shriners Hospital-Greenville (orthopaedic)	950 West Faris Road Greenville, SC 29605-4277 864-271-3444
Shriners Hospital-Honolulu (orthopaedic) Job listing (Last updated March 27, 2001)	1310 Punahou St. Honolulu, HI 96826-1099 808-941-4466

Shriners Hospital-Houston (orthopaedic) Job listing (Last updated April 11, 2001)	6977 Main Houston, TX 77030-3701 713-797-1616
Shriners Hospital-Intermountain (orthopaedic)	Fairfax Road at Virginia Street Salt Lake City, UT 84103 801-536-3500
Shriners Hospital-Lexington (orthopaedic)	1900 Richmond Rd. Lexington, KY 40502 606-266-2101
Shriners Hospital-Los Angeles (orthopaedic) Job listing (Last updated March 30, 2001)	3160 Geneva St. Los Angeles, CA 90020 213-388-3151
Shriners Hospital-Mexico City (orthopaedic)	Suchil No. 152, Col. El Rosario Delg. Coyoacan, 04380 Mexico, D.F., Mexico 011-525-618-1120
Shriners Hospital-Northern California (orthopaedic, burn and spinal cord injury)	2425 Stockton Blvd. Sacramento, CA 95817 916-453-2000
Shriners Hospital-Philadelphia (orthopaedic and spinal cord injury) Job listing (Last updated April 06, 2001)	3551 North Broad Street Philadelphia, PA 19140 215-430-4000
Shriners Hospital-Portland (orthopaedic) Portland Hospital's Web site: http://www.shcc.org	3101 S.W. Sam Jackson Park Road Portland, OR 97201-5090 503-241-5090
Shriners Hospital-Shreveport (orthopaedic) Job listing (Last updated March 29, 2001)	3100 Samford Ave. Shreveport, LA 71103 318-222-5704
Shriners Hospital-Spokane (orthopaedic)	911 W. Fifth Ave. Spokane, WA 99204-2901 509-455-7844
Shriners Hospital-Springfield (orthopaedic) Job listing	516 Carew St. Springfield, MA 01104 413-787-2000

(Last updated April 06, 2001)	
Shriners Hospital-St. Louis (orthopaedic)	2001 S. Lindbergh Blvd. St. Louis, MO 63131-3597 314-432-3600
Shriners Hospital-Tampa (orthopaedic)	12502 North Pine Dr. Tampa, FL 33612-9499 813-972-2250
Shriners Hospital-Twin Cities (orthopaedic)	2025 E. River Parkway Minneapolis, MN 55414 612-596-6100

April 05, 2001

Please take a moment to let us know what you think about our site. Thanks!
If you'd like to be notified when this Web site is updated, you can join our mailing list.

Home | Shrine | Shriners Hospitals | Hospital Directory | What's New
Patient Success Stories | Patient Education | Prevention | Research
For Shriners Only | Message Board | Imperial Potentate's Message | Archives

International Shrine Headquarters
2900 Rocky Point Dr.
Tampa, FL 33607-1460
813-281-0300

For you---O---Muslims I am listing further the names of their Shrines:

- - - LINKS - - -

- - - LINKS - - -

Shrine H.Q. and Shriners Hospitals

The International Shrine Clown Association

Aahmes Temple
Abba Temple
Abdallah Temple
Abou Saad Temple
Acacia Temple
Afifi Temple
Ahmed Temple
Ainad Temple
Akdar Temple
Al Amin Temple
Al Aska Temple
Al Bahr Temple
Al Bedoo Temple
Al Kader Temple
Al Kaly Temple
Al Koran Temple
Al Malaikah Temple
Al Menah Temple
Al Shamal Temple
Al Sihah Temple
Alcazar Temple
Aleppo Temple
Algeria Temple
Alhambra Temple
Ali Ghan Temple
Alladin Temple
Aloha Temple
Alzafar Temple
Amara Temple
Amran Temple
Anah Temple
Anezeh Temple
Ansar Temple
Antioch Temple
Arab Temple
Araba Temple
Arabia Temple
Ararat Temple
Bahia Temple
Barak Temple
Bedouin Temple
Beja Temple
Bektash Temple

Ben Ali Temple
Ben Hur Temple
Beni Kedem Temple
Boumi Temple
Cairo Temple
Crescent Temple
Damascus Temple
Egypt Temple
El Bekal Temple
El Hasa Temple
El Jebel Temple(Site 2)
El Kahir Temple
El Kalah Temple
El Katif Temple
El Maida Temple
El Riad Temple
El Zaribah Temple
Gizeh Temple
Hadi Temple
Hadji Temple
Hasan Temple
Hejaz Temple
Hella Temple
India Temple
Isis Temple
Jaffa Temple
Jericho Temple
Joppa Temple
Kaaba Temple
Kalurah Temple
Karnak Temple
Kazim Temple
Kena Temple
Kerbala Temple
Khedive Temple
Khiva Temple
Kismet Temple
Kora Temple
Korein Temple
Lu Lu Temple
Luxor Temple
Marzuq Temple
Mazol Temple

Media Temple
Medinah Temple
Melha Temple
Midian Temple
Mizpah Temple
Mocha Temple
Moila Temple
Morocco Temple
Moslah Temple
Moslem Temple
Murat Temple
Nile Temple
Nur Temple
Oasis Temple
Osiris Temple
Osman Temple
Palestine Temple
Philae Temple
Pyramid Temple
Rajah Temple
Rameses Temple
Rizal Temple
Sabbar Temple
Sahara Temple
Sahib Temple
Salaam Temple
Scimitar Temple
Sudan Temple
Syrian Temple
Tebala Temple
Tehama Temple
Tehran Temple
Tigris Temple
Tripoli Temple
Tunis Temple
Wahabi Temple
Yaarab Temple
Zamora Temple
Zelzah Temple
Zenobia Temple
Ziyara Temple
Zuhrah Temple

Grand Lodge of Alberta

Scottish Rite of Canada

O you! who read! wake up---your---"Kaaba"---and---"Al-Koran" have been named as---Temples---shrines---!

CHILDREN'S ORGANS

To understand human brain functions, Brotherhood has used innocent children as guinea pigs without their parents' consent. This practice carried on for twenty years in only one hospital in UK. Finally when the news leaked out, first Liverpool's "Alder Hey Children's Hospital" denied any such possibility all together. The constant struggle of 146 families (parents of children) proved hospital's guilt and hospital had to admit that they kept certain organs. Finally the hospital admitted:

"It has found 146 cerebella (approximately 10 per cent of the brain). They were taken for use, by a student who was comparing the weight of children's brains for his Ph.D. the study was never published." (Metro Wednesday, August 16 2000)

What does this tell you? Was a Ph.D., more important then 146 children? Who was that special student that was above all the laws and human values and who researched for long 20 years for his Ph.D.? It was never revealed! All brain tissues were returned to children's parents. Parents had to undergo the agony of a second burial of their already buried children.

But still this was not enough---after some time more brain tissues were found which were purposely hidden and not returned. This increased the traumatic situation. More devastation---more pain. Parents started preparing for a third burial of---innocent children. More comfort was required---This time in a joint statement issued by the "Alder Hey NHS Trust and the university" they admitted:

"This tissue, had been stored separately as the subject of a research study". (Metro Wednesday, August 16 2000)

Amazingly, even this time the Hospital together with NHS Trust was---lying---! On 26-01-2001, finally they admitted:

"Selling children's organs to private organizations". (BBC1 Breakfast News)

Who are these private organizations that are above the law and human values? Were these, the only cerebellums left with them or they have some more stored? Well there was still more to it.

The final episode came on Wednesday January 31 2001 when a Dutch Pathologist "Dick van Velzen" was made an escape goat. He was named:

"The Baby Butcher"

He stole their hearts, brains, lungs, kidneys, livers, eyes, stomachs...everything but their souls. ." " More then 100,000 organs---including brains, hearts and lungs---body parts and entire bodies of stillborn babies were taken...Some children were buried as complete shells."(The Mirror Wednesday, January 31, 2001)

It seems very Masonic---only one person responsible for so much---This is exactly what Mary Allen---who lost her 18-month old daughter Kathleen 10 years ago---said:

"I have no doubt that van Velzen is an evil. But to blame this all on one man is outrageous. Other people have known what was going on at Alder Hey. Successive governments are to blame for letting this continue." (The Mirror Wednesday, January 31, 2001)

After providing various evidences in medical profession, Martin Short reaches the conclusion:

"Masonic yearbooks billow with the names of doctors and surgeons. Just two of Surrey's most prestigious lodges, the St George's (No.370) and the Surrey (No.416), together boast some nineteen Past Masters who are medical men, including 13 surgeons. Almost all London teaching hospitals have their own lodges, including 'Bart's', 'St Mary's', St Thomas's', 'King's College', the London and Westminster." (Inside the Brotherhood. By, Martin short P-354)

This is only London he is talking about. Freemasonry has approximately 10,000 Lodges in the UK. The law of human embryo cloning has been passed from the Parliament in January 2001. Amazingly those who opposed this bill were announced to public and those who favoured were not. Professor Winston was only brought to light because he openly favoured the cloning and not because he was disclosed.

MK ULTRA

There is an abandoned park (at least looks like a park) in Montreal, Canada. Its gates are closed to public, though this is a public park, still there is an all round fence preventing public from entering in it. Inside the park an old building can be seen, which does not look much from outside and can go unnoticed at a glance, just like Roslyn Chapel. That is the purpose for its dull structure, because this is where one of the most dangerous 'official', mind-manipulating U.S. game was set, the 'MK ULTRA'. 'M' stands for mind and 'K' stands for kontroll, taken from German spellings, deference to Nazi Eugenic Program.

This project was carried out through "RAND", the "Research and Development Corporation":

"RAND is THE think tank most beholden to 'Tavistock Institute' and certainly the 'RIIA's' most prestigious vehicle for control of United States policies at every level".
(10-240)

Ewen Cameron was the scientist who headed this project, at least officially. He was heavily funded by Rockefellers, and was in constant touch with the CIA and had regular meetings with Allen Dulles; then head of the CIA, Ewen Cameron was code-named as Dr White.

Beside, many people know about different kind of new technologies, but don't actually know, how these technologies have played a part to mentally enslave them, by the elite bosses. Accidents don't just happen; they are carefully planned and orchestrated in view of the after effects.

Murder of JFK is a fine example of MK ULTRA; his supposed killer was murdered afterwards to skip the inquiries and to close the file. Many eyewitnesses have reported that he was in a constant form of trance. If he was the one who shot JFK, then impact should have pushed Kennedy sidewise. Videos clearly show that Kennedy was pushed backwards, which proves that the bullet is shot from the front, and who was sitting on the front? His own bodyguard! More over, the car ahead Kennedy's had four guards surrounding it but his car was not guarded at all. Why?

Helmeth Scheerer the former CIA man from 1957 to 1975 believes the murder as well as the murderer's trial was a set-up and the actual story was never told or disclosed.

After Kennedy was killed, despite all the uproars, the case was closed. This was very devastating for the public as well as for the Kennedy family. His brother Robert Kennedy took over the responsibility to stand up and fight for his brother's cause and to bring the case to a fair trial. He promised to open a reinvestigation to Kennedy's murder. This slogan provided for him an enormous popularity and his chances of winning the next elections, as President of USA increased. This was not the agenda of the Brotherhood; it left them with no choice but to get rid of Robert Kennedy. His supposed suspect was Sirhan Sirhan, a lone nutter. On June the 5th, 1968 Sirhan apparently came and opened fire on Robert Kennedy, which caused Robert's death, yet investigations show that, there were more bullets found on the wall then Sirhan had in his gun all together. Who shot the rest of the bullets? Angles of the bullets that cost Robert his life could not be shot from Sirhan's gun. Map of the scene shows that the guard, standing behind Sirhan was at the best place to shoot those bullets! Later investigations revealed that gunpowder was found on Sirhan's neck. This is exactly where the guard was standing. Bodyguard?

All proofs and evidence of the case confiscated by police and the only photos taken by an independent journalist were ceased. When public pressure compelled Police for the release of the photos, they had to release them, guess what? On the way to the press those photos were stolen from the Police car. What a joke!

The third prime example of MK ULTRA is the famous murder of John Lennon. His killer took it so easy that after killing Lennon he stood opposite side of the road reading the 'Catcher in the Rye' to give enough time to the guard (another guard) of the building, To come out side of the building to a phone box and call the Police. Still, the Killer would not move and patiently wait for his arrest. Another nutter! John Lennon's son is 100% sure that it was CIA's job, what even he does not know is that who is behind the CIA. To turn this fact into a fiction, Holly-Wood changed it into a film starring Bruce Willis and Julia Robert and named it "Conspiracy Theory". So they have done in "End of Days", starring "big Arnie". In "End of Days", they have shown "Templars" as a religious cult striving for 1,000 years to resist and fight the birth of "Anti Christ". The fact is vice-versa! They are the ones striving to pave the way for "Dajjal". It is Templars/Freemasons, who are "everywhere, unnoticed"! Holly Wood is one of the most sophisticated brainwashing equipment! Those who think it as voice of people---they are wrong! Holly Wood is the voice of Freemasonry, right from David W. Griffith, the American film pioneer, "The Birth of a Nation" (1915)----- to "Madonna" and "Michael Jackson".

"Cecil B. DeMille" the director of "Ten Commandments" and "Samson and Delilah"----Oliver Hardy of "Loral and Hardy" films. ----David Sarnoff the "President of the Radio Corporation of America" and the "father of American Television", he entered the "Craft in Strict observance" Lodge No 94, New York City in 1921, so appropriate with its name of "observance". ----Jack L. Warner the founder of "Warner Brothers", initiated in "Mount Olive Lodge" No 506, Los Angeles, California, in 1938----Darryl F. Zanuck, co-founder of "20th Century Productions" in 1933, which became "20th Century Fox" in 1935. Zanuck was a member of "Mount Olive Lodge" No 56, Los Angeles----The famous stars like "John Wayne", "Clark Gable" and many others were Freemasons. This place is not enough to list them all; however, it should be sufficient to give an idea to readers that how they dominate this industry and the "Holy-Wood" is not so "Holy"!

In fact Fraternity has manipulated entertainment for a long time. It was behind many famous legendary artists of the times:

"In 'The Magic Flute', the Austrian composer 'Wolfgang Amadeus Mozart' (who wrote his 'Requim Mass' in the same year) celebrated the Masonic alternative to the mass of the church". (16)

Robert Neasland from Stockholm went to a local hospital for a minor operation, after the operation he felt that his personality was changing, strange thoughts started coming in his mind, he also noticed that few people are secretly monitoring his movements. When situation got worse he went to have x-ray, which showed that in his right nostril there was a transmitter implanted. He got this transmitter removed privately and took it to a lab for examination; there he was told to come back in 10 days for the results. After 10 days, you can guess what happened, the transmitter was lost ('Beyond the Truth' showed on BBC).

Same was the case of the Oklahoma shooting in 1995. In this case, the culprit/victim was an ex- army soldier, he told many of his colleagues that he has been implanted with a chip during his hospital treatments but no one believed him, as usually happens in such cases. He said, he has been hearing voices in his head (another lone nutter?), but he was left alone to carry on the massacre. His former colleagues also reported that on the particular day, many people were told not to go to work (B/The Truth BBC).

All this information is kept well secret by the US-Army, the same army that is responsible for the world's peace. In Norway, the navy is the head quarters for all these scientific operations.

Admiral Slanfield Turner, then Director of the CIA, in 1977, publicly admitted that millions of dollars (of your money!) have been spent studying voodoo, witchcraft and psychic. At the Senate hearing on August the 3rd 1977, he admitted that CIA has been mind-controlling people without their consent. Still don't believe it? Read this!

Bill Clinton----yes---the US President, admitted in an open conference in 1995 that the US Government has been involved in mind controlling and other unethical experiments on public without their knowledge for the last fifty years--- (yes---fifty years) and is highly ashamed of it (I am sure!).

After this confession, MK ULTRA is sorting out its papers for public release, in other words, what is appropriate for the naive American public to know or not to know. It is believed that MK ULTRA has been stopped: but still an ex-project worker proved that the "High Frequency Microwave Beams" are emitting from the location (B/The Truth BBC). These HFM Beams can tune into any individual and he will hear voices in his head (creation of lone nutters?). If a person is chipped, it does not take much effort to manipulate him and in that trance he/she will be like a human robot. If; a person is a drug addict or with psychic history it is even easier to "kontroll" his mind. The subject can kill, rape, and open fire on the public.

It is also believed that TVs at home can be used as a tool to pass these signals. **"Short Vision"** is another successful experiment carried out by the manipulators. The moving picture that we see for one second on a screen i.e. TV or cinema: consists of around 45 photos. In other words 45 still photos make one second's moving image. If in between this one second---one still photo is shown, it only makes 45th part of a second, thus: not see-able with naked eye. Although it is not notice-able by a naked eye, it is noticed by our sub-conscious, which is sharper than our conscious, and it receives the message! Unknowingly we take inspirations from this message! An experiment; carried out in which they showed a bottle of Coca-Cola in short vision at a cinema house before break proved it effective when: majority of people bought Coca-Cola during the break! This technique is also used during the elections in developing countries. During elections, national TV stations cast their best programs people get glued in front of their TV sets. Within the transmissions elections are promoted, thus: creating people's interest in "Democracy" and in some cases short vision is used to "elect" a certain candidate. If you look back in early days of Democracy and TV, you will realise what I am talking about when elections were a big event on National TV channels. Now this agenda is taken over by satellite channels.

Another manipulation technique is called **"Back Tracking"**; this is when a record or cassette is played in reverse. This is where the actual message is hidden! What we hear is the forward play of the track, along with this is the track-message hidden in reverse which: our sub-conscious, de-code's and accepts. This message can be heard if we play the track backwards. To experience this manipulation: do it your self or listen to the audiocassette called "Shadows".

Every few months we hear stories of lone nutters in particularly America opening fire on public and now even in Europe. Dunblane school children were a satanic example of these mentally enslaved people or shall I say products of MK ULTRA?

Double Square

The double square, one square on top of another in any form, is more secret society symbolism. In the secret language, one square by itself means control of what is right and just. From this we get phrases like "fair and square" and a "square deal". One square on top of another means control of all that is right and all that is wrong, all that is just and all that is unjust, all that is positive and all that is negative. In other words "we control everything". The double square, or eight pointed star, can be seen in the lobby at the heart of the British Parliament and a long list of world police forces surround their badge with the same symbol.

The First Degree Tracing Board

The Second Degree Tracing Board

The Third Degree Tracing Board

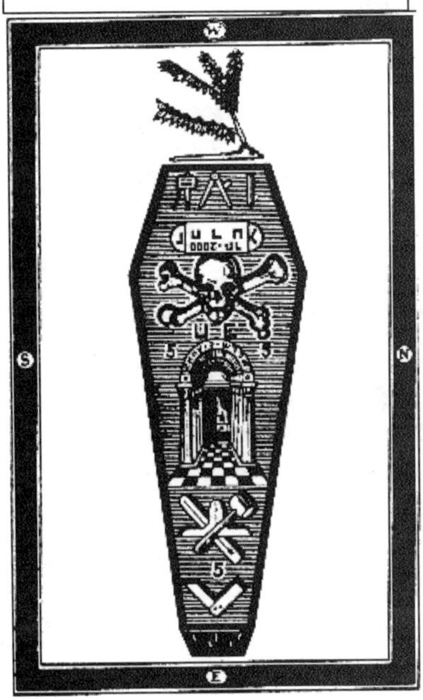

HRH Duke of Kent giving 3rd Degree Handshake

DAJJAL AND QAYAMAH

CH-22 AL-MASIH AD-DAJJAL

KNOWLEDGE OF THE HOUR

"They ask thee about the (final) Hour-when will be its appointed time? Say: 'The knowledge thereof is with my Lord (alone) none but He can reveal as to when it will occur. Heavy were its burden through the heavens and the earth. Only all of a sudden will it come to you'. They ask thee if thou wert eager in search thereof: say: 'The knowledge thereof is with God (alone), but most men know not.'" (Q- 7:187)

The knowledge of the "Judgement Day" is with Allah alone no Human being, Angel, Jinn or Shaytan knows about it. So far, many predictions of so-called anticipators have been proven wrong.

When Gabriel (AS) came to the Prophet (PBUH) in the guise of a Bedouin, and asked him about Islam, Iman and Ihsan; the Prophet (PBUH) answered his questions. But when he asked him about the Hour, he (PBUH) said:

"...The one questioned about it, knows no better than the questioner, but I will describe to you its portents. When the lady slave gives birth to her mistress, that will be of its portents; when the bare-footed naked people become the chiefs of the people, that will be of its portents." (Sahih Al-Bukhari 6.300 narrated by Abu Hurayra)

This Hadith is from Sahih Bukhari, which proves its authenticity. The Prophet Mohammad (PBUH) has told many other signs of Qayamah, which are recorded in form of his sayings by a chain of narrators: "the Hadith"! Some signs of Qayamah have been mentioned in Qur'an, and more in Hadith. **Dajjal (Anti Christ) has not been mentioned in Qur'an, by name, but only in Hadith,** he is too insignificant in the eyes of Allah. But on the other hand, this proves the authenticity of Hadith. Qur'an refers to certain signs before The Hour:

"...The day that certain of the signs of thy Lord do come, no good will it do to a soul to believe in them then, if it believed not before nor earned righteousness through its faith..." (Q-6: 158)

What these signs are, is explained in Hadith which we will explain Insha-Allah. One of them is "Al-Mahdi" and other is "Ad-Dajjal". Those who reject Hadith; also will have to reject Mahdi and Dajjal, thus refrain from allegiance to "Mahdi" (as he is also mentioned only in Hadith) and fall prey into "Dajjal's" hands.

Worthwhile is a quote from one of the self-made modern scholars, who in the pride of his own knowledge discarded these Ahadith as mere suspicions of Prophet Mohammad (PBUH). He wrote:

"Regarding these matters (Dajjal)*, the narrations of Prophet Mohammad (SAW) are in fact his (SAW) guesses, about these guesses he (SAW) was himself doubtful."*
(Rasael O Masael First Edition Sep 1951 p-55)

On page 57 he writes:

He (SAW) had doubts even in his own time that Dajjal may appear now or in the time near after him. But 1350 years have gone past; doesn't this prove that this was a suspicion in vain?

Wouldn't you like to know this scholar's name who considered, he had more knowledge than Prophet's (SAW)? In fact so much more that he could reject Prophet's Hadith on the basis of his own knowledge! He was the founder of "Jama'te Islami" in Pakistan, Maulana Modoodi!!!

We are only happy to announce that the present leader of "Jama'te Islami" has detached this organisation from Modoodi's claim. He also announced that "Jama'te Islami" is with "Ahle Sunnah Wal Jam'at" in Aqeeda (faith) about Dajjal.

As a Muslim, we all have to follow our Prophet Mohammad (PBUH) and his "Sunnah" (the practices, he established), to follow him and his "Sunnah", we have to know about him, to know about him, we have to know Hadith. This makes Hadith a vital element of our Iman (faith).

Among the greater and clear signs of Qayamah, the first one is Mahdi; he will come when human kind is in great tribulations. Second is Dajjal, who will come after Mahdi and spread mischief right and left. Third is Isa ibn Maryam (AS--Jesus), he will come after Dajjal and kill him. Fourth of the greater signs will be Ya'juj and Ma'juj (Gog and Magog). The scholars differ about the order of the rest of the other greater signs, which are:

The destruction of the Ka'bah.
The rising of the sun from the West.
The emergence of the Beast from the earth.
The smoke.
A wind that will take the soul of all believers.
The Qur'an will be taken up into heavens.
A fire will drive the people to their last gathering place.
The Trumpet will be blown.

I will describe as many signs of Qayamah as much Allah grants me ability. If anything is left because of my lack of knowledge, readers are requested to consult the books written by our great Islamic Scholars like Ibne- Kathir and others. To make it easy for readers I will quote only parts of Ahadith under different topics, which will clarify the only related subject. ("..."Means there is part of Hadith before/middle or after the quote. For complete Ahadith please read the Hadith books your-selves. All Ahadith are quoted from "The Alim CD", otherwise the name of the book is mentioned.)

AL-MAHDI

"Al-Mahdi" is the first among the greater signs of Qayamah after the Last Prophet Mohammad (PBUH). Prophet Mohammad (PBUH) was also one of the greater signs of The Day. Al-Mahdi will be only recognised by knowledgeable people. Others will either dispute or oppose him. Coming of Al-Mahdi is proved from Ahadith and Muslim scholars have no doubts concerning this.

"And what state you will be in when Ibn-e-Maryam (Isa, Jesus) will descend into you and your Imam will be from amongst you". (Narrated by Abu Hurairah. Sahih Bukhari Vol-1, p-490. Sahih Muslim Vol-1, p-87)

The Hadith above is a Mutawater (recurring) Hadith and there is no dispute in it. The eminent traditionist Badre Alam Madani writes:

"This is a prediction which all the prophets of Allah, from Noah to the last of the prophets had been telling and it is proved from the statement of the Prophet Mohammad (PBUH) that the graph of the evil up to that stage never occurred on earth. So it is necessary to believe that Antichrist is a central power. It was divine wisdom that a central be-faced by a central power." (Tarjuman Al-Sunnah Vol 3 P-562)

Ibne-Kathir mentions another Hadith in his book "Al-Badayah Wa-Nahayah":

"Hajjaj said that he heard Ali say, the Prophet (PBUH) said, 'even if there were only one day left for the world, Allah would send a man from among us to fill the world with justice, just it had been filled with oppression and injustice". (Ahmad Musnad Quote from 20-20)

This Hadith shows the definite coming of Al-Mahdi. In another Hadith:

"Abd Allah ibn al-Harith in Juz al-Zubaydi said, The Prophet (S) said, 'A people will come out of the East who will pave the way for Mahdi'" (Ibn Majah Kitab al-Fitan 3088 Quote from 20-22)

This means that there will be a group who will keep fighting and opposing the non-believers and paving the way for Al-Mahdi. Their struggle will be fruited by the leadership of Al-Mahdi.

Following Hadith gives the scenario of the time, when Al-Mahdi will come, and the mission he will complete. At that time Muslims will be oppressed and have disputes amongst each other. This Hadith also shows that Al-Mahdi will not claim himself to be Al-Mahdi but *"will be forced against his will"* to take up the lead of Muslims. So any one who claims him self to be Al-Mahdi is in fact a liar!

"The Prophet (peace be upon him) said: Disagreement will occur at the death of a caliph and a man of the people of Medina will come flying forth to Mecca. Some of the people of Mecca will come to him, bring him out against his will and swear allegiance to him between the Corner and the Maqam. An expeditionary force will then be sent against him from Syria but will be swallowed up in the desert between Mecca and Medina. When the people see that, the eminent saints of Syria and the best people of Iraq will come to him and swear allegiance to him between the Corner and the Maqam. Then there will arise a man of Quraysh whose maternal uncles belong to Kalb and send against them an expeditionary force; which will be overcome by them, and that is the expedition of Kalb. Disappointed will be the one who does not receive the booty of Kalb. He will divide the property, and will govern the people by the Sunnah of their Prophet (peace be upon him) and establish Islam on Earth. He will remain seven years, then die, and the Muslims will pray over him." (Sunan of Abu Dawood 4273 narrated by Umm Salamah)

As we see from the Hadith above that Al-Mahdi will establish the Law of Allah on earth and will be helped by Allah in destroying the enemies. So far all the people who have claimed to be Mahdi do not resemble even one bit of any prophecies about Al-Mahdi, and that stamps their false claim.

When pagans of Makkah heavily troubled our Prophet (PBUH), he was ordered to make Hijra (migration) from Makkah to Medina. From Medina he carried on the invitation and spread Islam. Al-Mahdi will reverse the Hijra (migration) process by migrating from Medina to Makkah, thus completing the cycle of Islam. He will enforce Shari'ah (Islamic Law) on earth and fill the earth with prosperity, just like Mohammad (PBUH) did.

Another Hadith tells not only Al-Mahdi's namebut his father's name will also be same as Prophet's (SAW) and his father's and again ascertains the completion of his mission.

"The Prophet said, 'if there were only one day left for the world, that day will be lengthened until a man from among my descendants or from among the people of my household, was sent. His name will be the same as my name and his father's name will be the same as my father's name. He will fill the earth with justice and fairness, just as it will have been filled with injustice and oppression...'" (Abu Dawood narrated by Abd Allah ibn Mas'ud Quote from 20-21)

According to some scholars he will be present when Ad-Dajjal appears and also be present when Isa ibn Maryam (Jesus AS) will descend from heaven. The following Hadith strengthens this idea, when Prophet (PBUH) was describing the tribulations, Dajjal will spread on the earth. Umm Sharik bint Abi'l- Akr said, "O Messenger of Allah, where will the Arabs be at that time"?

"...He said, at that time they will be few; most of them will be in Bayt al_maqdis (Jerusalem), and their Imam will be a righteous man. Whilst their Imam is going forward to lead the people in praying Salat al-Subh (the morning-prayer), Jesus son of Mary will descend..." (Ibn Majah Kitab al-Fitan 4077 Quote from 20-58)

DAJJAL (Antichrist)

First of all we will explain the meanings of "Dajjal", so it becomes easy to understand who actually Dajjal is! In Arabic, every word consists of a "root" that contains "three alphabets". The word "Dajjal" has a root of "D-J-L" or more appropriately "Da-Ja-La". In reading we will pronounce it as "Dajl", which means an ointment to patch up or to coat over the skin to hide a skin disease. When "Dajl" transforms into "Dajjal" this means "the one who hides the disease by patching it over" or in short and compact, "the impostor".

The basic faith (Aqeeda) about Ad-Dajjal (The Antichrist) according to the scholars of Ahle-Sunnah Wal-Jamaat", ordained by the companions of Prophet through their followers and their followers is stated in "Sahih Muslim":

"It has passed in the opening preface of this book and its commentary that Qazi says; the Ahadith, Imam Muslim has mentioned in context of Ad-Dajjal, are 'The Base' of the school of thought of Ahl-Al-Haq (the seekers of the righteousness). In the reality of Dajjal's existence that he in fact is a person. Through whom Allah will testify his pious and non-pious slaves. By granting Dajjal, powers of those powers, that Allah ultimately has. Such powers will be the ability to resurrect and bring back to life, those that Dajjal killed and from apparitions of the world such as miragified looks of paradise and hell. Dajjal's empowering on the treasures of the world. The ability to cause rain, 'Thus it will rain, and to grow, and it will'! Dajjal will have all the powers that will enable him to enact, with the powers of Allah and Allah's will.

Then Allah will disable him to do so; thus Dajjal will no longer have those powers. Then Dajjal's problems will multiply up to the point that Isa bin Maryam (Jesus) will kill him.

By this method, Allah will establish those who kept faith in Allah, in the path and the religion of Ahl-Al Sunnah. All Mohadithin, Fuqaha (jurists) and the far-sighted Muslims have this faith (Aqeedah) in contrast to the 'Khawarij', ' Jahmia', and most 'Mo'tazalia', who have likemindedly believed contrary to the Ahl-Al-Sunnah.

The above sects deny Dajjal's physical actualness and being. Their arguments are that these actualities are near to impossibility, due to these powers have been the miracles of prophets only. This is absolutely incorrect because Dajjal will not claim prophethood. The powers that will be in his possession will verify his claim of an even greater position, the claim of lord-ship or god-ship. Whilst he will be wrong in his claim with the apparantness of the situation that will occur. The deficiency of his powers and his inabilities will be evident, as Allah will take back his powers finally. The very powers that Allah enabled Dajjal in the first place.

The disability on Dajjal's face will also be a factor, which will appear to the believers who will see between his eyes the evidence of an unbeliever ("Ka Fa Ra") that will be written therein.

These will be the matters and problems that people of that time will endure through the calamities, which will split their hearts with the pace of such ferocious speed, that will paralyse minds." (Translation from Sahih Muslim Sharah of Imam Nawawi, p-399. Published by Saeed H M Company Adab Manzil, Karachi, Pakistan)

"Allah's Apostle said, "The Hour will not be established ...till thirty Dajjals (liars) appear, and each one of them will claim that he is Allah's Apostle..." (Sahih Al Bukhari 9.237 narrated by Abu Hurayra)

The Hadith above is explicit that not only there will be other Dajjals**in person** before "Al-Masih Ad-Dajjal", but also verifies that any one who claims to be a prophet after the Last Prophet Mohammad (PBUH) is a Dajjal. However, all these false prophets i.e. Musailma Kazzab, Baha-ullah, Mirza Ghulam Ahmad and the modern western prophets are not "The Dajjal", but only Dajjals.

WHO IS "AD-DAJJAL"? AND WHAT WILL HE LOOK LIKE?

There are many theories about the Dajjal (Anti Christ) itself. Some suggest America is the Dajjal, others believe Dollar is the Dajjal, having no doubt about their Dajjalic characteristics and donations towards paving the way for "Al-Masih Ad-Dajjal", they are not "Ad-Dajjal". "Al-Masih Ad-Dajjal (Anti Christ)" will be a man; he is described in Hadith as:

"...He (The Dajjal The Anti Christ) will be a young man with twisted, cropped hair, and a blind eye..." (Sahih Muslim 7015 narrated by An-Nawwas ibn Sam'an)

In the dream of Prophet Mohammad (PBUH) he was shown a vision of Dajjal while he (PBUH) was performing Tawaf around Ka'ba:

"...Man with a huge body, red complexion and curly hair and blind in one eye. His eye looked like a protruding out grape..." (Sahih Al Bukhari 9.242 narrated by Abdullah ibn Umar)

On the account of Tamim Dari, Prophet Mohammad (PBUH) described Ad-Dajjal as:

"...Well built person..." (Sahih Muslim 7208 narrated by Fatimah bint Qays)

In another Hadith Prophet (PBUH) said:

"...The word 'Kafir' (unbeliever) is written between his two eyes..." (Sahih Al Bukhari 9.505 narrated by Anas)

"...On his forehead will be written the word Kafir, and every believer, literate or illiterate, will be able to read it..." (Ahmad Masnad 3-367/368 Quote from 20-51)

These Ahadith clearly describe the personality of "Al-Masih Ad-Dajjal". According to these Ahadith:

Al-Masih Ad-Dajjal will be a young man.
He will be a well-built person with a huge body.
He will have red complexion.
His hair will be curly/twisted and cropped (cut very short).
He will be blind from one eye.
His one eye will be like a protruding grape (out of socket). Either this eye or the other one will be blind.
On his forehead or between his eyes will be written the word "Kafir". (NATO tanks used in "Gulf War" and "Kossovo" had **"KOFR"** written on them)

Very important is that; this word "Kafir" will be readable only by a believer, literate or illiterate. Non-believer: let be educated from "Oxford" or "Harvard" will not be able to read it.

According to Ibn Kathir:

"...It will be written perceptibly, not abstractly, as some people say". (20-62)

In case it is written abstractly then: The possibility of a believer recognising Ad-Dajjal is either through his evil acts or through the "symbol language". When an illiterate person goes to "Mc Donalds", he can't read the words but recognises it by the sign; same is the case with all big companies. "Shell" service stations have nowhere written "Shell", there is only sign of "A Shell". Yet everyone knows this is "Shell Petrol Station". So in either case it will be easy for a believer to reed it.

AD-DAJJAL EXISTS!

*"...When Allah's Apostle (peace be upon him) had finished his prayer, he sat on the pulpit, smiling, and said: Every worshipper should remain sitting in his place. He then said 'Do you know why I have asked you to assemble'? They said 'Allah and His apostle know best'. He said 'By Allah, I have not made you assemble for exhortation or for a warning. I have detained you here because Tamim Dari, a Christian who came and accepted Islam, told me something which agrees with what I was telling you about the Dajjal. He narrated to me that he had sailed in a ship with thirty men of Banu Lakhm and Banu Judham and had been tossed by waves in the ocean for a month. Then these (waves) took them (near) the land within the ocean (island) at the time of sunset. They sat in a small rowing boat and landed on that island. There was a beast with long thick hair (and because of this) they could not distinguish his face from his back. They said: Woe to you, who can you be? Thereupon it said I am al-Jassasah. They said what is al-Jassasah? It said: O people, go to this person in the monastery as he is very much eager to know about you. He (the narrator) said when it named a person for us we were afraid of it lest it should be a Devil. Then we hurried on till we came to that monastery and found a well-built person there with his hands tied to his neck and iron shackles gripping his legs by the ankles. We said woe to you, who are you? He said you soon come to know about me, but tell me who you are. We said we are people from Arabia and we embarked upon a boat but the waves had been driving us for one month and they brought us near this island. We took to the rowing boats and landed on this island. Here a beast with profusely thick hair met us and because of the thickness of his hair his face could not be distinguished from his back. We said: Woe be to thee, who are you? It said: I am **al- Jassasah**. We said what is al-Jassasah? It said: You go to this very person in the monastery for he is eagerly waiting for you to know about you. So we came to you in hot haste fearing that that might be the Devil. He (that chained person) said tell me about the date-palm trees of Baysan. We said in which respect do you seek information about it? He said I ask you whether these trees bear fruit or not. We said yes. Thereupon he said I think these will not bear fruit. He said inform me about the lake of Tabariyyah? We said what do you want to know about it? He said, is there water in it? They said, there is an abundance of water in it. Thereupon he said, I think it will soon dry up. He again said, inform me about the spring of Zughar. They said, what do you want to know about it? He (the chained person) said: Is there water in it and does it irrigate (the land)? We said to him: Yes, there is an abundance of water in it and the inhabitants (of Medina) irrigate (land) with its help. He said, inform me about the unlettered Prophet; what has he done? We said, He has left Mecca and has settled in Yathrib (Medina). He said, do the Arabs fight against him? We said Yes. He said, How does he deal with him? We informed him that he had overcome those in his neighbourhood and they had submitted themselves before him. Thereupon he said to us: Had it actually happened? We said Yes. Thereupon he said, If it is so that is better for them that they show obedience to him. I am going to tell you about myself. I am the Dajjal and will be soon permitted to leave'..." (Sahih Muslim, Hadith 7208-narrated by Fatimah, daughter of Qays)*

JASSASAH

"Al-Jassasah is so called because he spies on behalf of the Dajjal (from jassa-to try to gain information, to spy out, etc.)." (20-52)

Remember all Ahadith are 1421 years old, so is this one! Each and every word of Hadith is verifying its authenticity.

In modern times, information is very important. All big businesses are carried-on on the basis of information. To approach the right clients you need to know their whereabouts, their names, addresses, phone numbers and e-mail addresses. This service is provided by "Data Companies" and is called "Data Services" or "Data Information". Modern businesses are relying on the information collected by the survey companies i.e. consumer survey, health survey and other surveys. All this information is finally stored in to a "Master Computer" that is in Brussels, Belgium. (Ibid.)

When a person goes to shopping, in a big store i.e. Asda, Tesco or Sainsbury's, he is offered a "loyalty card" subject to some discount. This loyalty card holds information about his address, phone number, shopping he makes brands he likes etc. The camera inside the store watches him all the time. This camera records his movements and interests, i.e. which products he picks up straight away and which ones he chooses with hesitation.

There are cameras everywhere in Europe, America and are expanding to other part of the world. Usually the presence of cameras is justified by prevention of crime, safety of public and to stop people from over speeding on the roads. But the actual purpose is "Surveillance", for this purpose there are satellites all around the earth. These satellites can zoom into one square yard of any part of earth and find a lost needle. Yet they can't see what is happening inside the houses and shelters. To know the activities under the roof they rely on "survey Information". You must have come across so many survey forms from different companies that by now you take it as a routine. This is what the "Brotherhood" want! To make you feel everything is normal, routine and cool. This is mass manipulation. You are watched as you go out of your home till you come back---by street cameras shop cameras and now even in the public busses and transport. The transport cameras are very sophisticated and button sized. "Big Brother"; is watching you everywhere!

And when you come back home---through satellite channels subscription and "pay as you watch", they know what channels interest you most. Through your telephone record, they know your friends and family. Through your computer they know the web sites you visit, e-mails you get, send and all your computer links.

There are "Key Words", fed into the communication system, which are suspicious i.e. "Ussama bin Ladin"; you utter or write those words any where on line, special surveillance auto-focuses on to you---you may be on the phone, e-mail or web-site.

This is al-Jassasah!

WHERE IS AD-DAJJAL?

"...Behold he (Ad-Dajjal) is in the Syrian sea (Mediterranean) or the Yemen sea (Arabian sea). Nay, on the contrary, he is in the east---he is in the east---he is in the east, and he (PBUH) pointed with his hand towards the east..." (Sahih Muslim, Hadith 7208-narrated by Fatimah, daughter of Qays)

Some western writers i.e. "David Iyke" (writer of "And the Truth shall set you Free") also believe that the head of Freemasonry is somewhere in the east. It can be a personal research or derivation from our Prophet's (S.A.W) Hadith.

BEFORE AD-DAJJAL APPEARS

"...During the three years just before the Dajjal comes, there will be one year when the sky will withhold one third of its rain and the earth one third of its fruits. In the second year the sky will withhold two third of its rain and the earth two third of its fruits. In the third year the sky will withhold all of its rain and the earth all of its fruits, and all the animals will die..." (Ahmad, Musnad, 6/455,456 Quote from 20-66)

In another Hadith it is quoted as:

"...And earth all of its fruits, so that nothing green will grow. Every cloven-hoofed creature will die except for whatever Allah wills..." (Ibn Majah Kitab al-Fitan 4077 Quote from 20-59)

APPEARANCE OF AD-DAJJAL

In all Ahadith it is quoted that Ad-Dajjal will appear and not that he will be born. This proves his pre-existence. Although some Ahadith quote about the birth of "Abd al-Uzza" (in time of Prophet Mohammad PBUH) as Dajjal but scholars do not agree, as Abd al-Uzza was not Ad-Dajjal but one of the lesser Dajjals. As far as Ad-Dajjal is concerned:

"Amr ibn Hurayth quoted Abu Bakr as-Siddiq as saying that Allah's Messenger (PBUH) told them that the Dajjal would come forth from a land in the East called Khurasan..." (Al Tirmidhi 5487 narrated by Abu Bakr as-Siddiq)

"...He will appear on the way between Syria and Iraq and will spread mischief right and left..." (Sahih Muslim 7015 narrated by An-Nawwas ibn Sam'an)

"Allah's Messenger (PBUH) said: Dajjal will come from eastern side with the intention of attacking Medina until he will get down behind Uhud..." (Sahih Al-Bukhari 9.239 narrated by Ans bin Malik)

"...He will encamp in one of the salt areas neighbouring Medina..." (Sahih Al Bukhari-9.246 Abu Said)

INVITATION OF AD-DAJJAL

"...He will come to the people and invite them (to a wrong religion); they will affirm their faith in him and respond to him..." (Sahih Muslim 7015 narrated by An-Nawwas ibn Sam'an)

As Ad-Dajjal has not appeared himself---yet, but his system is already here which is supported and implemented by his followers---the Freemasons! Muslims believe in democracy, modern education system and western economic system. Muslims also believe in tax system, the opposite to the system of Islam, which is Zakah (compulsory charity for the rich). Thus we have to be very careful about our belief because every path that diverts from "Sirat al Mustaqim" will lead us straight into the hands of Dajjal.

Freemasonry is the **only "Secret Organisation"** amongst all the others; that with its own belief, rituals, ceremonies and dogmas is in full form of a religion. Nearly all the "Conspiracy Theorists" believe that **"New World Order"** is also escorted with a **"New Religion"**.

Freemasonry is the**only** "Secret Organisation" that uses **EYE** as a symbol. This **EYE** is of the deity to whom they worship and call **JAHBULON**. Freemasonry is a society that invites people to join through its members. Not necessarily Dajjal has to appear himself to call people, his team is doing a fine job. Martin Short writes:

"We had been discussing whether or not Freemasonry was a religion, and I had run through my customary list of religious terms used in Freemasonry. Then I added, one comes across the phrase, 'the sacred tenets of Freemasonry'. This seems to imply that Masonry thinks of itself as a religion...The Holy Royal Arch. They are all expressions of religion in its fullest sense, not in a masonic sense". (22' p-238)

"...He will start by saying that he is a prophet, but there will be no prophet after me. Then he will say, 'I am your lord' but you will never see your Lord until you die..."(Ibn Majah, Kitab al-Fitan 4077. Quote from 20-56)

He will not come and claim that he is Ad-Dajjal! Rather he will appear, as an icon of modernism as a hero or a philanthropist; that is why people will believe in him. He will be the ointed one, the impostor! He will invite people to a wrong religion and they will believe in him. Not forced by him, but impressed by his powers. This is exactly what is happening. People are joining Freemasonry, believing they are joining a charity organisation or they are doing a good job secularly and spiritually.

"The Prophet (peace be upon him) said: Let him who hears of the Dajjal (Antichrist) go far from him for I swear by Allah that a man will come to him thinking he is a believer and follow him because of confused ideas roused in him by him." (Sunan of Abu Dawood 4305 narrated by Imran ibn Hussayn)

To claim to be lord he will have means to sponsor his claim. Some people thought that he will hold miracles, but now it is largely understood that these will not be miracles like prophets had, but means---and these are---scientific means---dominated by---"Brotherhood"! (See Powers of Ad-Dajjal)

FOLLOWERS OF AD-DAJJAL

"These followers of Dajjal will be faced by a group from among the Muslims, and the leader of these people will be Isa bin Maryam. The Prophet (PBUH), predicted that those people have been liberated from the fire of Hell" (Sunan Al Nasiye Vol-2, p-63)

"...Dajjal would come forth from a land in the East called Khurasan, followed by people whose faces resembled shields covered with skin..." Tirmidhi transmitted it. (Al Tirmidhi 5487-Abu Bakr as Siddique)

*"Allah's Apostle (peace be upon him) said: The Dajjal would be followed by seventy thousand Jews of Isfahan wearing **Persian shawls**." (Sahih Muslim-7034-Ans ibn Malik)*

At one point all non-believers will believe in him but Jews will be his first followers as they are waiting for the last Messiah (see chapter Hiram Abif, King Solomon PBUH). At present, Isfahan is a major producer of **textile**!

POWERS OF AD-DAJJAL

"The Prophet said about Ad-Dajjal that he would have water and fire with him: (what would seem to be) fire, would be cold water and (what would seem to be) water, would be fire." (Sahih Al Bukhari-9.244-Hudaifa)

"...He (Dajjal) will have a mountain of bread and a river of water with him (i.e. he will have abundance of food and water)." The Prophet said, "Nay, he is too mean to be allowed such a thing by Allah," (but it is only to test mankind whether they believe in Allah or in Ad-Dajjal). (Sahih Al-Bukhari-9.244-Al Mughirah bin Shuba)

"...The people think that he would have with him rivers of water and mountains of bread, whereupon he (PBUH) said: He would be more insignificant in the sight of Allah than all these things (belonging to him). (Sahih Muslim, 5352- Mughira ibn Shu'bah)

"...Then the Antichrist (Dajjal) will come forth accompanied by a river and fire. He who falls into his fire will certainly receive his reward, and have his load taken off him, but he who falls into his river will have his load retained and his reward taken off him..." (Sunan of Abu Dawood-4232-Ghudhayfah ibn al-Yaman)

"...We said: Allah's apostle (peace be upon him) how quickly will he walk upon the earth? Thereupon he said: Like cloud driven by the wind..." (Sahih Muslim 7015 narrated by Nawwas ibn Sam'an)

"...He (Dajjal) will be riding a donkey; the width between its (donkey's) ears will be forty cubits..."(Ahmad Musnad 3/367,368 Quote from 20-51)

"...Among the tribulations he will bring will be the Paradise and Hell he will offer; but that which he calls Hell will be Paradise, and that which he calls Paradise will be Hell..." (Ibn Majah Kitab al-Fitan 4077 Quote from 20-58)

"...He will then give a command to the sky: there will be rainfall upon the earth and it will grow crops. Then in the evening, their pasturing animals will come to them with their humps very high, their udders full of milk and their flanks distended. He will then come to another people and invite them. But they will reject him so he will go away from them; they will have a drought and nothing will be left with them in the form of wealth. He will then walk through the desert and say to it: Bring forth your treasures. The treasures will come out and gather before him like a swarm of bees. He will then call someone in the flush of youth, strike him with the sword, cut him into two pieces and (make these pieces lie at the distance, which is generally between the archer and his target. He will then call (that young man) and he will come forward laughing with his face gleaming (with happiness)..." (Sahih Muslim 7015 narrated by Nawwas ibn Sam'an)

"...Allah will send with him devils who will speak to the people..." (Ahmad Musnad 3/367,368 Quote from 20-51)

"...He will say to a Bedouin, what do you think if I bring your father and mother back to life for you? Will you bear witness that I am your lord? The Bedouin will say yes, so two devils will assume the appearance of his father and mother, and will say, 'O my son, follow him for he is your lord'..." (Ibn Majah Kitab al-Fitan 4077 Quote from 20-58)

"...Ad-Dajjal will come and it will be forbidden for him to pass through the entrances of Medina. He will land in some of the salty barren areas (outside) Medina; on that day the best man or one of the best men will come up to him and say, 'I testify that you are the same Dajjal whose description was given to us by Allah's Apostle.' Ad-Dajjal will say to the people, 'If I kill this man and bring him back to life again, will you doubt my claim?' They will say, 'No'. Then Ad-Dajjal will kill that man and bring him back to life. That man will say, 'Now I know your reality better than before.' Ad-

Dajjal will say, 'I want to kill him but I cannot.'" (Sahih Al-Bukhari 3.106 narrated by Abu Said Al Khudri)

Let us look at the powers of Ad-Dajjal one by one:

1. He will have manipulation over **living resources** i.e. water, fire, bread, enormous wealth and treasures of earth.
2. He will have manipulation over **natural resources,** i.e. rain, crops, droughts and famines.
3. He will walk on earth, like a cloud driven by the wind. The distance between his donkey's (**his ride**) ears will be 40 cubits.
4. He will bring a false **Hell and Paradise** with him.
5. He will be **helped by devils** that will assume the appearance of dead people and speak to humans.
6. He will have a command over **life and death**.
7. He will have a **limited power** over life and death, as he will not be able to kill the mo'min (believer) second time.

Living resources: We know that "International Bankers" is the group that runs "World Bank" and "IMF" and through them, "Freemasonry", which is waiting for Ad-Dajjal (Antichrist). With whole world's economy depending on these two organisations, these organisations can be called the main pulse of world economy.

How "World Bank" is manipulating the "living resources" via economic pressure on its under-debt countries is shown here:

Several years ago, Ismail Serageldin, Vice-President of the World Bank announced that the wars of the 21st century would be about water! He was referring to a survey report, which assumed that "the world is running out of fresh water sources at an alarming rate, and the conflict over what remains will be inevitable".

First phase of manipulation is the**creation** of a problem. Second phase is the **solution** for the problem, which is presented by the Brotherhood. Third phase is the **action**. "Creation-solution-action" (David Icke calls this "problem-reaction-solution") is the formula applied by Brotherhood to achieve their target of mass-manipulation. In this case, first they "created" a problem via survey (which does not affirm any certainty, this survey could have been done by their own people---who knows?). "Solution" came from the World Bank too, leaving "action" for the local government.

"To respond to the crises, the World Bank has recently adopted a policy of water privatisation and full-cost water pricing. This policy is causing great distress in many Third World countries, which fear that their citizens will not be able to afford the cost of privatised water.

Two years ago, the World Bank (whose official attends Bolivian Government cabinet meetings as a full participant), refused to guarantee a US$25-million loan to refinance water services in Cochabamba, Bolivia's third-largest city. Unless the government sold the public water system to the private sector and passed on the costs to consumers! Only one bid was considered, and the utility was turned over to a subsidiary of a conglomerate led by Bechtel—the giant engineering company implicated in the infamous Three Gorges Dam in China, which has caused the forced relocation of 1.3 million people.

In January 1999, before the company had even hung up its shingle, it announced the doubling of water prices. For most Bolivians, this meant that water would now cost more than food; for those on a minimum wage or unemployed, water bills suddenly accounted for close to half their monthly budgets.

To add insult to injury, the World Bank granted monopolies to private water concessionaires, announced its support for full-cost water pricing, pegged the cost of water to the US dollar, and declared that none of its loan could be used to subsidise the poor for water services. All water, even from community wells, required permits to access, and peasants and small farmers even had to buy permits to gather rainwater on their property.

This is a story unfolding in many parts of the world. Just as humanity is beginning to come to terms with the awesome dimensions of the looming fresh-water crises, a handful of transnational water and food corporations, backed by the World Bank, are moving in on Third World countries and, in the name of human charity, commodifying their water for profit. These corporations openly dominated the UN/World Bank—sponsored World Water Forum in The Hague in March.

The privatisation of municipal water services has a terrible record that is well documented. Customer rates are doubled or tripled; corporate profits rise as much as 700 per cent; corruption and bribery are rampant; water quality standards drop, sometimes dramatically; overuse is promoted to make money; and customers who can't pay are cut off. When privatisation hits the Third World, those who can't pay will die!" (Nexus, New Times magazine, Aug/Sep 2000 p6/7)

Bolivia's story had a happy ending at least this time, when hundreds of thousands Bolivians marched to Cochabamba in an anti-government protest. On 10th April people won and government had to kick "Bechtel" out of the country.

This is a small example of **"living resources manipulation"**, that failed in its full implementation for the first time. But remember there is always a second time, and in case of "brotherhood" this is time and again, till they achieve their target---Time to wake-up---!

"...He (Dajjal) will have a mountain of bread and a river of water with him (i.e. he will have abundance of food and water)." The Prophet said, "Nay, he is too mean to be allowed such a thing by Allah," (but it is only to test mankind whether they believe in Allah or in Ad-Dajjal). (Sahih Al-Bukhari-9.244-Al Mughirah bin Shuba)

No doubt it is only a test for mankind weather they believe in Allah or in Ad-Dajjal!

Natural resources: Earth has got its own defence system, that filters lethal sun rays and other radio active waves reaching from different planets and stars via light beams and star bursts. These dangerous beams are called "Ultra Violent Rays". This system is phenomenal as it is created by Allah (S.W.T).

In 1886-8, "Nikola Tesla" an American, invented system of Alternating Current (AC) power source and transmission system. As 60-pulse-per-second (Hertz) AC power grids spread over the land, Earth will eventually dance to a different beat than her usual 7-8 Hertz frequency. In 1900 Tesla applied for patent on a device to "Transmit Electrical Energy through the Natural Mediums".

In 1905, US patent "#787,412" issued for above. In 1940, Tesla announced "Death Ray" invention. In 1958 "Van Allen radiation Belts" were discovered (zones of charged particles trapped in earth's and other planet's magnetic field) 2,000+ miles up.

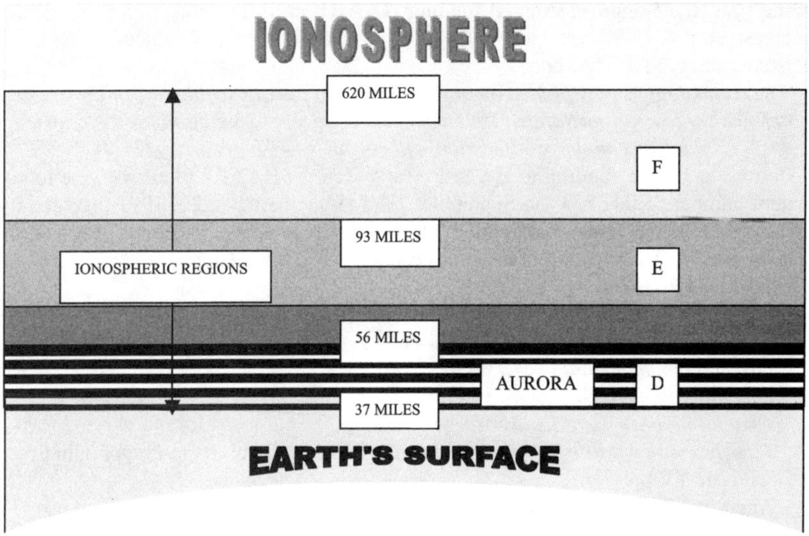

In 1958:

"White house advisor on weather modification says; Defence Department studying ways to manipulate charges 'of earth and sky, and to effect the weather'". (21-1)

In 1960s series of weather disasters began. Same year the dumping of chemicals (barium powder etc.) from satellites/rockets began. In 1972 were presented the:

"First reports on 'ionospheric heater' experiments with high frequency radio waves, at Arecibo.9 A 100 megawatt heater in Norway built later in decade can change conductivity of auroral ionosphere". (21-2)

In 1973 a documentation showed that the launch of "sky lab":

"Halved the total electron content of the ionosphere for three hours (by rocket exhaust)". (21-2)

In 1974, experiments were carried out that heated the "bottom side of ionosphere". These experiments took place at Plattesville, Colorado, Arecibo, Puerto Richo, and Armidale, New South Wales. Professor Robert Helliwell reported in 1975 that:

"Very low frequency (VLF) from power lines is altering the ionosphere". (21-3)

In 1975, Gaylord Nelson, a US Senator forced Navy to:

"Release research showing that extremely low frequency (ELF) transmissions can alter human blood chemistry". (21-3)

In later part of 1980's the US began:

"Net work of Ground Wave Emergency Network (GWEN) towers, each to generate very low frequency (VLF) waves for defence purposes. (21-3)

Between 1987-92 scientists from Arco Power Technologies Incorporated (APTI) built on Eastlund, patented of a new weapon capabilities (patent # 4,686,605—"Method and Apparatus for Altering a Region in the Earth's Atmosphere, Ionosphere and Magnetosphere" issued August 11, 1987. Invented by Bernard J. Eastlund). In 1994, military contractor "E-Systems" bought APTI holder of Eastlund patents and contracted to build the biggest ionospheric heater in the world. This project is called "High-frequency Active Auroral Research Project" (HAARP). The same year, the Congress stopped funding **HAARP** until the project planners would increase emphasis on earth penetrating tomography. In 1995, "Raytheon" bought E-Systems and old APTI patents.

"The technology is now hidden among thousands of patents within one of the largest defence contractor portfolios...1995, Congress budgets $10 million for 1996 under 'nuclear counterproliferation' efforts for HAARP project". (21-4)

Despite in 1994-6 funding to HAARP was frozen the HAARP planners were to test patent number "5,041,834" in September 1995 (Issued August 20, 1991 invented by Peter Koert. Titled "Artificial Ionospheric Mirror Composed of a Plasma Layer which can be tilted"). Their testing of first and second stage continued in 1995/6.

Finally year 2001 is:

"Projected date for fully operating HAARP system". (21-4)

The **full operation of HAARP** is described as:

Disrupt human mental processes.
Jam all global communication systems.
Change weather patterns over large areas.
Interfere with wildlife migration patterns. [We see animal micro-chipping in every wild life TV program]
Negatively effect your health.
Unnaturally impact the earth's upper atmosphere. (21-back page)

After creating serious weather disasters ("creation"), for last decade, elite of the philanthropists is holding a meeting in The Hague, on 20-11-2000 in strict privacy. Their agenda is to seek a way out ("solution") to the disastrous weather. The out come will be a suggestion to build a shield around the earth ("action"), which is exactly what Eastlund patent suggested. This shield will be able to carry on the **full operation** acquired by HAARP! BBC is already showing programs like "State of the Planet" (BBC1 22-11-2000) labelling global warming as a repeat natural process. In that they say; "although industry population and transport is playing some part in global warming but this is something that happened 10,000 years ago as well". This time scientists will defend the earth by creating a "magnetic shield" around it thus bringing the sea level down to normal and stop ice-burgs from melting.

Ride of Ad-Dajjal: He will travel with a speed "*cloud driven by the wind"* is no doubt the aeroplane, jet or the concord! The distance between his donkey's ears will be *40 cubits* and that is the approximate distance between two wings of an aeroplane.

Hell and Paradise: Just ask any one living out side Europe or America about the West; they call it---paradise---and---their own countries---hell! Ad-Dajjal will be having something similar to this with all the facilities and eases that he will call paradise. Areas or places without worldly comforts will be considered hell. (Allah knows best)

Helped by Devils: There is evidence of Shaytan's communication with righteous people and trying to lead them astray. This evidence is present in the story of Ayyub (A.S) (Prophet Job).

Our Prophet Mohammad (P.B.U.H) was the best of humankind. All the good characteristics of a human were gathered in him by mercy of Allah (S.W.T) and the symbol of these qualities appeared between his shoulders as the "seal of prophethood". This seal was admired by his companions so much that they used to kiss it whenever possible. Opposite of the goodness is badness, against the best person's (Mohammad S.A.W) followers (us), will be the worst and lowest of mankind. All the bad characteristics will gather in Ad-Dajjal and appear on his forehead as word "Kafir" and one eye will be the symbol of his defective personality. The angels helped Prophet Mohammed (S.A.W) on the contrary Ad-Dajjal will be helped by the devils. It will be only a test for Muslims; weather they believe in Ad-Dajjal or affirm their faith in Allah (S.W.T).

Life and Death: Life is the "presence of spirit in a body"; when this spirit is taken away, body stops functioning. We call it death! To over power the spirit is not possible because knowledge of the spirit is only with Allah (S.W.T)

"They ask thee concerning the Spirit (of inspiration). Say: 'The Spirit (cometh) by command of my Lord; of knowledge it is only a little that is communicated to you (O men!)'". (Q 17-85)

However Ad-Dajjal will be able to kill and resurrect on some occasions with *only a little* of *knowledge*. How is he going to do this is probably with the help of cloning!

The scientists have cracked the human genetic code, that is a combination of three-billion-letter DNA sequence found in every cell of a human body. It has been hailed as one of the biggest scientific breakthroughs of all time. This research the "Human Genome Project" was lead by Dr Mike Stratton, the brain behind cloning "Dolly" (first cloned sheep) in **"Roslyn Institute"** Scotland. At the moment it is presented as a cure from the genetic diseases, but once it has found a platform and accepted by the peoples---then will be the time to enforce the law of "human genome"! That means a total genetic birth control! (See One World Government, mass genetic testing of pregnant women on the way also see "End of Ad-Dajjal", last paragraph.)

DURATION OF AD-DAJJAL

ZERO POINT

It is believed that rotation of the earth, around its orbit; slows down by about 1.4 milliseconds every century, but recently the scientists have discovered that this can also happen in jumps. Gravitational forces from various planets play a part in slowing earth's spin by pulling it towards them. The latest discovery has revealed that beside all these factors, the major part in the 'slowing process' is played by the earth itself. That part is caused by the changes in the wind. In fact these 'wind changes' play 90% part in 'slowing process'. According to Dr. Jean Dickey from the 'Jet Propulsion Laboratory':

"Ninety percent of these variations are caused by changes in wind". Further he says that; *"If the atmosphere is speeding up, Earth is slowing down". (21-78)*

"HAARP"; directly related to the changes in the weather patterns; is heavily responsible for the 'slowing process'. Not only this but HAARP is also responsible for increment in earthquakes around the globe:

The movement of the atmospheric mass adds stress over new portions of the earth, and lowers stress in other parts. This shift in pressure or forces in the planet can increase earthquake frequency in all areas which experience changes in atmospherically created stresses". (21-78)

(1)-How they create stress in the atmosphere and, (2) do they really create stress in the atmosphere?

(1). They can create stress in the atmosphere by ionizing or de-ionizing the atmosphere.

(2). In 1958 the chief White House advisor on weather modification, Captain Howard T. Orville said the "Defence Department" was studying:

"Ways to manipulate the changes of the earth and sky and so affect weather" by using *"an electronic beam to ionize or de-ionize the atmosphere over a given area"* *(21-78)*

That was 1958 and now is---Dec 2000. Our Earth is like a giant magnet with different levels rotating to create a magnetic field, directly related to the Earth's rotation. Faster the Earth rotates, more powerful and dense the magnetic field is. There is another force that is directly related to the rotation of the earth and that is "Earth's resonant frequency", or its heartbeat if you like, which is increasing rapidly. This frequency, called "The Base Resonant Frequency" or "Schumann Cavity Resonance", was identified in 1899. Between then and the mid-1980s, it maintained a constant pulse of around 7.8 Hertz or 7 cycles per second. But from 1986- 87 (soon after the patent issued for—"Method and Apparatus for Altering a Region in the Earth's Atmosphere, Ionosphere and Magnetosphere" issued August 11, 1987. Invented by Bernard J. Eastlund) it apparently began to quicken. By the end of 1995 it had reached 8.6 according to some estimates and the last was heard it was said to be above 10 and still rising.

It is believed that when "earth's resonance frequency" reaches 13 cycles per second that will be the time when her magnetic field could be at or near zero. Gregg Braden the writer of ' *Awakening to Zero Point'* calls this Zero Point when the Earth's magnetic field will all but disappear because the planet's rotation will have stopped--!

This doesn't mean there will be no gravity because that is created by other phenomena, not the spin of the planet.

People like Braden estimate that the Earth will stop rotating for some days before it begins to spin in the opposite direction. As you can see when the flow of electricity through an iron bar is reversed, the poles reverse. As the planet spins in the other direction, the flow of electricity will reverse and so, therefore, must the poles. If the planet stopped rotating, one side of the Earth would be in constant sunshine and the other in darkness in this period—till earth slowly starts rotating in opposite direction-!

"...We said: O Allah's Apostle (peace be upon him), how long will he (Dajjal) stay on Earth? He said: For forty days, one day like a year, one day like a month, one day like a week, and the rest of the days will be like your days. We said: Allah's Apostle (peace be upon him) will one day's prayer suffice for the prayers of the day equal to one year? Thereupon he said: No, but you must make an estimate of the time (and then observe prayer)..." (Sahih Muslim 7015 narrated by Nawwas ibn Sam'an)

PROTECTION FROM AD-DAJJAL

"...If he comes forth while I am among you. I shall contend with him on your behalf, but if he comes forth while I am not among you, a man must contend on his own behalf; and Allah will take care of every Muslim on my behalf (and safeguard him against his evil)..." (Sahih Muslim 7015-An-Nawwas ibn Sam'an)

"Allah's Apostle (peace be upon him) said: If anyone learns by heart the first ten verses of the Surah al-Kahf, he will be protected from the Dajjal". (Sahih Muslim 1766 narrated by Abud Darda)

"...Whoever enters his (Dajjal's) Hell, let him seek refuge with Allah and recite the opening Ayat of Surat al-Kahaf, and it will become cool and peaceful for him, as the fire became cool and peaceful for Abraham..." (Ibn Majah Kitab al-Fitan 4077 Quote from 20-58)

"A man recited Surat-al-Kahf (in his prayer) and in the house there was a (riding) animal which got frightened and started jumping. The man finished his prayer with Taslim, but behold! A mist or a cloud hovered over him. He informed the Prophet of that and the Prophet said, "O so-and-so! Recite, for this (mist or cloud) was a sign of peace descending for the recitation of Qur'an." (Sahih Al-Bukhari 4.811Narratyed by Al Bara bin Azib)

MAKKAH AND MEDINAH SAFE FROM AD-DAJJAL

"The Prophet said, "The terror caused by Al-Masih Ad-Dajjal will not enter Medina and at that time Medina will have seven gates and there will be two angels at each gate guarding them." (Sahih Al Bukhari-3.103-Abu Bakra)

"The Prophet said, "Ad-Dajjal will come and encamp at a place close to Medina and then Medina will shake thrice whereupon every Kafir (disbeliever) and hypocrite will go out (of Medina) towards him." (Sahih Al-Bukhari 9.239 narrated by Anas bin Malik)

"The Prophet said: "There will be no town which Ad-Dajjal will not enter except Mecca and Medina. And there will be no entrance (road) (of both Mecca and Medina), but the angels will be standing in rows guarding it against him. And then Medina will shake with its inhabitants thrice, (i.e. three earthquakes will take place) and Allah will expel all the non-believers and the hypocrites from it." (Sahih Al-Bukhari 3.105 Anas bin Malik)

ISA IBN MARYAM (AS)---JESUS (PBUH)

Isa ibn Maryam (Jesus) PBUH was not crucified neither killed but raised up to heaven by Allah (SWT). Allah (SWT) says:

"That they said (in boast); We killed Christ Jesus son of Mary, the Apostle of God. But they killed him not nor crucified him, but so it was made to appear to them, and those who differ therein are full of doubts, with no (certain) knowledge, but only conjucture to follow, for of a surety, they killed him not. Nay---God raised him up unto Himself, and God is exalted in Power, Wise. And there is none of the people of the Scripture (Jews and Christians) but must believe in him (Isa ibn Maryam) before his (Isa's) death..." (Q- 4: 157-9)

Like many other signs of Qayamah, glimpse are shown in Qur'an, and explanation is provided in Hadith, so is with Isa ibn Maryam-Jesus (PBUH) that his second-coming is described in Hadith. Those who believe or believed that Jesus has passed away i.e. Sayyed Ahmed Khan, Mirza Ghulam Ahmad Qadyani and his followers, should had and should deny his second coming as well, because dead people don't come back, but not surprisingly they only accept those Ahadith partly that collaborate with their benefits. Here is clearly stated the second coming of Jesus (PBUH):

"...He (Jesus) will descend at the white minaret on the eastern side of Damascus, wearing two garments lightly dyed with saffron and placing his hands on the wings of two Angels. When he lowers his head, there will fall beads of perspiration from his head, and when he raises it up, beads like pearls will scatter from it..." (Sahih Muslim 7015-An-Nawwas ibn Sam'an)

"...I saw a reddish-white man with lank hair, and water was dropping from his head. I asked, 'Who is this? ' They replied, 'The son of Mary'..." (Sahih Al-Bukhari 9.242 narrated by Abdullah bin Umar)

Jesus (PBUH) will not come as a Prophet [as there will be no prophet after Mohammad (SW)...agreed upon] but as:

"...Jesus son of Mary will be a just ruler of my Ummah. He will break the cross, kill the pigs, and abolish the Jizyah (tax)..." (Ibn Majah Kitab al-Fitan 4077 Quote from 20-58)

Killing pigs and breaking cross means that; those who worship cross will stop worshipping it, and those who eat pigs will give-up eating it. Another important aspect of this Hadith is that Jesus (PBUH) will *abolish the Jizyah (tax)*. If you look at the world, every country has enforced tax on her subjects, be it Muslim or non-Muslim country. In fact Muslim countries are being forced by the West through "World Bank" and "IMF" to carry out these taxes because this is a part of "One World Government" and way of Al-Jassasah---the surveillance! To have details of every individual on the planet is only possible through tax system. This is "Antichrist" because Jesus (PBUH) will be against the tax and *abolish* it, so we can evidently say that---this "Tax-System" is "Dajjalic-System"---!

END OF AD-DAJJAL

*"...He (Dajjal) will then call someone in the flush of youth, strike him with the sword, cut him into two pieces and (make these pieces) lie at the distance which is generally between the archer and his target. He will then call (that young man) and he will come forward laughing with his face gleaming (with happiness). **It will be at this very time that Allah will send Christ, son of Mary**. He will descend at the white minaret on the eastern side of Damascus, wearing two garments lightly dyed with saffron and placing his hands on the wings of two Angels. When he lowers his head, there will fall beads of perspiration from his head, and when he raises it up, beads like pearls will scatter from it. Every non-believer who smells the odour of his body will die and his breath will reach as far as he is able to see. He will then search for him (Dajjal) until he catches hold of him at **the gate of Ludd** and kills him. Then a people whom Allah had protected will come to Jesus, son of Mary, and he will wipe their faces and inform them of their ranks in Paradise..." (Sahih Muslim 7015-An-Nawwas ibn Sam'an)*

Ludd is the place where, the biggest military air base of Israel is situated. Considering the "ride of Dajjal" (aeroplane); this will be an appropriate place for Dajjal to fly and seek refuge.

Why particularly: ***It will be at this very moment that Allah will send Christ, son of Mary?*** Why not any other time?

Because this power over life and death is something that people will have never seen in their lives and will convert masses of people thinking that Ad-Dajjal is their lord. In other words scientific achievements will be at their peak. On the other hand, Jesus (PBUH) being a prophet of Allah (SWT) has already performed this miracle (to bring the dead alive) by the Order of Allah (SWT) and may do it again. This will be the confrontation and triumph of miraculous powers over scientific powers! Thus, this time once again Allah (SWT) will save his true believers from straying and accepting Dajjal as their lord.

"...When the Dajjal sees Jesus, he will begin to dissolve like salt in water, and run away..." (Ibn Majah Kitab al-Fitan 4077 Quote from 20-58)

This may be an indication of partly fleshed and partly metalled human being, just like 6 million-dollar man or "terminator". This project is under way and Japan has already created a Robocop. On the other hand now this is possible to download the whole memory of a human brain on to a computer. In her lecture, Professor Susan Greenfield from Oxford declared to the other scientists that:

"We are now capable of downloading the entire human memory that consists of approximately 100 trillion cells out of which 100 billion cells are used for communication, on to a computer." (The Richard Dumbly Lecture BBC 1-1/12/99)

The strong possible fact that Professor Susan did not disclose is that a reverse action is even easier. The reverse action is "to upload memory onto a brain from a computer". With this ability comes the power of editing, subtracting and highlighting the areas of skills within the memory. For example memory of a man with a PhD in engineering or a distinguished engineer is up loaded with the memory of the best surgeon and scientist etc. That is the way to create a super human, a man who will be expert in all fields; best engineer, scientist, surgeon, politician, scholar, speaker, poet, you name it. An ideal man of the "New World Order"---the Dajjal---!

"Being" is the memory that one holds, if that memory is stolen he is no more a "being" that he was. Similarly, if that memory is transferred to any other "being" he becomes the one that; "memory was stolen from". This is the way to keep memory alive and a human being eternal. A narration also tells us that; "Dajjal would seem to be immortal for a while".

CH-23 QAYAMAH

THE HOUR WILL NOT BE ESTABLISHED UNTIL...

"Allah's Apostle (peace be upon him) said: The Last Hour will not come until the Romans land at al-A'maq or in Dabiq. An army consisting of the best (soldiers) of the people on Earth at that time will come from Medina (to oppose them). When they arrange themselves in ranks, the Romans will say: Do not stand between us and those (Muslims), who took prisoners from among us. Let us fight them. The Muslims will say: Nay, by Allah, we shall never turn aside from you and from our brethren so that you may fight them. They will then fight and a third (part) of the army, whom Allah will never forgive, will run away. A third (part of the army), which will be constituted of excellent martyrs in Allah's eyes, would be killed. The third who will never be put on trial will win and they will be the conquerors of Constantinople. As they are busy in distributing the spoils of war (amongst themselves) after hanging their swords by the olive trees, Satan will cry: The Dajjal has taken your place among your families. They will then come out, but it will be of no avail. When they reach Syria, he will come out while they are still preparing themselves for battle, drawing up the ranks. Certainly, the time of prayer will come and then Jesus (peace be upon him), son of Mary, descend and will lead them in prayer. When the enemy of Allah see him, it will (disappear) just as salt dissolves in water and if he (Jesus) were not to confront them at all, even then it would dissolve completely. Allah would kill them by his hand and he would show them their blood on his lance (the lance of Jesus Christ)". (Sahih Muslim-6924-Abu Hurayrah)

The fight between Romans (Westerners) or pagans and Muslims will take place that will result in the triumph of Muslims. These Muslims will be the conquerors of Constantinople, subsequently. As we know that the conquest of Constantinople (ancient name Qustuntunia and modern name Istanbul) has happened and Muslims rule this city, scholars believe that; this will be the second conquest. Muslims will win this conquest by saying "La Ilaha Illallah" and "Allah O Akbar". This is appropriate because, beside Constantinople is governed by Muslims but Freemasonry still rules Turkey (see ch-12, conclusion).

"Allah's Apostle (peace be upon him) said: You have heard of the city, one side of which is inclined and the other is on the coast (Constantinople). They said: Yes, Allah's Apostle (peace be upon him). Thereupon he said: The Last Hour will not come until seventy thousand people from ***Banu Isra'il attack it.*** *When they land there, they will neither fight with weapons nor shower arrows but will only say: "There is no god but Allah and Allah is the Greatest," and one side of it will fall. Thawr (one of the narrators) said: I think that he said: The area on the coast. Then they will say for the second time: "There is no god but Allah and Allah is the Greatest," and the other side will also fall. They will say: "There is no god but Allah is the Greatest," and the gates will be opened for them and they will enter. They will be collecting spoils of war and distributing them among themselves when a noise will be heard and it will be said: Verily, the Dajjal has come. Thus they will leave everything there and turn to (confront) him". (Sahih Muslim 6979 Narrated by Abu Hurayra)*

Although in this translation it is mentioned that **"Banu Israel"** will attack it. The actual Hadith writes the word **"Banu Ishaq"** (Jews' ancestry). "Qazi" the famous "Shareh" (commentator) of "Nawawi's Muslim", clarifies this part of Hadith regarding the faction of 70,000 people as being from "Bani Ismail" (The Prophet's ancestry) rather then "Bani Ishaq". Qazi says:

"This is the position of all the rules of Imam Muslim, that the most well known and preserved word here is 'Mim Bani Ismail', meaning from Bani Ismail. To which this Hadith indicates the victors to be from the Arabs". (Translation from Sahih Muslim Sharah of Imam Nawawi, p-396. Published by Saeed H M Company Adab Manzil, Karachi, Pakistan)

This explanation collaborates with the thought of the Ulama that; Arabs (Muslims) will conquer Constantinople once more! This time by waking the Iman (Faith) of Turks. Turks will revert to follow Prophet Mohammed (SAW), thus abandoning the "Ata Turk" and his "Secularism" Insha-Allah.

11 SIGNS

*"Allah's Apostle said, "The Hour will not be established (1) till **two big groups fight** each other whereupon there will be a great number of casualties on both sides and they will be following one and the same religious doctrine, (2) till about **thirty Dajjals (liars) appear**, and each one of them will claim that he is Allah's Apostle, (3) till the **religious knowledge is taken away** (by the death of religious scholars) (4) **earthquakes will increase** in number (5) **time will pass quickly**, (6) **afflictions will appear**, (7) Al-Harj, (i.e., **killing) will increase**, (8) till **wealth will be in abundance**--so abundant that a wealthy person will worry lest nobody should accept his Zakat, and whenever he will present it to someone, that person (to whom it will be offered) will say, 'I am not in need of it,' (9) till the people compete with one another in **constructing high buildings**, (10) till a man when passing by a grave of someone will say, 'Would that **I were in his place**,' (11) and till the **sun rises from the West**. So when the sun will rise and the people will see it (rising from the West) they will all believe (embrace Islam) but that will be the time when: (As Allah said,) 'No good will it do to a soul to believe then, if it believed not before, nor earned good (by deeds of righteousness) through its Faith.' (6.158) And the Hour will be established while two men spreading a garment in front of them but they will not be able to sell it, nor fold it up; and the Hour will be established when a man has milked his she-camel and has taken away the milk but he will not be able to drink it; and the Hour will be established before a man repairing a tank (for his livestock) is able to water (his animals) in it; and the Hour will be established when a person has raised a morsel (of food) to his mouth but will not be able to eat it." (Sahih Al Bukhari 9.237-Abu Hurayra)*

(1). **Two big groups fight:** There will be great many casualties on both sides and they both will be following the same religious doctrine. Many big fights have happened since i.e. war between Moawiah (RA) and Ali (RA), 1st World War, 2nd World War (both sides were Masonic Ibid.), or Iran-Iraq War.

(2). **Till about 30 Dajjals appear:** I am sure if we calculate the number of liars that claimed to be a prophet, it would be about 30, starting from Musailma Kazzab to the present day's modern false prophets.

(3). **Till the religious knowledge is taken away:** This will be either by the death of Ulama or by Qur'an, taken back into heaven. Death of Ulama in past few years is not hidden from anyone.

(4). **Earthquakes will increase:**

Earthquakes are sometimes caused by human activities. Such activities include the injection of fluids into deep wells, the detonation of large underground nuclear explosions, the excavation of mines and the filling of the large reservoirs.

"The number of earthquakes per year with magnitude 4.0 may reach 20,000." (16)

In the Matsushiro region of Japan, between August 1965 and 1967, there occurred a series of hundreds of thousands of earthquakes, some sufficiently strong (up to local magnitude 5) to cause property damage but no casualties. Such series of earthquakes are called swarms, but swarms also have been observed in many nonvolcanic regions. (Because of HAARP---?)

(5). **Time will pass quickly:**

"Allah's Messenger (peace be upon him) said, "The last hour will not come before time contracts, a year being like a month, a month like a week, a week like a day, a day like an hour, and an hour like the kindling of a fire."

Tirmidhi transmitted it. (Al-Tirmidhi 5448 narrated by Anas ibn-Malik)

The dramatic increase in solar flares is quickening the vibration of the Earth, and indeed the galaxy in general, which is giving the impression that the time is passing quicker and quicker. This is witnessed by every individual because of the increment in the "earth resonance frequency" (See Zero Point)---this is happening right now---!

(6). **Afflictions will appear!** Just a look around will tell you every thing about it, look at your city, town or country! Is it the same as it was a few years ago? Is the time coming, better than the time gone or is it worse? Just open any TV Channel or newspaper, look at films, neon signs, posters and you will see afflictions *falling like rain drops* everywhere, that is--- **if you can see---!**

(7). **Al-Harj (killing) will increase:** It doesn't need explanation, just look at any newspaper---!

(8). **Wealth will be in abundance:** The de-valuation of currency is a way to create this scenario. But more appropriately this will be the time of "Mahdi", when the world will be full of prosperity. There is no less-amount of wealth and provision even at this time on the planet, as Allah has created enough food for every living creature. But the problem is "distribution" of this provision, which is in the power of a hand full of the elite.

(9). **Competition in constructing high buildings:** Only a few decades ago our planet sustained her natural structure of billions of years i.e. hills, valleys, forests, deserts and grounds. All of a sudden this has changed utterly. Tall buildings have appeared which were never there since the beginning of the world. Look at any city---look at your own city---this evidence is sky high---!

(10). **I were in his place:** The increased number of suicides in the society is not hidden from any one. This suicidal trend is not just a fashion but fulfilment of the same very desire---I were in his place---!

(11). **Sun rises from the west:** This topic I have explained in "Zero Point". When the Earth will stop rotating for some days before it begins to spin in---the **opposite direction**---That means the sun will start rising from the west (Allah Knows Best). There are three events that will take place, one following the other, as they are explained in Hadith:

*"The Messenger of Allah (peace be upon him) observed: When three things appear faith will not benefit one who has not previously believed or has derived no good from his faith: the **rising of the sun** in its place of setting, **the Dajjal**, and the **Beast of the earth**." (Sahih Muslim 296 narrated by Abu Hurayra)*

This is the very time that Allah explains in Qur'an:

"...The day that certain of the signs of thy Lord do come, no good will it do to a soul to believe in them then, if it believed not before nor earned righteousness through its faith..." (Q-6:158)

After these signs appear, the door of repentance will be closed. No good will it do to believe---then---! **Now--- is the Time---!**

COPYING THE WEST

"The Prophet (SAW) said: 'The Hour will not be established till my followers copy the deeds of the previous nations and follow them very closely, span by span, and cubit by cubit (i.e., inch by inch)'. It was said, 'O Allah's Apostle! Do you mean by those (nations) the Persians and the Byzantines?' The Prophet said, 'Who can it be other than they?'" (Sahih Al Bukhari 9.241 Abu Hurayra)

In this Hadith: Prophet (SAW) gospeled his companions that Muslims will follow Persians and the Byzantines. Who do Muslims follow today? Europe and America! At that time America was not known to the other world. By giving an example of two big powers of that time Prophet (SAW) may have described the two big powers of today (Allah Knows Best). That means the main influential bodies of the world. Europe stands for Byzantine and America stands for Persia.

WHITE PALACE, OR WHITE HOUSE OF WASHINGTON?

"...A small force of the Muslims will capture the white palace, the palace of the Persian Emperor or his descendants..." (Sahih Muslim 4483 Jabir ibn Samurah)

DOLPHIN, APES COMMUNICATION AND MOBILE PHONES

"Allah's Messenger (peace be upon him) said: 'By Him in Whose hand my soul is. The last hour will not come before wild beasts speak to men, the end of a man's whip and the thong of his sandal speak to him, and his thigh informs him what his family have done since he left them.'"

Tirmidhi transmitted it. (Al Tirmidhi 5459 Abu Sa'id al Khudri)

During Second World War, United States used dolphins to carry out their army tasks. Dolphins were able to carry explosives and stick them on the enemy's marines and ships. On return, dolphins had to report back to their trainers about the completion or in-completion of the task. This; they would do by signal language, i.e. to touch a ball or a paddle accordingly. Further they were able to report the presence of any diver in the sea, this they would do by touching other paddles. Now this communication has reached up to 100 mutually understood signals among dolphins and human beings---! Apes; are the other specie, thought easy to communicate with. Now a special genetic breed of apes is being taught signal language and can express his various demands by pressing appropriate button. This is only a beginning---! (Video evidence is present for any challenges against the above)

In the time of Prophet (SAW) the equipments of nowadays did not exist. The language he used to describe them is exemplary. The beauty of Arabic language is in its vast meanings of words. One word has many grades of understandings that explain the variety of meanings according to the sentence it has been used in. The word "Fa-Kha-Za" in classic Arabic means "thigh and whatever is upon thigh". If we look at the best place we carry our mobile phones is on our thigh as we hang them on our belts. On leaving home we ring back and "whatever is on our thigh", "*informs us, what our family has done since we left them".* The "*end of man's whip",* may be the definition of mobile phone's antenna. The *"thong of his sandal"* may be interpreted as the leather cover of mobile phone or its stripe (Allah knows best).

"Imran ibn Husayn said, the Prophet (PBUH) said; 'some people of this Ummah will be swallowed up by the earth, some will be transformed into animals, and some will

be bombarded with the stones'. One of the Muslims asked, when will that be, O Messenger of Allah? He said 'when singers and musical instruments will become popular, and much wine will be drunk'." (Narrated by al-Tirmidhi Quote from 20-17)

US Military base in Porto Reco is one place that is carrying on the programme of mixing human gene with animals thus forming new species. Locals, who have witnessed these creatures, describe them so fast that they disappear like a bullet from your eyesight. I do not affirm this project only inform you with the possibility.

"Allah's Apostle said, "The Hour will not be established until you fight with the Turks; people with small eyes, red faces, and flat noses. Their faces will look like shields coated with leather. The Hour will not be established till you fight with people whose shoes are made of hair." (Sahih Al Bukhari-4.179-Abu Hurairah)

"The Prophet said, "One of the portents of the Hour is that you will fight with people wearing shoes made of hair; and one of the portents of the Hour is that you will fight with broad-faced people whose faces will look like shields coated with leather." (Sahih Al-Bukhari 4.178 narrated by Amr bin Taghlib)

"The Prophet said, "The Hour will not be established till you fight with the Khudh and the Kirman from among the non-Arabs. They will be of red faces, flat noses and small eyes; their faces will look like flat shields, and their shoes will be of hair." (Sahih Al-Bukhari 4.788 narrated by Abu Hurayra)

From above three Ahadith we get a description of different tribes or nations that Muslims or Arabs will fight.

Turks: The fight with Turks has happened at the end of Ottoman Empire, which I have described.

People with small eyes, red faces and flat noses: This is no doubt the description of Mangoles.

People whose shoes are made of hair: Again Mangoles used to wear these shoes, or it could be another fight.

People with broad faces like 'shield coated with leather': These could be the modern armies wearing defensive gas masks to immune from chemical weapons (Allah Knows Best).

"...When the lady slave gives birth to her mistress, that will be of its (The Hour) portents; when the bare-footed naked people become the chiefs of the people..." (Sahih Al-Bukhari 6.300 Abu Hurayra)

Children in the West are really masters of their parents. Parents can't stop them from doing any harm, can't beat them if they are going out of their way. Children are taught their rights in schools and threaten their parents to "call Police" on them if they shout and scream on children. It is getting worse and worse day-by-day.

"No locusts were seen in one of the years of Umar's caliphate, the year in which he died, and becoming very anxious on this account he sent a rider to the Yemen, another to Iraq and another to Syria to enquire whether any locusts had been seen. The rider who came from the Yemen brought him a handful and scattered it in front of him, and when Umar saw it he said, 'Allah is Most Great', and told that he had heard Allah's Messenger (peace be upon him) say: Allah who is great and glorious created a thousand species, six hundred in the sea and four hundred on the land. The first species to perish will be the locusts, and when they perish the species will follow one another like beads on a string." Bayhaqi transmitted it in Shu'ab al-Iman. (Al-Tirmidhi 5463 narrated by Jabir ibn-Abdullah)

According to a report billions of tonnes of food is consumed by locusts every year. This food can be useful and save the lives of thousands of people. Think tanks of humanitarian societies find this very depressing. To justify this injustice done by nature they have decided to mend the genes of this "plague" in such a way that their entire kind will disappear in **seven years time.**

"In order to extradite the plagues of locusts they will be genetically modified and with in 7 years, disappear". (Techno File, Sky News, 20-11-2000)

Allah (SWT) has made nothing in this world useless. Survival of every specie; relies upon the existence of others. For example birds and bees are means of plants' fertility. When they fly from one flower to other, they also carry their seeds, which are the only way for plants' re-growth. If we start thinking that every season billions of flowers die because of birds' and bees' suckling, thus start killing them, a day will come that we will have no flower on the surface of the earth. Locusts are useful to other species that rely on the re-production of locusts. Once locusts disappear this is going to cause unprecedented black hole on the face of earth, that will swallow all other creatures one by one---! **Time to act---!**

UNO (NATO FORCES)

"...Then a truce between you and Bani Al-Asfar (i.e. the Byzantines) who will betray you and attack you under eighty flags. Under each flag will be twelve thousand soldiers." (Sahih Al Bukhari-4.401-Auf bin Mali)

GOG AND MAGOG

There are various ideologies and questions about "Gog and Magog"; i.e. are they, on this planet or extraterrestrial (E.T)? Are they human beings or aliens? Do they visit us and abduct human beings? Are they interested in the planet called Earth? And finally, according to some modern western researchers (i.e. Elohimies), are they responsible for genetic mixing of the then local inhabitants of earth, the "chimpanzees" with their own, to bring human beings into existence? The latter is against intellect and Aqeedah (faith) anyway.

First of all we will check the Qur'anic version of "Zulqurnain" and "Gog and Magog", and then discuss the other stories and possibilities.

"Then followed he (another) way. Until when he reached (a tract) between two mountains he found beneath them a people who scarcely understood a word. They said: "O Zul-qarnain! the Gog and Magog (people) do great mischief on earth: shall we then render thee tribute in order that thou mightest erect a barrier between us and them?" He said: "(The power) in which my Lord has established me is better (than tribute): help me therefore with strength (and labor): I will erect a strong barrier between you and them: "Bring me blocks of iron." At length when he had filled up the space between the two steep mountain sides he said; "Blow (with your bellows)". Then when he had made it (red) as fire he said: "Bring me that I may pour over it molten lead." Thus were they made powerless to scale it or to dig through it. He said: "This is a mercy from my Lord: but when the promise of my Lord comes to pass He will make it into dust; and the promise of My Lord is true." (Q: 18: 92-98)

In Surah "Al-Kahf", Allah (SWT) tells the journey of "Zulqarnain". He travels three different directions. On the third excursion he reaches between two mountains that seem like two walls, between them is a valley. There he meets a nation that cannot understand his talks. Finally when he enables to communicate with them, they report him about two tribes called "Gog and Magog" that come from across the mountains through the valley and spread mischief on earth. On their demand, Zulqarnain fills the valley with iron sheets and burns them till they become like amber. Then he spills molten lead on top of the red iron. This way he stops the passage of "Gog and Magog" and builds a barrier between them and the tribe.

Many scholars believed that**Alexander** (Sikandr-e-Azam) from Macedonia was Zulqarnain. But the travelling paths of Alexander are well known to modern history, whereas Zulqarnain's are hidden in the pre-historic mysteries. Secondly, Zulqarnain was a rightly guided man who invited people to the path of Allah, whereas Alexander was a pagan and believed that he was son of a god.

On the other hand, some scholars believed that Zulqarnain built one or two iron gates as barrier, whereas Qur'an clearly states that he filled the path between two mountains with iron sheets and molten lead. If today through earth scanning equipment we can find out a thick layer of metal between two (after filling---one!) mountains, we might be able to trace out the exact location of the "Barrier". This is a barrier not a door or a window, that can be opened and shut as suggested by some modern computer science students (i.e. windows 95 or 2000 also called 'alien window areas'). Gog and Magog do not have any exit through it.

"And (Gog and Magog) were not able to surmount, nor could they pierce (it)." He said: "This is a mercy from my Lord: but when the promise of my Lord comes to pass He will make it into dust; and the promise of My Lord is true." (Q 18-97,98)

Gog and Magog have no power to make a hole into the barrier or to climb over it. When they come, they will swarm through every lofty place and this will be all of a sudden. The idea that; Gog and Magog (Aliens) randomly come to visit, abduct or communicate with terrestrials, is abrogated by Qur'an:

"Until the Gog and Magog (people) are let through (their barrier) and they swiftly swarm from every hill." (Q 21-96)

"...And then Allah will send Gog and Magog and they will swarm down from every slope. The first of them will pass the lake of Tiberias and drink out of it. And when the last of them passes, he will say: There was once water there..."(Sahih Muslim 7015. Narrated by An-Nawwas ibn Sam'an)

Lake Tiberias is also called "Sea of Galilee". A lake in Israel through which, Jordan River flows. Located 686 feet below sea level, it has a surface area of 64 square miles. The maximum depth is 157 feet. The Hadith above clearly defines raid of Gog and Magog on the earth and what they will do first (drinking water of the lake Tiberias). This demolishes the idea of their individual visits in UFOs. More over the order these events will take place is:

1. Appearance of Mahdi
2. Appearance of Ad-Dajjal
3. Descend of Jesus (PBUH)
4. Opening of Gog and Magog

"...Then a people whom Allah had protected [from Ad-Dajjal] *will come to Jesus, son of Mary, and he will wipe their faces and inform them of their ranks in Paradise. It will be under such conditions, that Allah will reveal to Jesus these words: 'I have brought forth from among My servants such people against whom none will be able to fight; you take these people safely to Tur'. And then, Allah will send Gog and Magog and they will swarm down from every slope. The first of them will pass the lake of Tiberias and drink out of it. And when the last of them passes, he will say: There was once water there..." (Sahih Muslim 7015-An-Nawwas ibn Sam'an)*

First we have to prepare ourselves for al-Mahdi, then worry about Ad-Dajjal, then witness the descend of Isa-ibn-Maryam (Jesus PBUH) and finally when Isa (PBUH) is present on earth, will come Gog and Magog with a warning from Allah (SWT).

ALIENS? --- UFOs?

Questions arise that if Gog and Magog are not the ones visiting us in UFOs, then what are UFOs and where do they come from? Who abducts human beings?

UFO sightings in America; began after 2nd World War. Prior to that Germany had developed forms of "Flying Saucers". British and American intelligence were deployed to spring the top Nazi scientists, engineers geneticists and mind manipulators from Germany to America. This project was code-named as "Project Paperclip".

"With a cost of $2,000,000,000 U.S government marshalled the manpower and resources needed to complete the project in four years that otherwise might have taken half a century. At the centre of the enterprise was a brilliant group of United States, British and refugee scientists". (16)

These *refugee scientists* were no other than the immigrants of "Paperclip". This cream of scientists brought America to a leading role in science. Even today the genius of the world, is absorbed by the west via Scholarships.

In 1938 actor "Orson Welles" claimed to be broadcasting live from the site of an alien landing in "New Jersey". In 1947 the famous incident of "Roswell" happened (the crash landing of a UFO). This incidence got extraordinary coverage by media. The concept of aliens comes from a novel called "War of the Worlds", written by H G. Wells a Freemason. In 1960s, a group of 15 experts presented the "Report from Iron Mountain", that "how to centralise power without wars". The "report" offered a "global threat" as a solution. This report was completed in 1966. One of the members leaked the contents of the report.

Threat from Russia and Hungary, on a small scale had united Europe in 1st World War. In 2nd World War this threat process succeeded to form "Allies", against Hitler. A bigger scale threat to the whole globe had to come from somewhere else and not earth to unite all human beings. Then a scientifically leading power would be considered as a leader automatically. America being the scientifically developed country had all the chances to take a lead in this situation. Freemasonry, working from the platform of America would no doubt have an upper hand to appoint their leader as the "messiah".

Interestingly in the USA the "UFO research", is funded by Rockefeller (a subsidiary of Freemasonry). Films like, "Independence Day" and "Alien Resurrection" were made by "20th Century Fox", owned by Rupert Murdoch, a Freemason, he also owns "Fox Television", the producer of "X Files". "Super man" was/is another part of mass manipulation, to introduce people with extraterrestrial!

Nevada is the constituent state of the United States of America. It borders California on the west, Oregon and Idaho on the north, Utah on the east and Arizona on the Southeast. It has an area of 110,567 square miles, which makes it the seventh largest of the 50 states. It contains vast semiarid grasslands and deserts. Nevada is divided into number of boxes starting from no1. Box 51, or **Area 51** is one of them. In the beginning, U.S government denied its existence totally and strictly refused any such evidences. But now Nevada is described as:

"Combined with the major scientific activity related to the federal government's atomic research facilities". (16)

Kelly Johnson was an aircraft designer who designed the first supersonic aircraft "U2". He needed someone reliable to test fly the plane. For this he turned to "Tony Le Vier", his civil aviation friend. Tony Le Vier is believed to be the father of Area 51. Tony consulted U.S government for the facilities he required for a test flight.

"U.S government across 30, 40 miles had all the facilities for this. CIA said; 'we will do it for you'." (Tony Le Vier recorded interview)

U2 was designed and tested successfully, completed its spying flights on USSR territory undetected by Soviet radars on a height of 26,000 feet. It went on for a while, photographed the Soviet atomic installations, unless all of a sudden it crashed in USSR and its captured pilot went for a trial in the court, sentenced to 10 years and exchanged for a Soviet prisoner in the U.S.

Second project, Area 51 had, was "B-2 Stealth Bomber". Its unique structure and speed was decades ahead. People could not expect such advance technology and named B-2 and other advance planes as UFOs. In 1988, U.S military officially unveiled the "B-2 Stealth Bomber" and "F-117 Stealth Fighter". People witnessed their mass destruction in Feb 1988 when; Gulf War proved their existence.

Present project is called "Aurora". It flies 6 times the speed of sound and attacks with a pinpoint accuracy. U.S government is constantly denying its existence too, just like B-2 and F-117.

The State of Nevada officially dubbed route 375 (highway leading to Area 51), "The Extraterrestrial Highway", due to the constant sightings of UFOs. Residents as well as their guests witnessed these sightings. Now Area 51 has been moved from its original situation to an unknown place.

Human abduction is also a vital element to make people believe the existence of aliens. Let me tell you that we don't need aliens to abduct us we have enough human scientists to do the dirty work. Abduction is another program after "MK Ultra". This project is carried out by "EDOM" (Electronic Dissolution of Memory). After MK Ultra was leaked and Bill Clinton had to apologise openly to the public (Ibid.) they changed the strategy. Now people blame aliens for this inhuman act and not humans for this alien act! A part of EDOM is also to implant a microchip in abductees. These microchips; are developed by a consortium of engineers. The chip-engineers are from "Motorola", "General Electric", "IBM" and "Boston Medical Centre". Other programs under **"Microchipping"** include a global financial collapse after year 2000 to introduce "One-World Electric Currency".

THE LAST CIVILIZATON

After Gog and Mgog invade the earth:

"...Jesus and his companions will then be besieged here (at Tur, and they will be so hard pressed) that the head of the ox will be dearer to them than one hundred dinars. Allah's Apostle (peace be upon him), Jesus, and his companions will supplicate Allah, Who will send to them (Gog and Mgog) insects (which will attack their necks) and in the morning they would perish as one single person. Allah's Apostle (peace be upon him), Jesus, and his companions, then come down to Earth and they will not find on Earth as much space as a single span that is not filled with putrefaction and stench. Allah's Apostle (peace be upon him), Jesus, and his companions will then beseech Allah who will send birds whose necks would be like those of Bactrian camels and they will carry them away and throw them where Allah wills. Then Allah will send rain which no house of mud-bricks or (tent of) camelhair will keep out and it will wash the Earth until it resembles a mirror. Then the Earth will be told to bring forth its fruit and restore its blessing, and as a result thereof, there will grow (such a big) pomegranate that a group of people will be able to eat it and seek shelter under its skin. A dairy cow will give so much milk that a whole party will be able to drink it. The milking camel will give such (a large quantity of) milk that the whole tribe will be able to drink from it, and the milking-sheep will give so much milk that the whole

family will be able to drink from it. At that time Allah will send a pleasant wind which will soothe (people) even under their armpits. He will take the life of every Muslim and only the wicked will survive who will commit adultery like asses and the Last Hour would come to them. (Sahih Muslim 7015-An-Nawwas ibn Sam'an)

CONCLUSION

O Allah!
Guide us to
Al Sirat-Al Mustaqim
(The Only Straight Path)

Reference Books List

1. Freemason's Guide and Compendium. Author: Bernard E. Jones
2. Freemasonry, A Celebration of the Craft. General Editors: John Hamill, Robert Gilbert. Forwarded By: HRH the Duke of Kent.
3. The Temple and the Lodge. Authors: Michal Baigent & Richard Leigh.
4. And The Truth Shall Set You Free. Author: David Icke.
5. Biggest Secret. Author: David Icke.
6. Rothschild, A Story Of Wealth & Power. Author: Derek Wilson.
7. The Times London. (Newspaper)
8. The Guardian London. (Newspaper)
9. The Hiram Key. Authors: Christopher Knight & Robert Lomas.
10. Conspirator's Hierarchy, The Story Of The Committee Of 300. Author: Dr. John Coleman.
11. Twentieth Century World History in Focus. Author: Harry Mills.
12. In Side the Seraglio. Author: John Freely.
13. Encyclopaedia Britannica 1946 Edition, (The New Hutchinson 20th Century Encyclopaedia, Vol-22)
14. A History of the 20th Century. Author: Martin Gilbert.
15. The Closed Circle. Author: David P. Jones.
16. Britannica CD 2000 Deluxe.
17. Mutalea-E-Brailwiyyat. (A Study of Brailwism) Author: Dr. Allamah Khalid Mahmood.
18. The Money Masters. (Video Tape)
19. The Second Messiah. Authors: Christopher Knight & Robert Lomas.
20. The Signs before the Day of Judgement. (English Translation) By: Ibne-Kathir.
21. Angels Don't Play This HAARP. By: Jeane Manning & Dr. Nick Begich.
22. The Brotherhood. (Stephen Knight)
23. Inside The Brotherhood. (Martin Short)
24. Majmooah Ilhamat (First Edition: 1935) 2nd Edition by Abdul Latif Bahawalpuri.
25. The Muslims of British India. (P. Hardy)
26. Separatism Among Indian Muslims. (Francis Robinson)

First Flag of the USA

"It's the first version of the U.S. flag. You will find the All-Seeing-Eye (Eye of Horus) & a prismatic (pyramidal) pencil of 9 rays of light & seven stars (pentagram). I suppose (I can't be sure) the 9 rays symbolize the "Unknown Superiors" or "The Nine Unknown Men". Quote from Bruno from France www.davidicke.com
Bruno's supposition strengthens the idea that "Nine Unknown Men" do exist. Ironically there exists a lodge named as "Nine Unknown Men".

Reverse of the 1-Dollar Bill